GOOD THINGS

GOOD THINGS

recipes to share with
people you love

SAMIN NOSRAT
WITH PHOTOGRAPHS BY AYA BRACKETT

EBURY
PRESS

BY SAMIN NOSRAT
Good Things
Salt Fat Acid Heat

EBURY PRESS

UK | USA | Canada | Ireland | Australia
India | New Zealand | South Africa

Ebury Press is part of the Penguin Random House group of companies whose addresses can be found at global.penguinrandomhouse.com

Penguin Random House UK
One Embassy Gardens, 8 Viaduct Gardens, London SW11 7BW

penguin.co.uk
global.penguinrandomhouse.com

First published in the US by Random House in 2025

First published in the UK by Ebury Press in 2025

1

Copyright © Samin Nosrat 2025

Photography by Aya Brackett

The moral right of the author has been asserted.

No part of this book may be used or reproduced in any manner for the purpose of training artificial intelligence technologies or systems. In accordance with Article 4(3) of the DSM Directive 2019/790, Penguin Random House expressly reserves this work from the text and data mining exception.

Colour origination by Altaimage Ltd

Printed and bound in Italy by Graphicom

The authorised representative in the EEA is Penguin Random House Ireland, Morrison Chambers, 32 Nassau Street, Dublin D02 YH68.

A CIP catalogue record for this book is available from the British Library

ISBN 9781529106718

Penguin Random House is committed to a sustainable future for our business, our readers and our planet. This book is made from Forest Stewardship Council® certified paper.

Credits for US edition:

Editor: Andy Ward • Managing editor: Rebecca Berlant • Production editor: Loren Noveck • Editorial assistants: Julia Harrison and Azraf Khan • Designer: Alvaro Villanueva • Art director and cover designer: Jenny Davis • Production manager: Richard Elman • Food stylist: Lillian Kang • Assistant food stylist: Paige Arnett • Prop stylist: Amy Elise Wilson • Recipe tester: Laurie Ellen Pellicano • Photo assistant: Mark Davis • Copy editor: Kate Slate • Proofreaders: Kate Bolen, Terry Deal, Jayne Yaffe Kemp, Zora O'Neill, Tess Rossi, Bridget Sweet, and Rebecca Zaharia • Indexer: Gina Guilinger

For Pasha, Ebony, Amanda, Laurel, Josh, Hrishi, Sarah, Alexis, Cara, Robbie, Thao, Orion, Flora, Vega, and Fava—the family who's chosen me

Eating is a small, good thing in a time like this.
—Raymond Carver

contents

introduction 11

rules of thumb 23
first things first

good things come in small packages 43
condiments, components, and toppings

good things to welcome others 83
small gestures of hospitality

good things come in threes 111
*seven versatile dressings
(and three ways to use each)*

good things to keep up your sleeve 139
making the most of store cupboard staples

good things come to those who wait 189
seasonal produce

finger-licking good things 277
chicken, chicken, and more chicken

good things are better shared 317
recipes to cook and eat in community

good things take time 367
yeasted breads and waffles

all good things come to an end 395
a sweet note

references and influences 443

resources 444

acknowledgements 445

index 446

introduction

the treasure chest

When my neighbour's daughter, Miya, was about six years old, she transformed an old cigar box into what she called her "treasure chest." She filled it with all sorts of precious things: jewellery and coins, seashells, cake urchins and acorns, and notes from Queen Zoe, the mischievous fairy who watches over our courtyard.

Any time I'd drop by, she'd sit me down in the living room and take me, piece by piece, through the box. She had a story for every little thing. A collection of pine cones from around her mom's childhood home. A geode, not yet cracked open. Tiny paintings. Each of these things told a story about who she was and what she cared about, a brief chance to view the world through her eyes.

This book is my cigar box. Inside, you'll find my most useful and beloved everyday recipes. You'll encounter my favourite ingredients, tools, and techniques, as well as stories about the ways cooking continues to be a source of meaning and beauty in my life. Like Miya and many other kids (and some adults), I've always had an unbridled enthusiasm for things others might consider useless—apricot stones, the liquid from a can of chickpeas, or the oil left behind after frying a pot of shallots.

I've obsessively collected and refined these treasures, large and small, over a lifetime of cooking. And because I believe sharing life's pleasures only magnifies them, I'd like to share my Good Things with you. Welcome.

the value of time

From a young age I was told, "Time is money." I learned to prioritise output, convenience, efficiency, and profit over all else. So I built my life around work. I measured my self-worth and happiness by how much I could produce. "If only I can make something extraordinary," I thought, "then I'll finally be happy and my life will mean something."

I held up my end of the bargain. For four decades, I single-mindedly poured myself into my work. I cooked at world-class restaurants in both California and Italy. I made the book and television show I'd always dreamt of creating. For my effort I was rewarded with praise and acclaim. But happiness and meaning continued to elude me. Instead, all I felt was emptiness.

Six years ago, in the wake of the success of *Salt Fat Acid Heat*, I began to grieve, though at first I wasn't sure why. Then, the pandemic hit. And then I suffered a series of tremendous losses—including the deaths of several people close to me. Finally, clinical depression, potent and ravenous, swallowed me whole. And the sense of joy I'd always found in cooking, eating, and more generally in life no longer felt attainable.

This period of turmoil and melancholy led me (slowly, slowly) to recalibrate my values—it was either that or perish. I began asking myself, "What is a good life?" The various answers to this, from the cosmic (a good life is built on a foundation of meaning) to the quotidian (a good life is one where I never have to frantically search for a phone charger), help me navigate my way. And my North Star—as simple as it is profound—is the hard-won understanding that our most precious currency is time.

This newfound appreciation for the one thing I can't restock or replace has become a much-needed antidote to the short-sighted beliefs upon which I'd built my life. It has reminded me that something as simple as cooking for my loved ones can carry as much meaning, as much worth, as any achievement or career milestone. I now consider a good life to be one where I feel deeply rooted in both my community and the natural world. It's one where beauty and pleasure are paramount, and I do meaningful work that creates joy and connection. A good life is one where time—and its fast companion, attention—are the most precious gifts I can give or receive.

The beauty of cooking is that it's a vessel for both time and attention. Cooking for someone, or sitting down for a meal together, is about more than nourishment—it's a way to share what's most valuable to you with the people you care about.

the problem with recipes

A few years ago, a friend suggested that I put together a book of my favourite recipes. No high concept, no subversion of the entire genre. "Just the simple things you cook at home for yourself and your friends," she said. "The things you most love to eat."

"Have you even *met* me?" I replied. "I hate recipes!"

A week later, I stood in my kitchen, dressing a cabbage slaw I'd made a dozen times during the pandemic. It was based on a salad from a fancy deli near my house, with a creamy miso dressing, coriander, and peanuts. It took about five minutes to pull together, cost practically nothing, and lasted for days. Each time I made it, I was shocked by how good it was. The slaw's bright flavours and crunchy texture reverberated across my palate, revealing new dimensions of pleasure with each bite. And since anytime I encounter something good, my instinct is to share it with others, I couldn't help but think, "If only I had some way to tell people about this recipe."

My next thought? "Uh-oh."

Ever since that moment, a struggle has raged inside me. I'd be lying if I didn't admit that at times it's felt like a betrayal—to myself and to you—to assemble a book of recipes after writing *Salt Fat Acid Heat,* which is a veritable manifesto designed to free cooks from relying on them. For as long as I've been cooking, I've had a complicated relationship with recipes—I could never escape the feeling that each was an attempt to capture, quantify, and define the ineffable.

I've always thought that a cook's relationship to a written recipe is akin to the way a musician relates to notes on a page. When asked about the experience of performing the same sheet music night after night, over the course of his long career, Yo-Yo Ma answered, "In a world where we can measure everything—or we think we can measure everything—how wonderful it is that you could have the poetry of music, or poetry, or music that actually makes you think you are touching infinity." I may not be a world-class cellist, but I do believe that the practice of cooking is another way to touch infinity. Just as no two performances of Bach's cello suites are ever the same for Yo-Yo, neither are any two preparations of a particular recipe—because each instance is shaped not only by its own context but also by all the ones that precede it.

Language simply isn't expansive enough to capture the essence of a practice as corporeal or sensory—not to mention brimming with as much history, tradition, memory, and nostalgia—as cooking. The value of any one dish is so much more than one list of ingredients and another of numbered steps. This is why you must trust yourself, your own judgement, and your own senses over anything anyone (including me) might instruct. After all, you're the one who's going to have to eat the darned thing.

No matter how many times I might test a recipe or how precise I might be in my measurements—and I worry myself sick over precision—it's inevitable that you and I will do some things differently. We may live in different parts of the country or the world. We may buy different brands of ingredients. Our pots and pans might be made of different metals and constructed in slightly different shapes. Our ovens and hobs may be calibrated differently, and we may use different heat sources. Maybe we're cooking at different times of year, at different altitudes, with different ambient temperatures or humidity.

Any of these variables—along with countless others—affects the way your dish and mine may differ. But in cooking, just as in life, differences aren't anything to fear.

We've learned to expect the wrong things from recipes. We've been trained to believe that if we just follow what's on the page, word for word, we'll get the same result every time. But good cooking isn't about mindless repetition. It's about being completely present with an experience as it unfolds. I believe it's the job of a good recipe to guide and empower a cook to use all of her senses—including common sense—to make the best choices in the moment. Standing in my kitchen, tasting that slaw, I realised it just might be possible to write a book of recipes while staying true to myself. Especially if I focused on sharing the things I love and the things I've learned—about cooking, but also about how it brings meaning to our lives.

Since usefulness to you is my priority, I've used various recipe formats and chapter structures throughout the book. Some recipes require more precision, while others leave room for flexibility. The precise weight of a head of cauliflower, for example, doesn't matter nearly as much as how thickly you slice it. Some techniques are so simple that a paragraph or two of description is plenty—no numbered steps required. Regardless of the format, my team and I have tested and retested every recipe in this book to ensure your success.

I've come to think of recipes not as rigid prescriptions but as "rituals that promise transformation," as the poet and pie-maker Kate Lebo so beautifully put it. I love this definition because it expands a recipe's value by taking it off the page. Recipes, like rituals, endure because they're passed down to us—whether by ancestors, neighbours, friends, strangers on the internet, or me to you.

    I'm offering you these Good Things with the sincere hope that cooking your way through them brings you as much joy as they've brought me. Happy cooking and eating!

rules of thumb

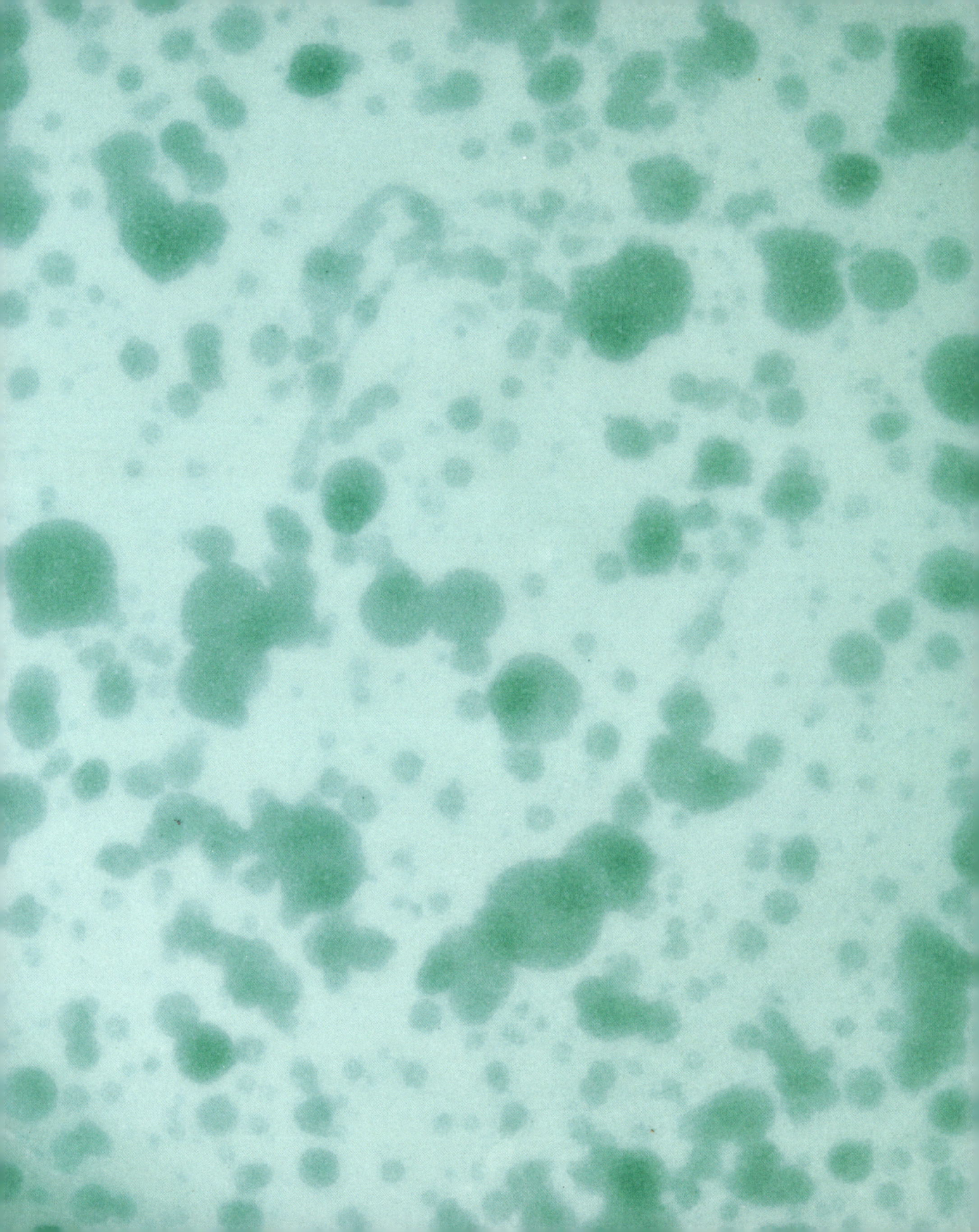

notes on ingredients

PRODUCE SIZE AND PREPARATION

Unless otherwise noted, I've tested recipes using medium sizes of produce (i.e., "1 onion" means 1 medium onion, so if all you've got is a humongous onion, use half of it!). And always wash produce and trim away peels, roots, ends, and any rotten bits before using, unless a recipe offers other directions.

KOSHER SALT AND FLAKY SALT

In this book, "kosher salt" refers specifically to the brand Diamond Crystal. I've used it exclusively to test these recipes. I prefer Diamond Crystal because it's lightweight and flaky, so it readily adheres to food and dissolves quickly.

Other brands of kosher salt may weigh up to twice as much per teaspoon, which means that your food may turn out inedibly salty if you blindly follow the recipes without adjusting for salinity or tasting along the way. To that end, I've included gram measurements where applicable so that you can use whatever salt you've already got if you don't want to seek out (or can't find) Diamond Crystal. The rest of the time, taste and adjust regularly as you cook!

Flaky salt, also known as pyramid sea salt, has a light, crunchy texture. Besides Maldon Salt, Blackthorn from Scotland and Jacobsen from Oregon are two of my favourite producers of flaky sea salt, which is ideal for sprinkling over food at the last moment.

OLIVE OIL

Olive oil is always extra-virgin. If the olive oil you base your cooking on doesn't taste good, your cooking will never taste good. It's as simple as that. So it's worth investing some time, energy, and money in finding a reliable source for olive oil. Leila's Shop in London, Honey & Co. and Ottolenghi online all carry delicious olive oils from across Europe and the Mediterranean.

Olive oil labels can be hard to decipher. Furthermore, price isn't an indicator of quality or a guarantee that the oil in a particular bottle isn't rancid. The single most important piece of information on an olive oil label is the harvest date (sometimes called the production date). If the oil is produced in the northern hemisphere, the production date will typically be in October or November. In the southern hemisphere, the date will generally be in April or May. And unlike wine, olive oil has a firm expiration date of eighteen months from the harvest date, so ignore any suggested expiration dates that exceed this length of time.

Keep oil away from air, light, and heat, which is to say, away from the range and any kitchen windows. Choose oils that are packaged in dark glass, metal, or bag-in-a-box to reduce exposure to light, which dramatically reduces shelf life. I like to decant oil from larger containers, which I'll store in cupboards, into ultraviolet-filtering glass bottles from Infinity Jars for everyday use. Once you open a bottle of olive oil, use it within six months, as oxidation will begin to occur, degrading both flavour and quality. And finally, always taste your olive oil before using it to make sure it's not too bitter or—even worse—rancid.

NEUTRAL OIL

"Neutral oil" simply refers to any oil that won't impart any flavour of its own to a dish. Examples include rapeseed, grapeseed, sunflower, safflower, peanut, and rice bran oils; since sunflower oil tends to yield the creamiest, thickest texture in aquafaba-based dressings, it's become my neutral oil of choice. Look for oils that specify "expeller pressed" on the label. This means that a press physically squeezes the oil from the nuts, seeds, or fruits. In contrast, commercially produced oils tend to be extracted chemically. Here, the raw matter is ground and then bathed in chemical solvents to draw out the fat. Then, the fat-and-solvent mixture is heated to allow the solvents to evaporate, but there's no way to ensure that the oil ends up free of solvents.

Neutral oils tend to have high smoke points, which makes them ideal for deep-frying and other high-heat uses. And since fat can be an important source of flavour at the base of any dish, choose a neutral oil when you don't want to influence that flavour in the wrong direction. For example, a peppery olive oil will set the stage beautifully for an Italian, Spanish, French, or Californian dish, but it's not the best choice for evoking, say, Korean or Filipino flavours in your cooking. Do your best to use the traditional cooking fats of any particular cuisine. And when in doubt, choose a neutral oil and let the other flavourings in a dish influence its direction.

VINEGAR

I like to keep several different types of vinegar on hand so that I can always achieve the precise flavour I'm after in a dish. In my European-influenced cooking, I reach for aged sherry and wine vinegars. When cooking Japanese- or Korean-influenced dishes, I rely on seasoned rice vinegar for its sweetness, salt, and delicate acidity (this is probably my favourite vinegar of all). I use raw apple cider vinegar for a nice, neutral taste in classic American dishes and dressings, as well as for pickling. And I always keep a little bottle of syrupy aged balsamic vinegar from Modena around to drizzle over salads and toasts.

GARLIC

There are a few important things to know about garlic: First, the smaller its form, the more intense its flavour. That means a clove of garlic added whole to a pot of soup will lend only a light, delicate bit of aroma and flavour to the pot, whereas thinly sliced or minced garlic sizzled in oil will impact the whole dish much more forcefully.

Second, garlic can support the growth and production of botulinum toxin, which is very dangerous and undetectable to the human eye, nose, and palate. Moisture, room-temperature storage of prepared garlic, lack of oxygen, and low-acid conditions all allow the bacterium that produces the toxin to thrive. To prevent food safety mishaps, refrigerate dishes containing

• Salt: kosher and flaky • Olive oil • Neutral oil • Vinegar •
• Garlic • Parmesan • Herbs • Citrus •
• Calabrian chillies and chilli paste • Labne • Miso paste • Tahini •
• Chicken stock • Nonstick cooking spray • Vanilla pods and extract • Cocoa and chocolate •

rules of thumb

raw garlic and consume them within a week, unless there is abundant acid present (as with a vinaigrette).

And finally, even though it's available to us year-round, garlic is harvested only once a year—in the summer. As the year goes by, the flavour of the garlic intensifies, so a summer clove is much milder than a winter clove, and you may need more or less garlic for any particular recipe depending on the time of year. I've done my best to write these recipes so they hit an any-time-of-year sweet spot, but please adjust them to your own liking. And as for the germ, or the little green sprout that appears in the autumn or winter in the centre of each clove, it's up to you to remove it if you like. I tend to, especially when I'm grating the garlic, but it's not necessary and won't affect the flavour of your cooking.

PARMESAN

There is no substitute for real Parmigiano-Reggiano, which is made in northern Italy in accordance with centuries-old traditions. Parmesan made in other places won't taste the same or add the same flavour to your cooking. This is one of the few ingredients where spending a little more money can make a big difference.

When a recipe calls for finely grated Parmesan, use the fine shredding holes on a box grater (or something that produces a similar result) rather than a rasp grater, which reduces the cheese to the consistency of papery, dried-out snow. Parmesan grated on a rasp grater will also completely throw off your recipe's flavour, since a cup of rasp-grated Parm is so fluffy that it's only about a third the weight of a cup of cheese grated on a box grater. And of course, save your rinds—I like to freeze mine—to add to soups, ragus, and pots of stock.

HERBS

I rely heavily on soft herbs—delicate herbs with tender, rather than woody, stalks—in my cooking. I use these fresh herbs, including basil, chervil, chives, coriander, dill, mint, parsley, shiso, and tarragon, somewhat interchangeably, relying on a combination of availability, cultural influence, and whimsy to guide my choices. (Throughout this book, herbs are fresh unless otherwise specified.)

With all fresh herbs, use the leaves or fronds and only the tenderest stalks. Parsley is always flat-leaf (also called Italian) and I recommend using only the leaves and the most delicate stems. Tender coriander stalks, on the other hand, are rarely fibrous and tend to be the most flavourful part of the herb.

FRESH CITRUS

Along with fresh herbs, fresh citrus is a permanent fixture on my grocery list. I use so much citrus juice and zest that I feel mildly alarmed when I don't have any lemons or limes around. There's no substitute for freshly squeezed—shelf-stable juices are pasteurised and often contain citric acid, while fresh citrus juice will lose flavour and develop a bitter edge if it sits for longer than a few hours. To finely grate citrus zest, use a rasp grater to remove the colourful zest in long strokes, rotating the fruit as you go. To produce long, wide strips of zest, use a Y-shaped vegetable peeler. And no matter how you remove the zest, take care to avoid the bitter white pith.

CALABRIAN CHILLIES AND CHILLI PASTE

If I could only keep one type of hot pepper on hand, it would be Calabrian chillies. To borrow a phrase from the late poet Thomas Lux, these southern Italian peppers are "a lit-from-within red." Fruity and moderately spicy, their warmth comes on slowly and fills your mouth as you eat. I add dried chillies to pots of beans and braises and keep a jar of crushed chilli paste in the fridge so I can stir a spoonful into pastas, soups, stews, sauces, or anywhere I want to add some chilli flavour, bright colour, and well-balanced heat. These days, you can find dried Calabrian chillies and jars of chilli paste at many specialist food shops, larger supermarkets, and online.

LABNE

Labne is to Greek yogurt as Greek yogurt is to natural yogurt. I like to think of it as the thick, creamy love child of yogurt and soured cream. And much like soured cream, it does beautifully in baked goods and makes a wonderful base for dips, in addition to all it offers as a garnish.

Many supermarkets these days carry labne alongside Greek yogurt, but you can also easily make your own.

To make **Homemade Labne**, all it takes is Greek yogurt, muslin, and patience. Line a fine-mesh sieve with a double layer of muslin, leaving plenty of overhang (or line the sieve with paper coffee filters or a mesh straining bag—often sold as a nut milk bag). Place over a medium bowl. Empty 240g of natural full-milk Greek yogurt into the sieve and cover with the excess muslin. Set a lightweight plate atop the muslin and place the bowl in the refrigerator for 24 to 72 hours (the longer, the better!). Discard the whey or use it in place of yogurt or buttermilk in the marinade for **Joojeh Kabob Roast Chicken** (page 284).

MISO

Miso is a salty, extraordinarily savoury paste made by fermenting soybeans or other pulses, salt, and a fungus called koji. Variables including the type of pulses, the variety of koji, and the length of the fermentation period affect the taste, texture, flavour, and colour of the final product. While there are more than thirteen hundred types of miso produced in Japan and beyond, the kind I use most often is shiro, or white, miso. Mild and sweet, shiro miso is ideal for use in sauces, dressings, and marinades. When shopping, avoid shelf-stable miso pastes, which are typically pasteurised and tend to be less flavourful due to accelerated fermentation. Instead, look for a refrigerated miso that contains only soybeans, salt, and koji. Hikari Miso, Clearspring, and Miso Tasty all produce wonderfully flavourful miso.

TAHINI

Sadly, all tahini is not created equal. At its best, tahini is rich in sesame flavour and, once stirred, has a smooth, creamy texture. But bad tahini can be gritty or pasty, unpalatably bitter, metallic tasting, or even rancid. To avoid disappointment, it's worth finding a brand you like and sticking to it. My favourites are Al Yaman and Al Arz.

CHICKEN STOCK

Chicken stock is such an important element in my cooking that I always use homemade. In fact, when my freezer stockpile (!) dwindles to just 2 or 3 litres, I immediately make more. While making stock isn't costly, I understand that the constraints of time or freezer space may limit your capacity to hoard it like I do. But good stock makes for good cooking, so I encourage you to abandon canned and boxed stock. Instead, look for high-quality stock or bone broth from your local butcher or grocer (it's often available in the freezer). I've also included a recipe—and an option for using an electric pressure cooker—on pages 314–15. (And while I don't consider chicken bouillon paste a replacement for homemade stock, I also always keep a jar around because it's a fantastic way to boost flavour in soups, sauces, and even the occasional pot of rice.)

NONSTICK COOKING SPRAY

I used to pooh-pooh nonstick cooking spray. I assumed it was just an expensive repackaged version of the neutral cooking oil I already had in the store cupboard. Then a pastry chef friend set me straight. She explained that aerosolised fat particles in cooking spray are much, much finer than their non-spray counterparts. The smaller the particles, the more evenly and thoroughly they can coat a surface, thus preventing sticking. I'm now a convert—I spray all my baking tins before and after lining them with parchment and every cake (and focaccia) slips out without incident.

VANILLA PODS AND EXTRACT

Real vanilla pods are not cheap, and for good reason! Grown on the only orchid that produces edible fruit, vanilla pods are incredibly labour- and time-intensive to cultivate. When a vanilla orchid blooms, the flower must be pollinated within twelve hours in order to produce a bean. In Mexico, the Melipona bee does the work of pollination; elsewhere, vanilla flowers need to be carefully pollinated by hand. Then, a single pod can take upwards of nine months to reach maturity. Finally, it must undergo a multi-step curing process for another four months to properly develop flavour. Apart from all of this time and labour, warming climates and climate disasters are a major threat to vanilla pod cultivation across the world.

For all these reasons, I consider vanilla a precious gift and use it accordingly. In a dessert, I let its aroma and flavour stand out so it can be properly appreciated. I also make sure to fish the pod out of any liquid in which it may have been steeped and rinse it off. After drying, I'll add it to the bottle of homemade vanilla extract I've had going in my store cupboard for more than ten years so I can make use of every last bit of flavour.

To make your own **Vanilla Extract,** halve 6 vanilla pods lengthways with a sharp paring knife and scrape out the seeds. Place the seeds and pods in a sterilised 500-millilitre or 1-litre canning jar (see **Sterilising Jars,** page 38) and add 240 millilitres vodka. Cover and set in a cool, dark place until the extract is a rich brown colour and deeply fragrant. Give the jar a good shake every week or whenever you think of it. Though the extract will be ready to use around the 3-month mark, it'll only get better with time. Once a year or so, decant the extract into another bottle for using, then add more pods and spirits to the jar to keep the process going.

Purchase vanilla pods from purveyors who prioritise regenerative agriculture and ethical labour practices, including Littlepod, Terre Exotique, and the Vanilla Bean Project.

COCOA AND CHOCOLATE

Quality cocoa and chocolate make all the difference in baking. I call for Dutch-process cocoa in my recipes because I prefer its darker, smoother flavour to that of natural cocoa, which tends to be lighter and more acidic. I'm a huge fan of the Dutch-process cocoa from Valrhona for its deep, dark, chocolaty flavour.

With added stabilisers and a lower percentage of cocoa butter, chocolate chips retain their shape when heated. Hence, a chocolate chip cookie made with chips will emerge with intact chip-shapes of chocolate distributed throughout the cookie.

Meanwhile, baking chocolate in the form of bars, wafers, and discs is free of stabilisers and has a higher percentage of cocoa butter to encourage melting. In a chocolate chip cookie, chopped baking chocolate will melt into the dough, creating gooey pockets of chocolate throughout the cookie.

I love both the Jivara and Manjari chocolate chips from Valrhona. With respective cacao percentages of 40 per cent and 64 per cent, neither is too light or dark for my tastes. They're just right for baking.

When it comes to baking chocolate, Guittard, Valrhona, Cacao Barry, and Callebaut all have excellent options. Since the "milk chocolate" and "plain dark chocolate" nomenclature isn't standardised across brands, I prefer to recommend using chocolate with cacao somewhere in the range of 54 per cent to 66 per cent for baking because it'll yield plenty of deep chocolate flavour without being too sharp. I also usually keep some unsweetened chocolate around. And, for the rare occasion when I want to bake with white chocolate, I'll use a caramelised white such as Valrhona Dulcey for its toasted, buttery flavour.

As with vanilla, the long-term production of chocolate is also seriously threatened by climate change. Historically, labour practices across the chocolate industry have been devastatingly exploitative, especially of women and children. It's worth familiarising yourself with the ethics and sustainability guidelines of any chocolate producer you patronise to ensure they meet your standards.

eating with your eyes

Take a moment to look at any ingredient before you decide how to trim, slice, or otherwise prepare it, because we eat first with our eyes, as the saying goes. As a rule, avoid straight lines and blunt cuts to yield the loveliest pieces, crumbles, and swirls. Let the natural shape of an ingredient guide your choices about how to approach it: Cut asparagus on a sharp bias to mimic the shape of the whole spear, crumble pecans into large pieces instead of chopping them to leave their curved sides intact, and instead of slicing a halved avocado for a salad, scoop out asymmetrical spoonfuls. Use this small arsenal of techniques to make all of your food more visually interesting and appealing.

ROLL-CUT

Roll-cut long vegetables—including cucumbers, courgettes, celery stalks, and parsnips—to produce unique-looking pieces that are, above all, fun to eat. And since roll-cut pieces have more surface area than sliced ones, they'll cook (and brown!) more quickly and evenly.

To roll-cut, place a carrot, for instance, on the chopping board horizontally in front of you. Hold your knife about 2.5cm from one end at a 60-degree angle relative to the carrot and make your first cut. Roll the carrot a quarter-turn away from you so that the longest point is at the topmost position. Keeping your knife at the same angle, bring it up another 2.5cm and repeat the cut.

Continue rolling and cutting, always with the longest point at the topmost position. As you work your way to the thicker end, adjust the angle of your knife closer to 45 degrees relative to the carrot in order to end up with pieces that will cook evenly.

TEAR

Take every opportunity you get to tear an ingredient instead of cutting it. Tear soft fruits, including figs, apricots, and dates, for fruit plates, salads, or crostini. Tear stale bread into croutons to create more nooks and crannies to nestle dressings and bits of cheese. Tear lettuces and herbs to avoid the straight lines slicing will yield. And tear fresh mozzarella and burrata into large, craggy bites before drizzling them with olive oil and flaky salt.

PEEL

A vegetable peeler can be an artistic tool as well as a practical one. While it makes sense to entirely peel certain types of produce—including carrots, potatoes, and anything else with tough, fibrous skin—let aesthetics as well as texture guide how you peel thin-skinned varieties of cucumbers, aubergines,

and winter squash. Peel skin in alternating strips—I call this a stripy peel—to create a vibrant visual contrast. Or use a peeler to shave long, wide ribbons for a salad.

CRUMBLE

To create charmingly irregular pieces of soft nuts and cheeses, crumble them. When crumbling cheese into a salad, make your pieces a bit larger than you'd like, knowing they'll continue to break down as the salad is tossed and the bowl is passed around the table. Use the tip of a table knife to gently chip crumbles from a block of hard cheese, such as Parmesan or aged Gouda, for a cheese platter or to add to a chopped salad.

SPOON AND SMEAR

Most of the time, I find imperfection and unevenness much more appetising than flawless smoothness. Instead of focusing on smoothing spreads perfectly onto toasts or platters, use the back of a spoon to

create pools and ridges upon which other ingredients can sit. And scoop out bite-sized rustic spoonfuls of avocado for a salad in order to avoid the straight lines slicing or dicing would produce.

BIAS CUT

The bias cut is a simple way to add a little visual flair to slices of any ingredient. With the ingredient placed horizontally in front of you, hold your knife at a 45-degree angle, or bias, and slice pieces of whatever thickness you'd like. For longer slices with greater surface area, use a sharper angle—this is a great way to dramatically slice a baguette.

The bias cut is ideal for particularly dense or fibrous vegetables, including asparagus, carrots, parsnips, sweet potatoes, and celery because it shortens their tough fibres, making them easier to eat.

a few basics

TOASTING NUTS AND SEEDS

For the most even results, toast nuts and seeds in the oven (or toaster oven) rather than on the hob, and make sure to use a timer! Adjust an oven rack to the centre position and preheat to 190°C. Spread the nuts or seeds in a single layer on a parchment-lined baking sheet (use a different tray for each type of nut or seed to ensure the most even cooking). Bake for 4 minutes, then rustle the nuts around and rotate the tray. Continue checking the tray and stirring every 1 to 2 minutes until they're fragrant, evenly golden, and pleasantly toasty throughout (bite into a nut to make sure it's toasted all the way through). Immediately transfer the toasted nuts or seeds to a plate to prevent overcooking.

While every batch is different, seeds and small or light nuts, including pine nuts, walnuts, pecans, and pistachios, take 5 to 8 minutes to toast. Denser nuts, including hazelnuts, macadamia nuts, and almonds, take longer—anywhere from 8 to 18 minutes—so don't forget to reset the timer every time you close the oven door!

TOASTING SPICES

Toast whole spices in a small dry frying pan over medium heat, swirling the pan constantly to ensure even cooking. Toast until the seeds are aromatic and just beginning to pop. Immediately transfer the spices to a bowl to prevent burning. If desired, grind in a mortar or spice grinder before using.

GRINDING AND BLOOMING SAFFRON

To get the most out of precious saffron, grind it and then bloom it in hot water before adding it to food. Use a small mortar and pestle to grind saffron threads into a fine powder with a pinch of salt. Add 1 to 2 tablespoons of boiling water and allow the saffron to steep for 10 minutes. Carefully add the bloomed "tea" to your recipe, using a little more hot water to swirl every last drop of saffron out of the mortar.

MAKING CROUTONS

To turn any stale bread (including **Fluffy Pitta Pockets,** page 385, and **Sky-High Focaccia,** page 372) into croutons, adjust an oven rack to the centre position and preheat to 200°C (if using more than one tray, adjust the racks to upper-middle and lower-middle positions). Use a serrated knife to remove any excessively leathery crust. Then, tear the bread into rustic 2cm pieces (or dice it into approximately 2cm cubes). Toss the croutons with a generous amount of extra-virgin olive oil to evenly coat the pieces, then spread them out in a single layer on a baking tray. Use a second tray as needed to avoid crowding, which would trap steam and prevent the croutons browning.

Place the tray(s) in the oven and bake. After 8 minutes, use a thin flexible metal spatula to turn and stir the croutons. Rotate the tray front to back, and if using more than one tray, also switch racks. Once the croutons begin to brown, check them every few minutes, continuing to stir, turn, and rotate.

Some croutons might be ready before others, so remove them from the tray and let the rest finish cooking. Bake until the croutons are golden brown and crunchy on the outside, with just a tiny bit of chew on the inside.

Depending on the type and density of the bread, croutons can take anywhere from 15 to 22 minutes to toast. Continue using a timer throughout the cooking time to prevent burning. Cool toasted croutons in a single layer, then use immediately, or store at room temperature in an airtight container for up to 3 days. Refresh stale croutons in an oven or toaster oven at 200°C for 3 to 4 minutes.

BRINGING EGGS TO ROOM TEMPERATURE QUICKLY

If you forget to bring eggs to room temperature before baking (or for any other use), place them in a bowl and cover them completely with the hottest water you can coax from the tap. Let the eggs sit for 5 minutes, then proceed with the recipe.

STERILISING JARS

To sterilise jars for canning and storing condiments, line a large pot with a rack or a few tea towels to prevent the jars jostling and cracking while they boil. Arrange the jars atop the rack or towels and fill them with hot water, then add enough water to the pot to cover the jars by at least 2.5cm. Bring the water to a boil, then set a timer for 10 minutes (if you are not at sea level, add a minute for each additional 300m of elevation). When the jars are finished boiling, turn off the heat and use a jar lifter to carefully remove them from the pot.

Boiling water can damage jar lids and rings, so simply wash them with warm, soapy water. Set lids, rings, and jars on clean tea towels to dry.

suggested substitutions

In my cooking, I tend to rely on a few specialist ingredients and many of the pickles, sauces, dressings, and other components I developed for this book, but my ultimate goal is to get you cooking with the least amount of fuss. So if you're itching to try a recipe that calls for something you don't have on hand, here are some ideas for substitutions:

Beans or chickpeas: Substitute 1 x 400g tin drained beans or chickpeas for every 240g of beans or chickpeas you've cooked yourself (or vice versa)

Bright Pickled Onions (page 52): Thinly sliced shallot or red onion, macerated in red wine vinegar for 15 minutes

Cardamom Ghee (page 61): ¼ teaspoon freshly ground cardamom stirred into 2 tablespoons of ghee, brown butter, or melted butter

Chilli Vinegar (page 76): Seasoned rice vinegar plus chilli flakes or fresh jalapeño or serrano chilli to taste

Dried Calabrian chillies: Chillies de árbol or chillies japonés

Garlic and Herb Labne (page 48): Natural labne or natural whole-milk Greek yogurt

Ghee (page 62): Melted butter, brown butter, or olive oil

Marinated Feta (page 71) **or Goat's Cheese** (page 74): Plain feta-style or goat's cheese

Pickled Thai Chillies (page 76): Fresh jalapeño or serrano chilli, seeded, to taste

Preserved Meyer Lemon Paste (page 79): Puréed or finely chopped shop-bought preserved lemons

Shallot Oil (page 55): Neutral oil or olive oil

essential kitchen tools
BASIC

• Box grater • Stand mixer • Food processor • Measuring cups and spoons • Silicone spatulas • Tongs • Lots of bowls • Lots of baking trays • A few good knives—chef's, serrated, paring • Parchment paper • Cake tins in all the right sizes • Cast-iron and stainless-steel frying pans • Casserole dishes with lids: small (3- to 4-litre), medium (5- to 6-litre), and large (7- to 9-litre) • A very large (10- to 12-litre) pot or stockpot •

UNEXPECTEDLY ESSENTIAL

· Japanese mandoline · Digital kitchen scales with gram weights · Fine-mesh skimmer ·
· Wide-mouth canning jars and canning funnel · Digital thermometer · Offset spatula · Immersion blender ·
· Microplane (rasp) grater · Mortar and pestle · Fine-mesh sieve · Food mill · Pastry brush · Citrus juicer ·

condiments, components, and toppings

It's taken me years to unplug my professional brain when cooking at home. In restaurants, I learned to think like a chef when creating dishes and menus. And it felt natural to apply the same rigour to my home cooking, even when I was only making a late-night quesadilla. But for every restaurant-quality outcome, there were a dozen other disappointments. Discouraged when I couldn't source the same heirloom produce or aged balsamic vinegar I cooked with at the restaurant, I'd often give up on cooking entirely and eat toast for dinner instead. Or, after several days spent shopping for, prepping, and cooking a particular meal, I'd be left with a chaotic aftermath that would take days to clean up. I was never quite sure whether the effort was worth the results.

I can now clearly see that it's silly—even destructive—to hold ourselves to professional standards when cooking at home. And yet, it seems completely acceptable to compare a dish you've just cooked to something made in a fully stocked and staffed kitchen by a trained professional with decades of experience.

Professional cooking serves a completely different purpose from home cooking. In restaurant kitchens and glossy magazine spreads, on social media, and even in many cookbooks, food is meant to dazzle and impress. As customers, viewers, and readers, we're being convinced that what's on offer is worth our money, time, and attention. But home cooking is about nourishment, care, and, ideally, enjoyment. To that end, the simple and familiar tends to be not only comforting but indispensable.

Most nights, the food I cook is extraordinarily simple. Often, it's a heap of boiled broccoli, asparagus, or another vegetable, drizzled with olive oil or toasted sesame oil. Sometimes the broccoli tops a bowl of rice along with a fried egg, a bit of tofu, or some fish. When it's too hot to cook, I'll assemble a crunchy, refreshing salad topped with Spanish or Italian olive oil–packed tuna and eat it straight from the mixing bowl. On other nights, I get a pot of rice or lentils going while I figure out the rest. Or I'll cook a pan of chicken thighs to add to soba or tuck into a quesadilla over the coming days.

"There are no new ideas," wrote Audre Lorde. "There are only new ways of making them felt." Most of what I cook on a daily basis may not be particularly innovative. But it feels new because I stock my store cupboard and fridge with condiments, toppings, and herbs that allow for all sorts of possibilities.

Sometimes I know exactly what to reach for—garlic and herb labne, say, to dollop atop a bowl of lentils. Other times, I'll notice the giardiniera (Italian pickled vegetables) in the back corner of the refrigerator and be struck by the desire to make chicken schnitzel so I can turn every bite into a "best bite" by eating it with the right amount of little pickles. Some marinated goat's cheese stirred in at the last moment will turn a simple pasta with broccoli purée into a luxurious, creamy treat. A spoonful of Calabrian chilli crisp adds textural excitement to practically everything I make, regardless of whether the recipe originated in Sichuan, Rome, or Veracruz. And a shower of crispy fried shallots can dress up, well, anything.

    These little flourishes allow me to take the dishes and preparations in my regular rotation in all sorts of different directions. Some take a few minutes to throw together, while others are more of a weekend project. But they all have the power to make what's old feel new again.

garlic and herb labne

MAKES ABOUT 360G

450g container labne or 360g homemade (see page 29)

1 or 2 finely grated garlic cloves

3 to 4 tablespoons finely chopped dill, parsley, coriander, and/or mint in any combination

½ teaspoon (2g) kosher salt

Growing up, I topped everything from rice to soup to spaghetti (gasp!) with a spoonful of natural yogurt. (What can I say? We Persians are a yogurt-loving people.) These days I use labne instead. At any given time you'll find a jar of it—doctored up with chopped fresh herbs and a hint of garlic—in my fridge. It's my all-purpose creamy accompaniment to vegetables, rice, chicken, and fish. Served alongside crudités, potato crisps, crackers, or **Fluffy Pitta Pockets** (page 385), it also makes an excellent dip. Or, smear a generous amount onto a platter before plating grilled or roasted vegetables, fish, or chicken for an elegant upgrade.

• • •

In a medium bowl, combine the labne, garlic, chopped herbs, and salt. Taste and adjust the seasoning, keeping in mind it may take a little while for the salt to dissolve thoroughly. Cover and refrigerate for up to 5 days.

VARIATIONS

To make **Cucumber and Herb Labne:** Add 2 finely diced or coarsely grated **Persian cucumbers**.

•

To make **Shallot and Spring Onion Labne:** Omit the garlic and herbs. Instead, stir 2 finely sliced **spring onions** and 2 tablespoons of **Shallot Oil** (page 55) into the labne and top with a handful of **Crispy Fried Shallots** (page 55).

•

For a touch of brightness, stir in the finely grated zest of 1 **lemon**.

•

For a little heat, stir in a secret amount of **Calabrian Chilli Crisp** (page 56).

green sauce

Herb sauce, salsa verde, chimichurri, zhoug, chutney: Whatever you call it, there's nothing like a good green sauce. This is my take on a legendary version made by the Cheeseboard Collective in Berkeley, California (old-timers may still call it Papi Chulo sauce). A hint of mustard along with an immersion blender or food processor helps emulsify this creamy coriander sauce. Use it on pizza, tacos, rice and noodle bowls, grilled or roasted fish, chicken, and vegetables. Fold some into cabbage slaw or a summer salad of grilled courgette and corn. Or stir a spoonful or two into **Whipped Tahini** (page 63), yogurt, or labne to lend it a spicy, herby, acidic edge.

• • •

In a food processor, combine the coriander, garlic, and chillies (if using) and pulse until finely chopped. Add the sugar, salt, oil, vinegar, lemon juice, and mustard and purée until the herbs are minced and the sauce comes together into a creamy, uniform texture. Taste and adjust with salt and vinegar as needed.

Cover and refrigerate for up to 1 week.

MAKES ABOUT 250ML

- 85g coarsely chopped coriander
- 2 garlic cloves, sliced
- 1 to 2 serrano chillies or **Pickled Thai Chillies** (page 76), stalks removed (optional)
- 1 tablespoon sugar
- 1 teaspoon (3g) kosher salt
- 110g extra-virgin olive oil
- 4 tablespoons **Chilli Vinegar** (page 76) or seasoned rice vinegar
- 3 tablespoons freshly squeezed lemon juice
- 1 tablespoon Dijon mustard

NOTE

To use an immersion blender instead, combine all the ingredients in a wide-mouth jar or similar container and blend until creamy and uniform in texture, then taste and adjust with salt and vinegar as needed.

bright pickled onions

MAKES 1 LITRE

680g red onions (about 3)

400ml apple cider vinegar

120ml water

2 tablespoons (18g) kosher salt

50g sugar

1 bay leaf

1 dried Calabrian chilli

½ teaspoon dried oregano (optional)

A few black peppercorns (optional)

At some point over the last few years, I noticed that I'd been omitting raw onions and shallots from my everyday cooking because I couldn't handle macerating them. Let me be clear: Macerating isn't hard. It's just another word for softening the harsh fire of alliums by soaking them in some acid—usually vinegar or citrus juice—for 15 to 20 minutes. But sometimes, the last thing I can bear is another step—especially one that might delay my meal by even 15 minutes.

Enter this life-changing jar of lightly pickled onions. Now I always have them at hand to add to slaws, salads, tacos, rice bowls, bean and grain salads, and sandwiches. When chopped, they lend a welcome crunch and punch of acid to any salsa, relish, or salad dressing. Use them wherever you need a little extra brightness.

• • •

Use a sharp knife or mandoline to thinly slice the onions and tightly pack them into a sterilised 1-litre canning jar (see **Sterilising Jars,** page 38). Set a canning funnel over the mouth of the jar.

In a nonreactive medium saucepan, combine the vinegar, water, salt, sugar, bay leaf, chilli, oregano (if using), and peppercorns (if using). Bring to a boil over medium-high heat, whisking to encourage the sugar to dissolve. Once the sugar has dissolved, pour the boiling brine into the jar and allow it to cool. Cover and refrigerate overnight before using.

As long as you're very careful to not cross-contaminate the pickles (in other words, use a clean utensil every time you dip into the jar), they'll keep indefinitely in the refrigerator.

crispy fried shallots
(and shallot oil)

These shallots add a burst of sweetness, crunch, and character anywhere they're employed. Shower a handful of them over beetroot and avocado salad, pasta or rice, bean gratin, roasted carrots heaped atop a cloud of **Whipped Tahini** (page 63), or flaky fish poached in tomato sauce. Make sure to save the shallot oil, too—it's liquid gold! Add it to labne, salad dressing, and pasta sauce, or use it to make refried beans and sauté green beans.

• • •

Use a mandoline to slice the shallots into 4mm-thick rings. Line a baking tray with kitchen paper. Set a fine-mesh sieve over a heatproof medium bowl and set aside.

In a small saucepan, combine the shallots and oil. Place over medium-high heat and cook, stirring frequently, until the shallots begin to bubble, 2 to 3 minutes. Reduce the heat to medium, ensuring the shallots remain at a constant bubble (it should look like a rapid simmer). Continue cooking, stirring constantly to ensure that the shallots fry evenly, until they turn a pale golden brown, 18 to 22 minutes longer. (Resist the urge to increase the heat—you might save a few minutes, but the shallots won't cook as evenly.)

Carefully and quickly pour the oil and the shallots through the prepared sieve. (Beware—they will continue to cook and darken as they cool, and if you pull them too late you will end up with acrid, bitter shallots.) Spread the shallots out on the prepared tray. Save the **Shallot Oil** for another use. Season the shallots with salt and allow to cool. They will crisp up as they cool.

Once the shallots and oil have cooled to room temperature, store them separately in airtight containers and refrigerate. Shallots will keep for up to 3 weeks. Oil will keep for up to 6 weeks.

MAKES ABOUT 60G

- 6 large shallots (about 425g), peeled
- 320ml neutral oil
- Kosher salt

calabrian chilli crisp

MAKES ABOUT 875G

- 5 large shallots (about 350g total), peeled
- 3 to 4 heads garlic, peeled
- 7 to 10 dried Anaheim, New Mexico, or California chillies (about 50g total)
- 4 to 6 dried guajillo chillies (about 30g total)
- 25 to 30 dried Calabrian chillies (about 20g total)
- 40g toasted white sesame seeds
- 30g toasted black sesame seeds
- 35g granulated sugar
- 1 tablespoon (4g) Sichuan peppercorns, partially ground in a mortar and pestle
- ¾ teaspoon (2g) freshly ground black pepper
- 5cm piece of cinnamon stick, broken into 2 or 3 pieces
- 27g kosher salt, plus more for sprinkling
- 90g salted dry-roasted peanuts
- 295g neutral oil

recipe and ingredients continue

I first learned about crispy chilli condiments when I tasted Jing Gao's Sichuan chilli crisp in 2018. I was immediately hooked and started trying every version that money could buy. Then, at the height of the pandemic, a care package arrived on my doorstep from pastry chef Carolyn Nugent. Inside was a jar of her homemade chilli crisp, teeming with crunchy shallots, garlic, peanuts, and black and white sesame seeds. It had an ideal balance of spicy, salty, sweet, and savoury. And every spoonful was so packed with crispy goodness that my plate was never overrun with grease. Flavourwise, it lay somewhere on the spectrum between a Chinese chilli crisp and a salsa macha from Veracruz. It was such a revelation that it inspired me to make a chilli crisp of my own.

More than anything, I dreamt of an all-purpose condiment—one that would complement Mexican, Sichuan, Japanese, and Italian flavours equally well. It'd be spicy, but not too spicy, a little tingly, and packed with flavour and crunch. Carolyn gladly shared her recipe with me, mentioning it was a variation on Sohla El-Waylly's version. With their recipes as my touchstones, I began to tweak things.

All along, I'd known I wanted to incorporate Calabrian chillies into my version. Layered atop a base of rich, mild Anaheim and guajillo chillies, the Calabrians round out the symphony of spice. While I enjoyed the tingle in Carolyn's condiment, I cut down on the amount of Sichuan peppercorns in mine. I wanted the tingle to support, rather than overwhelm, the chillies' gentle burn. Then I pumped up the salt and sugar and peanuts and followed Carolyn's suggestion to pack in as many shallots as possible. After about a year of experimentation—and many iterations that were far too tingly, spicy, or garlicky—I finally had a condiment I reached for at every meal.

I now fret any time the jar of chilli crisp in my fridge is less than a quarter full. I put it on toast, on eggs, on pasta and rice. It's salty and savoury and sweet and crunchy and will add a nice, rounded amount of richness to an otherwise lean bowl of brothy soup. This recipe is a weekend project, for sure, but

95g extra-virgin olive oil, plus more as needed

½ teaspoon toasted sesame oil

½ teaspoon (2g) MSG (optional)

it brings me so much daily pleasure that I'd gladly spend twice the amount of time it requires for half the yield.

• • •

Use a mandoline to slice the shallots into 4mm-thick rings. Slice the garlic crossways into very thin chips, about 2mm thick. You should end up with about 200g of shallots and 100g of garlic. Set aside.

Preheat a cast-iron frying pan over medium-high heat. Once it's hot, reduce the heat to low, add 4 or 5 of the dried chillies, and toast, flipping with tongs occasionally, for 1 to 2 minutes per side, until they soften slightly, change colour, and become fragrant. Be careful not to let them burn or smoke. Repeat until you've toasted all the chillies.

Wearing disposable gloves, seed, de-stalk, and remove the ribs from the Anaheim and guajillo chillies. Remove the stalks from the Calabrian chillies but leave the seeds behind. Working in batches, use a spice grinder to grind the chillies down to the size of chilli flakes. Transfer to a large heatproof bowl or pot along with both sesame seeds, the sugar, Sichuan peppercorns, black pepper, cinnamon stick pieces, and salt. Set aside.

If there is any skin on the peanuts, place them on a clean tea towel and gather the ends to form a pouch. Rub the pouch of peanuts between your hands. The friction will encourage the peanuts to shed their skins. Place the peanuts in a colander or sieve and shake off as much skin as possible. Pound the peanuts in a mortar with a pestle until no whole pieces remain. Add to the bowl of chillies and set aside.

Line a baking tray with kitchen paper and set a fine-mesh sieve over a medium saucepan. Set aside.

In a second medium saucepan, combine the shallots and neutral oil and place over medium-high heat. Cook, stirring frequently, until the shallots begin to bubble vigorously, 3 to 4 minutes. Reduce the heat to medium and, with the shallots constantly bubbling, continue frying: The constant bubble is key; the oil temperature will hover right around 100°C until the water in the shallots evaporates, and then it will climb to about 115°C. Stir regularly to ensure even cooking, until the shallots turn pale golden brown, 18 to 22 minutes longer.

Quickly and carefully pour the shallots and the oil into the prepared sieve, draining the oil into the medium saucepan below. (The shallots will continue to cook to a deep golden brown as they cool and crisp up.) Carefully spread out the shallots to cool on the prepared pan and sprinkle lightly with salt. Set aside.

Reset the now-empty sieve over the pan you cooked the shallots in and set aside. Place the saucepan with the strained oil over medium heat and heat to 120°C. Add the garlic (it will bubble a lot) and reduce the heat to medium-low. Cook, stirring, until the garlic begins to take on the faintest hint of colour, 4 to 5 minutes.

Quickly and carefully pour the garlic and the oil into the sieve, draining the oil into the empty saucepan. (The garlic will crisp up and darken slightly as it cools—the final colour should be about that of a lightly toasted sliced almond. It is of the utmost importance that the garlic does not brown any further. If it does, discard the garlic and the oil, which will both taste acrid and ruin the entire chilli crisp, and start with new garlic.) Carefully break up any clumps and spread out the garlic to cool alongside the shallots; sprinkle lightly with salt. Set aside.

Return the oil to 120°C over medium heat and pour it over the bowl of chillies. Stir to combine, then set aside and allow to cool to room temperature.

Add the shallots, garlic, olive oil, sesame oil, and MSG (if using) to the bowl with the chillies. Stir, taste, and adjust the salt as needed. Pour into a 1-litre jar (see **Sterilising Jars,** page 38), top with more olive oil if desired, cover, and refrigerate indefinitely, though it won't last that long!

cardamom ghee

Once, during a brief but stifling heat wave, a pastry chef friend gave me six kilograms of European-style butter she could no longer use. I left the butter on the worktop until I could make some room to put it away. Then I got distracted—for two days.

When I finally noticed, the butter was *very* soft. The only thing I could think to do to extend its shelf life was to turn it into ghee. The South Asian cooking fat is made by browning milk solids to yield a form of clarified butter with slightly caramelised and nutty background notes. What's more, it can be kept for up to 6 months in a cool, dark spot (and even longer in the refrigerator).

I unwrapped the butter and threw it all into a huge pot. As it began simmering, I decided to try adding my jar of cardamom seeds. "Cardamom ghee," I thought. "That sounds good!" While I had no clue how I'd use it, I suspected the ideas would eventually reveal themselves to me. And they did. I drizzled it on popcorn, made baked goods and marshmallow treats with it, tossed winter squash and root vegetables in it before roasting, rubbed it onto couscous, browned chicken in it, added it to my soups by the spoonful, and gave away jars of it to chef friends who delighted me with the creative ways they used it. Later, I learned about niter kibbeh, the spiced ghee essential to the Ethiopian pantry. As happens so often in cooking, I thought I'd stumbled upon a culinary invention, only to learn that traditional cuisines across the world have been doing the same thing, or something similar, for ages.

• • •

Line a fine-mesh sieve with three layers of muslin. Set aside, along with a 1-litre glass jar (see **Sterilising Jars,** page 38).

In a spice grinder or mortar and pestle, break up the cardamom pods to release the seeds. Transfer them to a small bowl, fill the bowl with water, and agitate it. Let it sit for a minute: The seeds will sink and the pods will float. Use a fine-mesh skimmer to skim the pods off the surface of the water and discard. Drain the seeds in the sieve and blot dry on a tea towel, then return them to the spice grinder or

MAKES ABOUT 660G

25g green cardamom pods

912g unsalted butter, preferably grass-fed, organic, and/or European-style (such as Plugrà or Kerrygold)

mortar and pulse or pound for a moment, just long enough to crack the seeds open.

Place the cardamom and butter in a medium casserole over medium heat. As the butter melts, it will separate into whey proteins (the foam at the top), fat (the clarified butter in the middle), and milk solids (at the bottom of the pan). Use a fine-mesh skimmer or a slotted spoon to gently skim the foam away from the top so you can more easily see down to the bottom of the pot.

Once the butter comes to a simmer, reduce the heat to very low. Stirring every minute or so, keep cooking until the milk solids that have settled on the bottom of the pot turn toffee brown. This will take 20 to 25 minutes, but the goal here is to let the cardamom steep for as long as possible without letting the milk solids burn, so try to push it to 40 minutes. But if you sense the milk solids are getting too dark, pull the ghee from the hob and strain it to avoid a burnt flavour.

Remove the pan from the heat and allow the contents to settle for a moment before straining through the muslin into the jar, careful to leave the milk solids behind. Store the ghee in a cool, dark place for up to 6 months or in the refrigerator for up to 1 year.

VARIATION

To make plain **Ghee:** Omit the cardamom and cook the **butter** over low heat, as above, until the milk solids turn toffee brown, 20 to 25 minutes.

While testing a tahini dressing a few years ago, I absent-mindedly left the food processor running after drizzling in the liquid. The tahini broke, as it always does at the beginning, becoming a greasy, gloppy mess. But since I was busy with another task, I left the machine running instead of rushing to stabilise the emulsion with more liquid or ice. When I turned my attention back to the tahini, it'd transformed into something miraculous—fluffy and spreadable, almost marshmallowy. Holding a soft peak as if it were a meringue, it was entirely unlike any tahini sauce I'd ever seen.

Use this tahini fluff in any number of ways: Smear a bed of it on a platter before mounding grilled fish, chicken, or roasted vegetables on top. To make a spur-of-the-moment dip for crudités, sprinkle a bowl of whipped tahini with chopped herbs or nigella seeds. Or spread it liberally onto steamed sweet potatoes, **Fluffy Pitta Pockets** (page 385), or **Olive Oil–Fried Bread** (page 94) for a satisfying afternoon snack.

• • •

In a food processor, combine the tahini, salt, and cumin and pulse until blended. With the food processor running, stream in 5 tablespoons of the lemon juice. As you begin adding the liquid, the tahini will break into an oily mess—don't worry! It'll eventually come back together and begin to lighten in colour and texture as you add more liquid. Stop the machine and taste the tahini. It should be lightly seasoned and gently balanced in acid. If it's not, add the remaining tablespoon of lemon juice and salt as needed. Once you're happy with the way the tahini tastes, continue running the food processor and add a tablespoon of water. Check the texture of the tahini, considering that it'll continue to set up a bit in the refrigerator. If it's delightfully light and fluffy, then you're done. If you want to push it a little, add the remaining water, 1 tablespoon at a time with the machine running. You'll know it's done when it's light and fluffy and can hold a soft peak.

recipe continues

whipped tahini

MAKES ABOUT 200G TO 300G

120g well-stirred tahini

1 teaspoon (3g) kosher salt

1 teaspoon ground cumin

5 to 6 tablespoons freshly squeezed lemon juice

1 tablespoon to 120ml cold water

NOTE

Though I've successfully tested this with several different brands of tahini, some brands simply refuse to whip to a soft peak. I wish I could offer an explanation for this, but if your tahini won't whip, try again with Seed + Mill tahini, which fluffs up perfectly every time.

Cover and refrigerate for up to 3 weeks. If the tahini stiffens or separates a bit when chilled, simply return it to the food processor, add a few ice chips, and pulse until it returns to a smooth, whipped consistency.

VARIATIONS

To make **Whipped Green Tahini:** Add 4 tablespoons finely chopped **soft herbs** and 1 finely grated **garlic** clove to the **tahini** and **salt** when you blend them. Then reduce the **lemon juice** to 3 tablespoons and add 2 tablespoons **Green Coriander Vinegar** (page 233) to the food processor when you blend in the lemon juice. Note that the raw garlic will reduce the shelf life to 5 days.

•

To make **Toasty Whipped Tahini:** Add 1 teaspoon **toasted sesame oil** along with the tahini.

•

To make **Spicy Whipped Tahini:** Add 2 or 3 minced **Pickled Thai Chillies** (page 76) to the **tahini, salt,** and **cumin** when you blend them. Then reduce the **lemon juice** to 3 tablespoons and add 2 tablespoons **Chilli Vinegar** (page 76) to the food processor when you blend in the lemon juice.

a small, good thing: whipped ricotta

Whipping ricotta with salt turns it into an evenly seasoned, lustrous spread or filling. My favourite way to use it is smeared atop a piece of grilled **Sky-High Focaccia** (page 372) or **Olive Oil–Fried Bread** (page 94). Sprinkle it with a little **flaky sea salt**. Or top it with torn **fresh figs** or sliced ripe **peaches** and a drizzle of **aged balsamic vinegar**.

Or fill a shallow bowl with **whipped ricotta** and use the back of a spoon to make a divot in the centre. In the spring, fill the divot with lightly **Stewed Spring Vegetables** (page 207), then top with chopped **parsley**, finely grated **lemon zest** and **flaky salt**. In the summer, fill it with bite-sized chunks of **ripe tomatoes** tossed with **salt** and **olive oil**, then drizzle with **Basil Pesto** (page 67). Serve with a heap of warm **focaccia**.

You can also use whipped ricotta in place of regular ricotta in **Ricotta Custard Pancakes** (page 145), lasagne filling, or **Creamy One-Pot Pasta with Ricotta and Peas** (page 182).

If your ricotta is the consistency of cottage cheese, drain it before whipping: Transfer 450g full-fat-milk ricotta to a mesh strainer bag and use your hands to squeeze out as much whey as possible. (Alternatively, scrape the ricotta into a fine-mesh sieve lined with muslin, cover with a plate, and weight it down with a tin of beans for 30 minutes.) Place the drained ricotta in a food processor, add a large pinch of salt, and blend until smooth, 30 to 60 seconds. Taste and adjust the seasoning as needed.

Cover and refrigerate for up to 1 week.

basil pesto

I've made every imaginable variation of pesto (carrot top, kale, and rocket and walnut, to name a few) using every imaginable tool (a mortar and pestle, food processor, and blender). It may not be the most traditional method, but I keep returning to this streamlined recipe. Generous amounts of pine nuts, Parmesan, and extra-virgin olive oil yield a sauce with a rich, creamy texture and plenty of umami. Carefully chopping the basil at the last second, then adding it to the already-ground base will discourage oxidation and ensure your pesto ends up a vibrant shade of green.

• • •

In a food processor, combine the Parmesan, pine nuts, garlic, and salt and pulse until the nuts break down into a fine meal, about 10 seconds.

Run a knife through the basil to chop it coarsely, then add it to the nut mixture. Pulse a few times to break the basil down a bit, then stop and scrape the bowl with a silicone spatula. Add 120ml of the oil and continue pulsing, stopping and scraping until the pesto begins to come together. Avoid overprocessing the basil, which will cause it to turn brown. When the pesto is thick and uniform, taste it, adjusting the seasoning for salt. Add up to 60ml more oil to achieve your desired consistency—I prefer thicker pesto for pasta or spreading on toast, while thinner pesto is better for drizzling over roasted vegetables and salads.

Cover and refrigerate for up to 3 days or freeze for up to 3 months.

MAKES ABOUT 400G

100g finely grated Parmesan

65g pine nuts, lightly toasted (see page 37) and cooled

1 to 2 garlic cloves, finely grated

½ teaspoon (2g) kosher salt

60g basil leaves

110 to 160g extra-virgin olive oil

mark's giardiniera

My friend Mark Gordon may have been a chef in the San Francisco Bay Area for nearly three decades, but his Midwestern roots run deep. He's taught me about Chicago-style butter crust pizza (so flaky that it melts on the tongue), shown me the "right way" to eat a hot dog (no ketchup!), and given me my first taste of frozen custard (richer and denser than ice cream could ever be). Most important, he shared his recipe for giardiniera—an essential element in Chicago-style Italian beef sandwiches. While you can technically start eating it after a week, Mark says he personally wouldn't touch it for at least a month, and it really starts getting good after a year. The longer it sits, the better—so go ahead and make a double batch!

• • •

To prepare the vegetables, place them in a large bowl and weigh them—you should have about 900g. If you're a little short, add more carrots, celery, and cauliflower to make up the difference. If you have a little more than called for, that's fine!

Toss the vegetables with the salt until combined. Add just enough cold water to submerge the vegetables, then place a plate over them to weight them down. Cover the bowl and set in a cool, unrefrigerated spot for 12 hours or overnight. (If the room temperature is warmer than 21°C, refrigerate the vegetables for the same length of time to prevent spoilage.)

Drain the vegetables and rinse them well.

To make the vinaigrette, in a large bowl, vigorously whisk together all the ingredients except for the bay leaves. Add the drained vegetables.

Place 1 bay leaf into the bottom of each of 2 sterilised wide-mouth 1-litre canning jars (see **Sterilising Jars,** page 38). Use a canning funnel and a large spoon to evenly divide the vegetables and vinaigrette into the jars (it helps to fill

MAKES 2 LITRES

Requires overnight soaking and at least 1 week ageing (3 years if you're Mark)

FOR THE VEGETABLES

- 3 serrano chillies, thinly sliced in rounds
- 2 large celery stalks, finely diced
- 2 carrots, peeled and finely diced
- 2 garlic cloves, thinly sliced
- 2 red peppers, finely diced
- ½ head cauliflower, trimmed into tiny florets
- ½ large fennel bulb, finely diced
- 144g kosher salt

FOR THE VINAIGRETTE

- 360ml white wine vinegar
- 160g extra-virgin olive oil
- 180ml neutral oil
- 140g coarsely chopped Nocellara olives
- 1 tablespoon dried oregano
- 1½ teaspoons coriander seeds, lightly toasted (see page 37)

recipe and ingredients continue

1½ teaspoons fennel seeds, lightly toasted

1 teaspoon chilli flakes

1 teaspoon crushed black peppercorns

½ teaspoon celery seeds

2 bay leaves

each of the jars a little at a time to ensure both jars get even amounts of vegetables and vinaigrette).

Seal the jars with sterilised lids, label the jars with the date, and refrigerate for at least 1 week before serving. As long as you're very careful to not cross-contaminate the pickles (in other words, use a clean utensil every time you dip into the jar), they'll keep indefinitely in the refrigerator.

As kids, when my brothers and I asked our mom for cheese, it was safe to assume we meant feta. All other cheeses required names or descriptors. Feta was always the default.

The problem was that each family member preferred a slightly different type. At my mom's favourite Middle Eastern grocery, she'd order 225g each of mild Danish feta, creamy French feta, and salty, tangy Bulgarian feta to suit everybody's tastes. (I should note that in 2002, Greek feta was given a Protected Designation of Origin; throughout this book, I'll refer to non-Greek salty, brined white cheeses as "feta-style.") She'd bring them home, rinse them, make new brines, and store them in the fridge. Each morning, she'd pull out the cheeses along with a variety of jams, butter, and all sorts of traditional breads she'd squirrelled away, while a samovar of black tea scented with bergamot and rose brewed on the hob.

For years after I moved away, I'd buy a block of cheese on autopilot while grocery shopping. I'm partial to the creamy, rich tang of a French white cheese (my favourite brand, Valbreso, is made exclusively with the milk of Lacaune sheep, high in protein and butterfat—the same used for Roquefort). I also love the saltier, sharper kick of the Bulgarian cheese called sirene (I'm partial to the Zergüt brand). But even when I took the time to make a new brine, like my mom had taught me, I could rarely eat the whole block before it went bad.

When I stopped buying feta-style cheese to avoid wasting it, I regularly found myself wishing I had some to add to a salad, crumble over roasted vegetables, or spread on toast. After I bought a fancy jar of marinated goat's cheese on a whim and used it for weeks to improve my salads and breakfasts, I tried marinating my own feta-style cheese to see if that might extend its lifespan. And it worked! The cheese now remains pristine for weeks, so I can use it at my convenience in salads, frittatas, **Kuku-Kopita** (page 330), or the occasional Persian breakfast.

· · ·

marinated feta

MAKES A 500ML JAR

120ml neutral oil

2 dried chillies, such as chiles de árbol or Calabrian, stemmed and seeded

1 teaspoon black peppercorns

2 bay leaves

8 kumquats, thinly sliced crossways and seeded

1 teaspoon flaky sea salt

225g French feta-style cheese, cut into 1-inch cubes

About 55g extra-virgin olive oil

recipe continues

NOTES

If kumquats aren't available, you can substitute 4 long, wide strips of lemon, orange, or Meyer lemon zest. But whereas I insist you eat the kumquats, I wouldn't recommend trying the same with the zest!

Strain and save the oil—you can repurpose it for a second batch or use it to marinate chicken or lamb, to add in a vinaigrette, or to make **Butter Beans Braised with Artichoke Hearts and Goat's Cheese** (page 162).

In a small frying pan, combine the neutral oil, chillies, and peppercorns and set over medium heat. You're just warming the oil here, so as soon as you see tiny bubbles emerge and envelop the edges of the chillies, reduce the heat to low and cook very gently, stirring, for 90 seconds.

Remove the pan from the heat. In a small heatproof bowl, combine the bay leaves, kumquats, and flaky salt. Pluck the chillies out of the pan and add to the bowl. Carefully pour the oil through a fine-mesh sieve into the bowl (discard the peppercorns, if you like). Allow the oil to cool to room temperature.

Place 1 of the bay leaves in the bottom of a wide-mouth 500ml jar (see **Sterilising Jars,** page 38) or similar container. Pack in one layer of cheese. Spoon the chillies and kumquats over, and add just enough steeped oil to cover everything. Use a chopstick or skewer to gently release any air bubbles that may have formed. Continue layering with the remaining bay leaf, cheese, and marinade. Add the rest of the steeped oil. Add as much olive oil as necessary to completely cover the cheese, again releasing any new air bubbles that may have formed.

Allow the cheese to marinate at room temperature if you'll be eating it within a few hours. Otherwise, cover the jar and refrigerate it overnight.

Keep refrigerated for up to 1 month.

marinated goat's cheese

MAKES A 500ML JAR

120ml neutral oil

   3 garlic cloves (see Note), halved lengthways

   6 sprigs thyme

4 x 7.5cm sprigs rosemary

   ½ teaspoon black peppercorns

   3 long, wide strips lemon zest

   2 bay leaves

   1 teaspoon flaky sea salt

285g goat's cheese, cut into 2.5cm-thick coins

   About 55g extra-virgin olive oil

This classic flavour combination is inspired by the iconic baked goat's cheese at Chez Panisse. In 1981, the upstairs Café began serving warm coins of creamy goat's cheese coated in breadcrumbs alongside a perfectly dressed leafy green salad. The dish, which changed the way Americans think about both salad and goat's cheese, has been on the menu nearly every day since.

As a young cook, I spent Sunday mornings unwrapping dozens of logs of goat's cheese. Then I'd slice them into coins and bathe them in a marinade rich with herbs and spices. So much olive oil was involved in the task that even some twenty-odd years later, just thinking about it makes my hands feel moisturised. For the home kitchen, I've replaced some of the olive oil in the recipe with a neutral oil, such as sunflower or rapeseed, to prevent the marinade from solidifying in the refrigerator. This way, you won't have to wait for the oil and the cheese to return to room temperature before using them, or risk breaking up the cheese as you dig through congealed oil.

• • •

In a small frying pan, combine the neutral oil, garlic, thyme, rosemary, and peppercorns and set over medium heat. You're just warming the oil here, so as soon as you see tiny bubbles emerge and envelop the edges of the garlic, reduce the heat to low and cook very gently, stirring, until the garlic is fragrant, about 90 seconds.

Remove the pan from the heat. In a small heatproof bowl, combine the lemon zest, bay leaves, and flaky salt. Carefully pour in the steeped oil through a fine-mesh sieve (discard the garlic, thyme, rosemary, and peppercorns). Allow the oil to cool to room temperature.

Transfer 1 of the bay leaves and half of the zest to a wide-mouth 500ml jar (see **Sterilising Jars,** page 38) or similar container, then pack in one layer of cheese. Add the remaining bay leaf and lemon zest and just enough steeped oil to cover everything. Use a chopstick or skewer to gently release any air bubbles that may have formed. Continue layering in the remaining cheese. Finally, add the rest of the steeped oil. Add as much olive oil as necessary to completely cover the cheese, again releasing any new air bubbles that may have formed.

Allow the cheese to marinate at room temperature if you'll be eating it within a few hours. Otherwise, cover the jar and refrigerate it overnight.

Keep refrigerated for up to 1 month.

USE

To make a Chez Panisse-style **Baked Goat's Cheese Salad,** carefully remove as many coins of **cheese** from the jar as you'd like to bake. Let the oil drain off the cheese. Pulse 40g **panko breadcrumbs** in a food processor to break them down a bit, then roll the cheese coins in the panko to coat them completely. Bake at 200°C on a parchment-lined baking tray for 5 to 6 minutes, until golden brown and bubbling. Serve alongside a **leafy green salad** dressed with **House Dressing** (page 117).

NOTES

It is of the utmost importance that you discard the garlic to avoid botulism!

Strain and save the oil—you can repurpose it in a second batch or use it in vinaigrettes, marinades, or salads.

pickled thai chillies (and chilli vinegar)

MAKES 1 LITRE

115g fresh red Thai chillies
1 bay leaf
400ml apple cider vinegar
360ml water
48g kosher salt
3 tablespoons sugar

The pickling liquid is just as valuable as the chillies in this recipe. A spoonful or two of the chilli vinegar will add a whisper of heat to sauces, vinaigrettes, roasted vegetables, and salads. But I also love the chillies themselves—they come in handy when I've forgotten, yet again, to buy a fresh jalapeño or serrano chilli for a dish. Both components are now staples in my cooking. I continue to find new uses for them, and I suspect you will, too.

• • •

Trim the dried ends from the chilli stalks and discard any rotten bits. Rinse the chillies and place them in a 1-litre canning jar (see **Sterilising Jars,** page 38) along with the bay leaf. Set a canning funnel over the mouth of the jar.

In a nonreactive medium saucepan, combine the vinegar, water, salt, and sugar and bring to a boil over medium-high heat, whisking to encourage the sugar to dissolve. Once the sugar has dissolved, pour the boiling brine over the chillies in the jar and allow to cool. Cover and refrigerate overnight before using.

As long as you're very careful to not cross-contaminate the jar of chillies (i.e., always use a clean utensil and don't double-dip!), they will keep indefinitely in the refrigerator.

preserved meyer lemon paste

I'm a sucker for any recipe where time transforms ingredients into something greater than the sum of their parts, so it makes sense that I enjoy preserving Meyer lemons. But I wasn't very good about using them up until my friend Chris Crawford gave me a jar of preserved lemon purée and told me to use it anywhere I'd use lemon juice or zest. Before that, I'd only ever thought to add preserved lemons to North African dishes or the occasional vinaigrette. I did as Chris instructed and was surprised by how reliably the paste highlighted the flavours of every dish.

When I asked Chris—the fermentation genius behind the Tart vinegar company—for the secret to her impeccably balanced paste, she responded simply, "I seed the lemons before I salt them." Of course! She explained that discarding the seeds yields multiple benefits: First, it streamlines the process, yielding lemons that are ready to purée without any fuss once they're preserved. But even more important, getting rid of the seeds eliminates the primary source of bitterness in a Meyer lemon. The final paste is savoury, slightly sweet, and funky—but never bitter. Over time, I've taken to slipping a few slices of fresh turmeric root into the jar to impart a marvellous marigold hue to the finished purée.

Stir a spoonful of this bright yellow paste into a chicken or lamb braise, swirl it into **Whipped Tahini** (page 63) or **Garlic and Herb Labne** (page 48), and use it to marinate chicken or fish before grilling. Add it to tuna salad, chicken salad, **Marinated Gigante Beans** (page 161), and **Whipped Baba Ghanoush** (page 100). Or sneak a tiny bit into mashed avocado, **Creamy Lemon-Miso Dressing** (page 122), or **Creamy Oregano Dressing** (page 125). Use it in any dish where you'd like to add a bit of salt, funk, umami, and floral acidity from Meyer lemon.

• • •

MAKES ABOUT 1 LITRE

- 10 Meyer lemons, preferably organic and unwaxed, washed
- Kosher salt
- 2.5cm piece fresh turmeric root, peeled and thinly sliced (optional)

recipe continues

Halve 8 of the lemons crossways and use the tip of a paring knife to remove the seeds (the remaining lemons will be for juicing). Slice into each lemon half from the cut side towards the end, leaving the two pieces connected by about 1.25cm of fruit.

Working over a bowl to catch run-off, rub a generous amount of kosher salt (about 2 teaspoons/6g per lemon half) over all of the exposed lemon flesh, then reshape the lemon halves.

Reserving the bowl of excess salt and juice, tightly pack the lemons into a sterilised wide-mouth 1-litre glass jar (see **Sterilising Jars,** page 38), breaking them apart as needed to fit them all in. If using turmeric, layer slices in as you go.

Squeeze the juice of 1 lemon into the reserved bowl of salt and top the jar off with the salty juice. Use a chopstick to remove air bubbles from between the lemons, gently tap the jar on the counter to let the juice settle, and add more lemon juice if needed to ensure the lemons are submerged, leaving 1.25cm of space at the top of the jar. Seal the jar with a sterilised lid (if using a metal lid, wrap it with plastic wrap to prevent corrosion).

Leave the jar at cool room temperature out of direct sunlight, shaking the jar daily and checking that the lemons remain submerged. The lemons are ready when the rinds are tender, about 3 weeks in moderate climates (in a cool climate this can take up to 1 month, while in a warm climate the lemons may be ready in about 1 week).

Reserving the brine, transfer the lemons and turmeric to a blender or food processor. Pulse to blend, adding a splash of brine if needed to encourage things along. When the lemons have mostly broken down, taste the paste and, if desired, add some or all of the brine to taste (otherwise, you can save the brine in a separate jar). Continue blending to achieve your desired texture—I prefer a smooth purée and usually end up using all of the brine. Transfer to a sterilised jar, cover with a sterilised lid, and refrigerate for up to 1 year, as long as you're very careful to not cross-contaminate (i.e., always use a clean utensil and don't double-dip!).

USES

To make **Spicy Meyer Lemon Relish:** In a small bowl, stir together 4 tablespoons **Preserved Meyer Lemon Paste**, 55g **extra-virgin olive oil**, 1 tablespoon finely chopped **coriander** leaves, 2 teaspoons finely grated fresh **ginger**, 1 tablespoon **maple or light agave syrup**, and 2 to 3 minced **Pickled Thai Chillies** (page 76). Taste and adjust the seasoning as needed. Spoon the relish over fish, roasted or braised chicken, or a platter of "nearly burnt" vegetables (see roasting vegetables, page 196) to add some freshness and zing.

•

For a refreshing **Salty Lemon Soda,** stir a spoonful of **Preserved Meyer Lemon Paste** into a large glass of chilled **sparkling water**. Sweeten with **agave syrup** to taste and serve over ice.

small gestures of hospitality

Until recently, I thought being a good host meant neurotically planning, buying, and preparing everything myself. I thought generosity meant taking care of it all, then cleaning up afterwards so that guests could feel completely at ease. Anytime anyone asked why I wouldn't sit still and enjoy my own party, I'd say, "I'm a cook. I'm happier in the kitchen than at the table."

Then, a ten-year-old showed me I've been missing the point all along.

I love making birthdays special for the kids in my life. I'll ask them to describe the birthday menu of their dreams, then do my best to bring their vision to life. When my buddy Orion turned ten, they asked for fish tacos and churros. "No biggie," I figured, and proceeded to plan the meal.

By the time their birthday arrived, the guest list had doubled from ten to twenty people. The increase didn't worry me, but it did mean there'd be twice as much fish to fry. So, once I was about halfway through cooking, I insisted that everyone begin eating—no one wants to eat cold fried fish, after all. As I kept frying, Orion's mom came in from the garden to report that they had piled a plate high with slaw, rice, beans, and tacos. Taking a bite of their first taco, Orion sighed with great satisfaction. Then a look of concern crossed their face. "Wait," they asked, scanning the table, "where's Samin?" Hearing this as I stood over a pot of bubbling oil, my heart fell.

It struck me that Orion hadn't asked for fish tacos and churros. They'd asked to eat fish tacos and churros with me and their entire chosen family. With a single comment, Orion upended my entire understanding of generosity. The act of cooking for someone is only a small part of a larger exchange—one of attention, which, as Simone Weil put it, "is the rarest and purest form of generosity." By focusing solely on cooking, I'd deprived myself and my guests of the opportunity to attend to one another. And isn't that ultimately what spending time together is all about?

I've been trying to put what I learned from Orion that day into practice. I spend less energy trying to do everything for everyone. Instead, I rely on a handful of recipes I think of as small, welcoming gestures and focus on spending quality time outside the kitchen with the people I love. Since I'm more present and less frazzled, my guests are more relaxed, too. These recipes—including velvety whipped baba ghanoush, devilled eggs spiked with tangy crème fraîche, and my favourite way to make popcorn—are warm and inviting. They're also uncomplicated enough to get you out of the kitchen quickly, so you can spend more of your precious time with your guests.

warm nocellara olives

Meaty, buttery, and mild, Nocellara olives—sometimes called Castelvetrano—are a joy to eat and an ideal way to begin any meal. When marinating these plump, gently brined olives, less is more. All they need is a quick rinse, a drizzle of oil, an aromatic or two, and a moment on the stove.

• • •

Place the olives in a large bowl and cover with warm water. Use your hands to swirl them around, then drain and rinse. Let the olives drain in a colander in the sink while you heat the pan.

Set a medium frying pan over medium-low heat and add the oil and garlic. When the garlic grows aromatic and begins to sizzle, add the lemon zest and chilli (if using). Add the olives and swirl to coat. Cook, swirling regularly, until the olives are warm and fragrant, 4 to 5 minutes. (At this point, you can leave the olives out at room temperature for up to 3 hours before serving.)

Serve warm, alongside a smaller bowl for discarding stones.

Cover and refrigerate any leftovers for up to 1 week. Bring to room temperature or reheat gently before serving.

MAKES ABOUT 125G

- 115g unpitted Nocellara (Castelvetrano) olives, drained
- 1 tablespoon extra-virgin olive oil
- 1 garlic clove, smashed and peeled
- 1 long, wide strip lemon zest or 1 teaspoon **Preserved Meyer Lemon Paste** (page 79)
- 1 dried Calabrian chilli (optional)

forever popcorn

MAKES ABOUT 65G
(WHICH IS ABOUT 1 SERVING IF YOU'RE ME)

30g nutritional yeast

1½ teaspoons (5g) kosher salt

1 tablespoon sunflower, safflower, grapeseed, or rapeseed oil

1 tablespoon coconut oil

55g popcorn kernels

Anyone who's ever had a taste of Bjorn Qorn knows it's the most utterly perfect popcorn you can buy. To my mind, there is no finer snack. And yet, anytime I scrutinised the packaging, looking for the secret to what makes it so utterly exceptional, I came away befuddled! Only four ingredients are listed! Popcorn, oil, nutritional yeast, and salt! "Why," one wonders to herself, "when I make popcorn with the exact same ingredients, do I end up with a pile of greasy, underseasoned Styrofoam atop another greasy pile of salted nutritional yeast flakes?"

The answer is threefold. Part one is so obvious it's upsetting: You must grind the nutritional yeast and salt to a fine powder in a spice grinder. The second trick is simply this: You must use a high-heat oil (I like a combination of sunflower and coconut). This will simultaneously produce a very crisp exterior on the popcorn and offer enough "glue" for the yeast-and-salt seasoning to adhere to when tossing. The third, and final, secret is: Shake, shake, shake until you're caught in a cloud of yeast. I suspect you'll be so thrilled with the result that this will become, as it has for me, the only popcorn you ever want to make, forever and ever.

• • •

Use a spice grinder or mortar and pestle to grind the nutritional yeast and salt into a fine powder. Sprinkle 2 tablespoons of the mixture evenly into a large bowl and set aside, along with another large bowl.

If, like me, you are popcorn-obsessed enough to own a hand-cranked popcorn popper, use that. Otherwise, wrap the lid of a large casserole with a clean tea towel (this will trap the steam and keep it from dripping back down into the popcorn and making it soggy).

Add both oils and a few kernels to the pot and set over medium-high heat. Cover and cook until the kernels pop.

recipe continues

Add the remaining kernels, cover, and cook. Either crank the handle or shimmy and shake the pot until the popping subsides (wear potholders or use clean tea towels to hold the pot—it will get HOT!).

Immediately uncover the pot and pour the popcorn into the prepared bowl. Sprinkle with another tablespoon of the yeast mixture. Invert the second bowl and use it to cover the bowl of popcorn. Holding the bowls together, shake vigorously to combine. Taste and adjust the seasoning with more salt and nutritional yeast as desired. Serve immediately. Store any remaining ground yeast mixture in an airtight container.

a small, good thing: kid crudités

I've always been far more likely to eat raw vegetables if someone else takes the time to peel and cut them up. Even as a kid, I never thought to make carrot or celery sticks, but anytime my Aunt Leyla prepared a plate of them I'd hungrily help myself. And while I now love few things more than assembling a stunning platter of crudités for my guests, it rarely occurs to me to do the same for myself.

Then, one night I watched my friend Aya cut up **carrot sticks and cucumber spears** for her kiddos. Instead of serving the vegetables unadorned, she piled them into a bowl and lightly drizzled them with **seasoned rice vinegar** and a bit of **flaky salt**. When I saw how enthusiastically the kids reached for them, I tried some for myself. The sweet-tart vinegar and salt functioned as a kind of lazy pickle brine for the vegetables. The salt elevated and balanced the innate flavours of the crudités, while the acid gave them a gentle mouthwatering pucker. They were irresistible, and I joined the kids in gobbling them up.

This has since become my favourite way to serve crudités—even just for myself. To make them extra refreshing, I like to chill the vegetables in the fridge for 15 minutes after dressing them with a few drops of vinegar, then season with flaky salt to serve.

miso and labne onion dip

A few small tweaks to the classic sour cream and onion number yield this truly exceptional dip. A little miso paste and vinegar take caramelised onions—already rich in character—to a whole new level. The salt, sweetness, umami, and acid balance out the onions' earthiness and dark caramel notes. Labne offers a welcome tangy counterpoint to the robustly flavourful onion mixture without sacrificing creaminess. If you're anything like me, you'll want to hoard this dip at your end of the table. And though it's best served with potato crisps, this dip also works beautifully as a sandwich spread or alongside steak, roast chicken, and roasted vegetables.

• • •

Set a large frying pan over medium heat. Once it's hot, add the oil. When it shimmers, add the onions and season with salt. Cook, stirring the onions and scraping the pan regularly, until the onions begin to brown. After about 20 minutes, once the onions have cooked off most of their water, bare spots in the pan might cause onions to start to stick and burn. Add a splash of water as needed to loosen any bits that are cooked on. As long as they're not burnt, you can scrape and stir them back into the onions. If they are burnt, don't add any water and instead scrape everything but the blackened bits into a new pan and continue cooking—you may also need to add another tablespoon or so of oil.

Continue cooking and scraping regularly until the onions are very well caramelised, 45 to 55 minutes total. Turn off the heat and stir in the miso and vinegar. Taste and adjust the seasoning with salt and vinegar as needed.

Allow the onions to cool, then chop them finely. Transfer the onions to a large bowl and add the labne, onion powder, chives, and a few grinds of pepper. Taste and adjust the seasoning with salt. Add sugar if needed to balance out the salt and vinegar. Transfer to a serving bowl and garnish with more chives.

Serve with potato crisps, warm pitta, crudités, or crackers.

Cover and refrigerate leftovers for up to 1 week.

MAKES ABOUT 625G

55g extra-virgin olive oil, plus more as needed

2 brown onions, thinly sliced

Kosher salt

2 tablespoons white miso

1 tablespoon red wine vinegar or aged sherry vinegar

335g labne

1½ teaspoons onion powder

3 tablespoons minced chives, plus more for garnish

Freshly ground black pepper

1 teaspoon sugar (optional)

Potato crisps, **Fluffy Pitta Pockets** (page 385), crudités, or crackers, for serving

a small, good thing: olive oil–fried bread

To perform a bit of everyday alchemy, fry a slice of **farmhouse-style bread** in an obscene amount of **extra-virgin olive oil**. What you'll end up with isn't toast. It's more like a warm, golden crouton—crunchy on the surface, chewy on the inside, and rich with olive oil flavour.

Set a pan over medium-high heat—cast iron works especially well. Then add enough olive oil to coat the bottom generously—don't skimp! Lay in a slice or more of bread, leaving ample room between pieces. Once the first side is well coated with oil, flip it and add more oil as needed to saturate the second side. Cook over medium-high heat, rotating and tending to the bread to ensure even browning. After 2 to 3 minutes, when the bread is browned, flip it and repeat on the other side.

Fried bread makes an excellent snack on its own, sprinkled with a bit of **flaky salt**. But it's also an ideal blank slate for all manner of toasts and salads-on-toast. To make an **Avocado Toast,** mash ripe **avocado** together with **Preserved Meyer Lemon Paste** (page 79), minced **Pickled Thai Chillies** (page 76), and chopped **soft herbs**. Smear onto the fried bread and sprinkle with flaky salt.

Use fried bread as a canvas for **Whipped Baba Ghanoush** (page 100) or **Whipped Ricotta** (page 66). Simply smear on your chosen spread and top with flaky salt and a drizzle of good olive oil.

For a very satisfying breakfast, smear fried bread with **Rapini Pesto** (page 258) and top with a **fried egg**. Spread **Marinated Goat's Cheese** (page 74) onto a slice and top it with **Medjool dates** fried in olive oil. Or, smear fried bread with **Whipped Tahini** (page 63), flaky salt, and a drizzle of **honey**.

And for a variation on a classic **Roast Chicken with Bread Salad,** lay several slices of fried bread onto a platter, then spoon pan drippings from a **roast chicken** over them, along with a drizzle of **House Dressing** (page 117). Pile pieces of roast chicken on top, along with a handful or two of lightly dressed **radicchio or rocket**, and serve.

crème fraîche devilled eggs

Amalia Mariño, one of the chef friends I call my Culinary Brain Trust, makes the best devilled eggs I've ever had—perfectly balanced in both flavour and texture. To get her filling so airy and light, she insists on passing the yolks through a tamis, the type of very-fine-mesh drum sieve found in professional kitchens. I don't have a tamis—and I'm guessing you don't either—so I'm here to assure you that a civilian-style fine-mesh sieve will yield the same snowy yolks that make her filling so exquisitely smooth. Her other secret: substituting crème fraîche for most of the mayonnaise. It lends the rich filling a welcome tang that makes these eggs impossible to resist.

• • •

Prepare a bowl of ice water for the eggs and set aside.

Bring a medium pot of water to a boil. Using a slotted spoon or spider, gently lower the eggs into the pot to prevent breaking. Reduce the heat to keep the pot at a vigorous simmer and cook for 10 minutes (set a timer!). Drain and rattle the eggs around the pan to crack the shells, then transfer them to the bowl of ice water to chill completely.

Peel the chilled eggs, halve them crossways, and place the yolks in a fine-mesh sieve set over a medium bowl. Set the whites aside.

Use a silicone spatula to press the yolks through the sieve. Add the crème fraîche, mayonnaise, mustard, and paprika and mix vigorously to combine. If needed, add up to 1 teaspoon of ice water to thin the filling. Taste and adjust the seasoning with kosher salt. Transfer the filling to a piping bag or plastic zip-lock bag with a corner removed.

To fill the egg whites, trim a thin slice off the bottom of each egg half to create a stable base, lay them out on a parchment-lined tray, and season lightly with kosher salt. Pipe or spoon a generous mound of filling into each egg white, then shower with za'atar, flaky salt, and dill. Transfer to a platter and serve.

MAKES 16 EGG HALVES

- 8 medium eggs, straight from the fridge
- 4 tablespoons crème fraîche
- 2 tablespoons mayonnaise
- 1 teaspoon Dijon mustard
- Pinch of paprika
- 1 teaspoon ice water
- Kosher salt
- Za'atar, for garnish
- Flaky sea salt, for garnish
- Finely chopped dill, for garnish

roasted almonds with fried sage

MAKES ABOUT 225G

Extra-virgin olive oil
1½ teaspoons boiling water
¾ teaspoon (2g) kosher salt
220g raw whole almonds
6 to 8 sage leaves
Pinch of chilli flakes or cayenne pepper (optional)
Flaky salt

Sizzling sage in olive oil not only crisps up the leaves, it also infuses the oil with their unmistakable, woody fragrance. Toss just-roasted almonds with some of each to work in multiple facets of sage flavour. Add a little chilli and flaky salt and you'll get the consummate bar snack—perfect for enjoying with a glass of wine, beer, or **Vin d'Orange** (page 106).

• • •

Adjust an oven rack to the centre position and preheat to 190°C. Lightly coat a baking tray with oil.

In a medium bowl, stir the water and kosher salt together to dissolve. Add the almonds and toss to coat, then spread them out in a single layer on the prepared tray. (Hold on to the bowl.)

Roast, stirring the nuts and rotating the tray front to back every 5 minutes, until the almonds are fragrant, toasted, and golden throughout, about 15 minutes.

Meanwhile, line a plate with kitchen paper and set near the hob. Set a very small frying pan over medium heat and add enough oil to reach a depth of 6mm. When the oil shimmers, add a sage leaf to test the temperature—when it sizzles, add the remaining sage leaves to fry. After about 30 seconds, as soon as the bubbles subside, remove the sage from the oil with a slotted spoon and spread out on the kitchen paper to cool and crisp up. Season the sage with kosher salt and turn off the heat.

Wipe the bowl dry and add 1 tablespoon of the sage oil and the chilli flakes (if using).

As soon as the nuts are toasted, pour them into the bowl with the sage oil and toss, adding a little more oil if needed to coat them evenly (save and reuse remaining oil for **Olive Oil–Fried Bread,** page 94). While the nuts are still hot, taste and adjust the seasoning with flaky salt and chilli flakes as desired.

When the nuts are no longer hot, crumble in the sage and toss to distribute. Serve warm or at room temperature.

Store roasted nuts in an airtight container for up to 5 days.

whipped baba ghanoush

MAKES ABOUT 500G

900g globe aubergines (about 2)

120g well-stirred tahini

1 tablespoon **Chilli Vinegar** (page 76) or seasoned rice vinegar

1 or 2 **Pickled Thai Chillies** (page 76) or fresh serrano chillies, stemmed and chopped

1½ teaspoons (5g) kosher salt

3 to 4 tablespoons freshly squeezed lemon juice

I've spent some time over the last few years really getting to know tahini. I thought we understood each other intimately, but coming to learn its capacity to hold water and change from a paste into a cloudlike butter when whipped in the food processor was a revelation. That led, of course, to **Whipped Tahini** (page 63), one of my favourite condiments to keep around for daily use. But then I started to wonder if I could take advantage of tahini's remarkable capacity for textural transformation when making baba ghanoush. And what if I drained every bit of liquid from the aubergine before adding it to the tahini—might that allow the pectin left behind to give the dip a little shape once it sets? As it turns out, the answer to both musings is yes. Gone is any trace of the sliminess that puts some people off aubergines. Serve this dip with **Fluffy Pitta Pockets** (page 385), cucumbers, or crackers. Or use it as a sandwich spread or a base for a simple tomato and herb salad.

...

If you have a gas hob, cook the aubergines directly on the rings. Line the area around the rings with aluminium foil for easier clean up. Turn the extraction fan on high, or open the kitchen windows (this is the kind of thing that always sets off my smoke alarm). Use tongs to place the aubergines on the rings over medium-high heat and roast, turning every 3 minutes or so. Cook until the flesh is completely tender and no longer spongy and the skin is thoroughly blackened, 12 to 15 minutes. You can also use this method on a gas barbecue grill, or set the aubergines directly in a bed of live coals, which will yield the smokiest, most delicious result of all.

If you don't have a gas hob, heat the grill. Place the aubergines on a foil-lined baking tray and set the tray in the oven so that the aubergines are about 5cm from the heat source. Allow the skins to char and split, turning with tongs until the entire surface is blackened and the aubergines completely deflate, 15 to 25 minutes, depending on your grill.

recipe continues

Allow the cooked aubergines to cool in a single layer, then peel away the skin and scoop the flesh into a fine-mesh sieve set over a bowl. Avoid the charred skin as much as possible, but a little left behind is no big deal. Set a small plate over the aubergine flesh and weight it down with a tin of tomatoes or beans. Let the flesh drain for at least 20 minutes.

Meanwhile, in a food processor, combine the tahini, vinegar, pickled chillies, salt, and 3 tablespoons of the lemon juice and blend until puréed.

When the aubergines are well drained and feels like a dense mass of pulp, add them to the tahini mixture and blend until the mixture comes together into a light, airy purée. It will look and taste like a heavenly whipped cloud of aubergine. Taste and adjust the seasoning with salt and lemon juice as needed.

Though you can start eating it right away, this dip is best after 30 to 60 minutes in the refrigerator.

Cover and refrigerate leftovers for up to 5 days.

sekanjebin (sweet and sour mint shrub)

When it came to thirst-quenching summer drinks, my mom eschewed the Tang and Kool-Aid I lusted after as a kid. Instead, she made us sharbats—refreshing Persian drinks made with cordial-style syrups. Sometimes, she'd use the syrup left over from a jar of preserved sour cherries to make sweet-tart sharbat-e albaloo. And whenever the sharp, heady aroma of boiling vinegar weaved its way through the house, I knew the best sharbat of all wasn't far behind. Soon, we'd all be drinking sekanjebin from tall glasses filled with the sweet, mint-laced shrub, diced cucumbers, and ice water.

These days, I always keep a jar of sekanjebin syrup in the fridge. When it's hot, I'll treat myself to a glass. When heading out on a hike or for a day at the beach, I'll fill my water bottle with it. And anytime friends drop by, I'll make a pitcher and offer the adults a little splash of tequila, Pimm's, or gin, because, as it turns out, sekanjebin makes a great cocktail, too.

• • •

MAKES ABOUT 480ML SYRUP (ENOUGH FOR ABOUT 16 DRINKS)

FOR THE SHRUB

720ml water

400g sugar

240ml plus 2 tablespoons white wine vinegar

Large pinch of kosher salt

48 mint leaves

FOR SERVING

Finely diced or coarsely grated Persian cucumbers

Ice

Pimm's No. 1 Cup, gin, or tequila blanco (optional)

Cold water or sparkling water

To make the shrub, in a medium saucepan, combine the water and sugar and bring to a boil. Boil uncovered for 10 minutes to dissolve the sugar and reduce the volume a bit.

Add the vinegar and salt and continue boiling until the liquid has reduced by about half and the syrup is bubbling evenly across the surface, another 10 to 12 minutes (the temperature should read about 107°C). Add about three-quarters of the mint leaves, remove from the heat, and allow to cool to room temperature.

Pour the shrub through a fine-mesh sieve into a sterile glass jar. Add the remaining mint leaves, then cover and refrigerate until ready to use.

To serve, place a couple of spoonfuls of diced or grated cucumber into each glass, along with a large ice cube or a couple of smaller ones. Add 2 tablespoons of sekanjebin and 30 to 60ml of liquor, if desired. Stir to dissolve the shrub. Top off with water or sparkling water, taste, and add more shrub to taste. Stir to dissolve added shrub and serve.

Cover and refrigerate shrub for up to 6 months.

vin d'orange

MAKES THREE AND A HALF 750ML BOTTLES

Takes about 6 weeks

- 6 Seville or Bouquet de Fleurs oranges, preferably organic (see Note)
- 1 orange or blood orange
- 1 lemon
- 3 x 750ml bottles crisp, bright white wine or rosé
- 480ml vodka
- 335g sugar
- 1 vanilla pod

FOR SERVING

- Ice
- Twist of orange zest

This Provençal apéritif is traditionally made with the lumpy, seed-riddled sour oranges known as Sevilles, which come into season in peak winter. Marmalade makers around the world prize Seville oranges for their peels, which are particularly rich in aromatic oils. But I prefer to use them in vin d'orange, where those fragrant oils, along with some sugar and a vanilla pod, transform vodka-spiked wine into a subtly bittersweet cocktail. I usually make a double batch so that I can serve it over ice all summer long and still have plenty left to give away for the holidays.

While this recipe isn't complicated, it does take some advance planning. Traditionally vin d'orange steeps for at least forty days, then rests for at least another month after bottling. But all you need to make this stellar apéritif is a few basic ingredients, some patience, and a cool, dark place where you can store the container. Don't bother using the fancy stuff for this project—inexpensive table wine and decent vodka will do just fine. And finally, vin d'orange only improves with time, so let it age for as long as you can bear it. The best vin d'orange I've tasted was from a bottle a friend had squirrelled away and forgotten about for four years!

• • •

Rinse the fruit with warm water, taking care to scrub off any wax that may have been used to seal it. Cut each piece of fruit in half, and then quarter the halves.

Pour the wine, vodka, and sugar into a 6-litre container. Use a small knife to split the vanilla pod lengthways and scrape the seeds from the pod into the container, then add the pod. Stir to dissolve the sugar. Add the fruit, taking care not to jostle it too much—what you want here is maximum exposed surface area of fruit, pith, and skin without releasing juice, since juice will make the wine cloudy.

Place a bowl or small plate atop the fruit to keep it submerged, cover the container, and store in a cool, dark place (such as a cellar or garage). If the ambient temperature

NOTES

Seville oranges are generally available at farmers' markets or specialty produce markets in January and February, depending on your area. If you can't get them in your area, make **Vin de Pamplemousse** instead: Substitute 6 Ruby Red grapefruits for the Seville oranges and, if you like, use tequila blanco instead of vodka.

Bottles, corks, corkers, filters, and other winemaking supplies are available online from Oak Barrel Winecraft.

is warmer than 20°C, then refrigerate the vin d'orange for the same length of time to prevent spoilage. Every few days, give the mixture a stir and a taste. Add a little more sugar if necessary, and pluck out a few pieces of orange if it's already growing too bitter.

Somewhere between 40 and 42 days, when the vin d'orange tastes pleasantly orangey and bitter enough, remove the solids and strain through a triple layer of muslin into bottles, being careful not to pour in the sediment from the bottom of the container. If your batch is especially cloudy and you're feeling patient, try siphoning it out or strain it through a wine filter (see Note).

Bottle and store the vin d'orange in a cool, dry place at room temperature. As time passes, the flavours will mellow and meld. Serve chilled, poured over a couple ice cubes, with a twist of orange—the perfect summer apéritif.

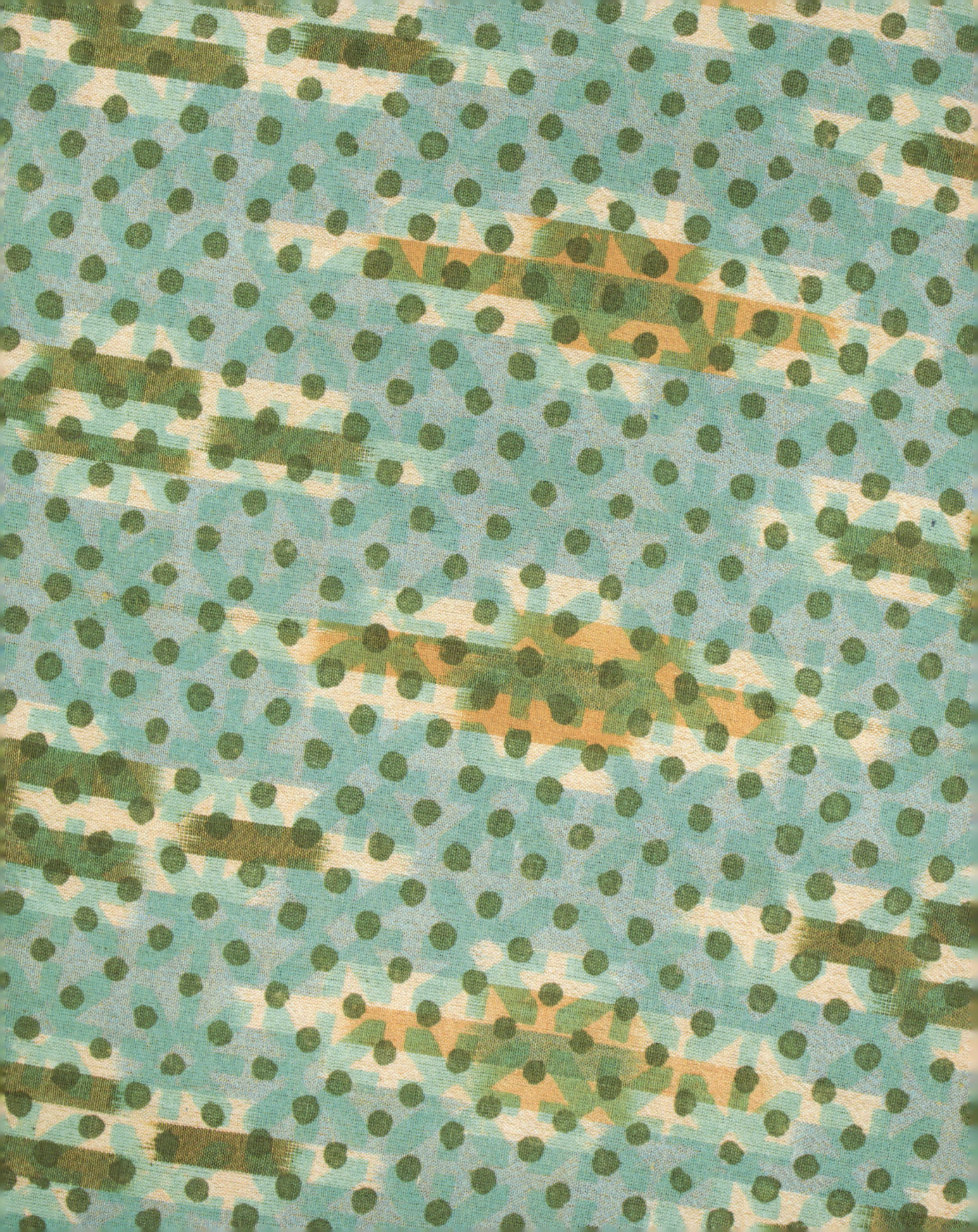

seven versatile dressings
(and three ways to use each)

As a young person, I was extremely salad averse. Eating it always felt like a chore, something my mom said I had to do. At every meal, I happily ate Shirazi salad, a classic Persian side dish of diced cucumbers, tomatoes, and onions dressed with lime juice and olive oil, but I thought of it as a condiment, not a salad. And my mom's only other salad was a romaine heart and sun-dried tomato number with a dressing so tart that it made my jaws cramp.

But in my early days at Chez Panisse, I had a total change of heart. In that kitchen, salad is religion, vinaigrette is gospel. Each day, tiny heads of baby lettuces are trimmed, washed, spun, and carefully laid between tea towels to dry until someone orders a salad. Cooks are taught to detect nuances in various olive oils and vinegars and then layer them to create delicate vinaigrettes.

And of course, day-old dressing is sacrilege.

For years, I held my own salad preparation at home to the standards I was taught at the restaurant: buying only the most perfect, locally grown organic produce (or better yet, growing it myself), washing lettuce daily, and making vinaigrette in one-salad-sized batches. In theory, this meant that every day I'd be enjoying the finest salads in town in the comfort of my own home.

But in practice it meant that I almost never ate salad. I set up so many hurdles for myself that, rather than violate my own impossible standards and use, say, bagged hearts of romaine or a batch of dressing I'd made a few days earlier, I'd give up on salad altogether and just eat a quesadilla or some Annie's mac and cheese. I knew it was time to rethink my approach when I realised I'd been thinking of salad as a special-occasion food.

It's taken me years, but I've finally stopped holding myself to restaurant standards at home. Yes, I still garden and shop at the farmers' market, but not because I feel like I have to, and not exclusively. I also love bagged romaine hearts and always keep Persian cucumbers on hand, no matter the season. Most important, I make sure I've got some truly delicious dressing made at all times.

The recipes in this chapter fit the bill. I started developing them because in recent years I've found that, as much as I love rich, creamy dressings, I just can't handle as much dairy or mayonnaise as I used to. So, using a variety of ingredients, including aquafaba, miso, mustard, and tahini, I've created a roster of all-purpose dressings that are unctuous, mostly plant-based, and easy to digest. I've also included an MVP vinaigrette for the occasions when you want something a little lighter to coat your tiny, perfect lettuces.

Now, at any given time, I've got a jar or two of dressing on hand so I can pack myself a fresh, crisp salad to brighten up a day at the office, turn a baking tray of roasted vegetables into a gorgeous side dish, or make a huge chopped salad for dinner with ease. I'm including three serving suggestions for each dressing, but I'm sure you'll continue finding new ways to deploy each one.

a bit about aquafaba

The thing that initially piqued my curiosity about aquafaba was its Latin name. (What can I say? I'm a nerd—always have been, always will be.) In Latin, *aqua* is "water" and *faba* is "bean." Aquafaba, then, is bean-cooking liquid, and even though it sounds like an ancient term, it's not. Some other Latin-loving nerds coined the term in 2015.

    The proteins and starches in aquafaba make it an uncannily accurate substitute for egg whites. I've seen it used to make extraordinary meringues, mousses, brownies, and all manner of baked goods. And thanks to its ability to thicken sauces and dressings, aquafaba has allowed me to untangle creaminess from richness in my cooking. As an added benefit for those with dietary restrictions, most of my recipes that contain aquafaba are egg-free or completely plant-based.

    While any bean-cooking broth (or liquid from a tin of beans) will work fine, to keep the colour and flavour neutral I prefer using chickpea or white-bean cooking liquid. When testing the recipes for this book, I used various brands of tinned, as well as home-cooked, chickpeas—they all work fine. To use the liquid from beans or chickpeas you've cooked yourself, make sure it's the consistency of egg whites when it's at room temperature. If it's too thin, reduce it a bit, let it cool, and see how it feels (it should be sort of . . . snotty). And finally, for reference, one tin of chickpeas contains about 180ml of aquafaba.

house dressing

This perfect vinaigrette recipe comes from Via Carota, the charming West Village restaurant in New York City run by Jody Williams and Rita Sodi. Since I first wrote about it in 2019 in *The New York Times Magazine,* it's become indispensable not only for me but also for my entire Culinary Brain Trust, who now simply call it House Dressing.

The warm water in the recipe might surprise you. "We add warm water to make it more palatable," Jody told me. "Pure vinegar is just too strong—it assaults the taste buds. We want a salad dressing so savoury and delicious that you can eat spoonfuls of it. We want you to be able to drink it!" I recommend drizzling this dressing liberally over everything from boiled asparagus to farro salad to steak and fish and roast chicken. And if you don't have both types of mustard on hand, just use twice as much of whichever you do have.

• • •

Place the shallot in a fine-mesh sieve and quickly rinse with cold water. Allow to drain, place in a medium bowl, add the vinegar and warm water, and let the shallot mixture sit for 2 minutes.

Whisk in the oil, honey, both mustards, thyme, garlic, salt, and pepper. Taste and adjust the salt and vinegar as needed.

Cover and refrigerate remaining dressing for up to 1 week.

MAKES 360ML

- 1 large shallot, very finely diced
- 3 tablespoons plus 1 teaspoon aged sherry vinegar
- 1 tablespoon warm water
- 215g extra-virgin olive oil
- 1½ teaspoons honey
- 1½ teaspoons Dijon mustard
- 1½ teaspoons whole-grain mustard
- 2 sprigs thyme, leaves picked and finely chopped (about ½ teaspoon)
- 1 garlic clove, finely grated
- 1 teaspoon (3g) kosher salt
- ½ teaspoon freshly ground black pepper

THREE WAYS TO USE HOUSE DRESSING

1 To make a **Crunchy and Refreshing Green Salad,** toss **Little Gems** (or your favourite variety of baby lettuces), thinly shaved **fennel**, tender **dill fronds**, whole **coriander and parsley** leaves, 2.5cm pieces of **chives**, and dressing. Season with **salt** and freshly ground **black pepper**. Delicately mound onto a serving platter and serve immediately.

2 Make an **Autumn Chicory Salad:** Toss **radicchio** torn into bite-sized pieces, crumbled **Parmesan or Roquefort**, toasted **walnuts or pecans**, and sliced seasonal fruit—**pears, persimmons, or apples**—with this dressing. Season with **salt** and **pepper** to taste and serve immediately.

3 Generously drizzle the dressing over a platter of just-boiled **broccoli, tenderstem broccoli, carrots, cauliflower, or string beans**. Garnish with **flaky salt** and serve immediately.

creamy sesame-ginger dressing

This is the recipe that inspired this book. And my entire palate still puckers with pleasure every time I make it. After I've balanced and adjusted the flavours and dipped a bit of lettuce or cabbage into the dressing for a final taste, I always marvel at the way it manages to take every element—salt, acid, umami, fiery ginger, garlic, and spice—right to the edge . . . without stepping over.

. . .

In a measuring jug or wide-mouth jar, combine the lemon juice, vinegar, miso, honey, sesame oil, garlic, ginger, and chilli and use an immersion blender to purée until smooth. With the immersion blender running, add the neutral oil in a thin stream. (Alternatively, you can use a countertop blender.) Taste and adjust with salt, lemon juice, and vinegar as needed.

Cover and refrigerate remaining dressing for up to 1 week.

MAKES 360ML

- 4 tablespoons freshly squeezed lemon juice
- 4 tablespoons seasoned rice vinegar
- 5 tablespoons white miso
- 2 tablespoons honey
- 2 teaspoons toasted sesame oil
- 6 garlic cloves, thinly sliced
- 7.5cm piece fresh ginger, peeled and thinly sliced
- 1 **Pickled Thai Chilli** (page 76) or fresh jalapeño, stalk removed (seeded if desired) and sliced
- 120ml neutral oil
- Kosher salt

good things come in threes

THREE WAYS TO USE CREAMY SESAME-GINGER DRESSING

1 To make a **Crunchy Cabbage Slaw,** combine ½ head thinly sliced **cabbage**, 2 coarsely grated **carrots**, 4 tablespoons finely chopped **coriander**, 2 **spring onions** sliced thinly on a sharp bias, 3 tablespoons **toasted sesame seeds**, and 150g **salted roasted peanuts** in a large bowl. Toss with a generous amount of dressing. Taste and adjust the seasoning. Chill for 30 minutes before serving.

2 Toss just-boiled **string beans, sugar snap peas, asparagus, broccoli,** or **tenderstem broccoli** with a light drizzle of **toasted sesame oil** and **flaky salt**. When cool, toss with the dressing. Taste and adjust the seasoning, then transfer to a platter and garnish with toasted **sliced almonds**.

3 Make a **Brown Rice Bowl** topped with **Mara's Tofu** (page 187), **Chicken Thigh Schnitzel** (page 309), or **Teriyaki-ish Chicken Thighs** (page 306). Add whatever vegetables you have around, blanched (**string beans, asparagus, broccoli, or cauliflower**) or raw (thinly sliced **sugar snap peas, cucumbers, carrots, or cabbage**). Drizzle generously with dressing and garnish with chopped **salted roasted peanuts**, sliced **spring onions**, and **coriander**.

creamy lemon-miso dressing

MAKES ABOUT 480ML

- 4 tablespoons aquafaba (see page 115)
- 1 tablespoon Dijon mustard
- 4 tablespoons cider vinegar
- 180ml neutral oil (see Note)
- 50g sugar
- 2 packed teaspoons finely grated lemon zest
- 4 tablespoons freshly squeezed lemon juice
- 3 tablespoons white miso
- 2 garlic cloves, thinly sliced
- 1 teaspoon onion powder
- ¼ teaspoon celery seeds
- 1 teaspoon (3g) kosher salt
- 2 tablespoons poppy seeds (optional), lightly toasted (see page 37)

If I were a singer-songwriter, I would write a power ballad about my love for Kismet Rotisserie in Los Angeles. The shoebox-sized, mostly take-away restaurant serves the kind of food I'd eat every day if I lived in the neighbourhood: golden roast chicken, fluffy pitta, and perfectly seasoned side dishes piled high with vegetables. But what I love most are their sauces and dressings. Especially their Miso Poppy Seed dressing, which I set out to recreate a couple of years ago. At some point, though, my journey took a detour, landing me here, at what just might be my new favourite all-purpose dressing. Tangy and sweet, creamy and rounded out with umami, it manages to hit every note you could want in a dressing without being cloying. Add some poppy seeds for that classic flavour or leave them out to make the dressing more versatile for drizzling over roasted vegetables, in potato salad, or anywhere else you can imagine.

• • •

In a measuring jug or wide-mouth jar, combine the aquafaba, mustard, and 1 tablespoon of the vinegar. With an immersion blender running on high speed, drizzle the oil in a thin stream to purée and emulsify and make aquafaba "mayonnaise."

In another wide-mouth jar, blend together the remaining 3 tablespoons vinegar and the sugar, lemon zest, lemon juice, miso, garlic, onion powder, celery seeds, and salt until smooth. Return the blender to the aquafaba mayonnaise and with the blender running at high speed, drizzle in the lemon-miso mixture. Stir in the poppy seeds, if desired. Taste and adjust with salt, vinegar, and lemon juice as needed.

Cover and refrigerate remaining dressing for up to 1 week.

THREE WAYS TO USE CREAMY LEMON-MISO DRESSING

1 For a **Shaved Fennel and Apple Salad,** use a mandoline to thinly shave 1 **fennel** bulb (halved and cored), 1 small crisp **apple** (halved and cored), and 1 **celery** stalk into a salad bowl. Crumble in 30g toasted **pecans** and 40g **aged Gouda,** crumbled into pea-sized pieces. Toss with the poppy seed variation of the dressing and season with freshly ground **black pepper** and **salt** to taste. Serve immediately.

2 Gently massage finely grated **lemon zest** onto dark-roasted **broccoli** and **cauliflower** when you take it out of the oven, then let it cool a bit. When it's nearly room temperature, transfer to a serving platter, drizzle generously with the dressing (the Preserved Meyer Lemon variation—see Note below—is especially nice here), garnish with finely chopped **parsley or chives,** and serve.

3 For a **Spring Chopped Salad,** combine diced, lightly blanched vegetables with herbs and crunchy raw greens to make a hearty lunch. In a large bowl, toss diced **romaine** and **red cabbage,** thinly sliced **cucumbers,** blanched bites of **tenderstem broccoli** and **asparagus,** sliced raw **sugar snap peas,** cooked **chickpeas, coriander** leaves, and torn **croutons** with the dressing. Taste, adjust with salt, and add a squeeze of **lemon juice** if needed, then serve immediately.

NOTES

Sunflower oil will make the thickest aquafaba mayonnaise, so if you can find it, use it here.

For a funky, salty variation on this dressing, omit the salt and use 2 tablespoons of **Preserved Meyer Lemon Paste** (page 79) in place of the fresh lemon juice and zest.

If you'd like a slightly thinner dressing, simply omit the aquafaba. Blend all the ingredients besides the oil with an immersion blender until smooth and drizzle in the oil in a thin stream to emulsify. Add **poppy seeds,** if desired.

creamy oregano dressing

This dressing started with a simple dream—one of a classic chopped salad. The kind that's on the menu in every classic red sauce joint. Radicchio and iceberg, kidney beans and chickpeas, pickled artichokes and peperoncini, cheese, tomatoes, salami, and seasoned croutons. And the more I made that salad for myself, the more I craved a creamy dressing instead of the classic lemony vinaigrette with dried oregano. So, with the help of ever-trustworthy aquafaba, I whipped up this dreamy creamy dressing. And, just when I was worried it'd only have one use, summer rolled around and it became an all-purpose Mediterranean miracle sauce for anything I could think of—Greek salad, chicken skewers, grilled fish and vegetables, beans and grains, salads of all kinds. I can't wait to see what you do with it.

• • •

In a measuring jug or wide-mouth jar, combine the aquafaba, vinegar, and mustard. With an immersion blender running, add the oil in a thin stream. Once all the oil is incorporated, add the lemon zest, lemon juice, garlic, sugar, oregano, onion powder, salt, and pepper and blend into a smooth, creamy dressing. (Alternatively, you can use a countertop blender.) Taste and adjust with salt, lemon juice, and vinegar as needed.

Cover and refrigerate remaining dressing for up to 1 week.

MAKES ABOUT 360ML

75g aquafaba (see page 115)
1 tablespoon red wine vinegar
1 teaspoon Dijon mustard
145g extra-virgin olive oil
1 packed tablespoon finely grated lemon zest
4 tablespoons freshly squeezed lemon juice
2 garlic cloves, thinly sliced
1 tablespoon sugar
2 teaspoons dried oregano, crumbled
1 teaspoon onion powder
1½ teaspoons (5g) kosher salt
½ teaspoon freshly ground black pepper

THREE WAYS TO USE CREAMY OREGANO DRESSING

1 To make a **Classic Chopped Salad,** start with a base of torn **radicchio** and **romaine**. Add **Bright Pickled Onions** (page 52), **chickpeas, kidney beans,** whole **bocconcini mozzarella or aged provolone** crumbles, **tomato** chunks, and thin batons of **Genoa salami**. If you like, add **pickled artichoke hearts,** sliced **hearts of palm,** and **peperoncini** too. Dress, taste, adjust seasoning, and serve.

2 To make a **Greek Salad with Farro and Souvlaki-ish Chicken Skewers,** season 3.8cm pieces of boneless, skinless **chicken thighs** with kosher **salt** and freshly ground **black pepper**. Place the chicken in a zip-lock plastic bag and add enough dressing to coat it generously. Seal the bag and squish the chicken around a bit. Refrigerate for 30 minutes to 2 hours, then thread onto bamboo skewers and cook in a griddle pan or on a grill over medium-high heat until browned on all sides and cooked through, about 6 to 8 minutes.

Meanwhile, in a large bowl, combine roll-cut **Persian cucumbers,** halved **cherry tomatoes** (or larger tomatoes cut into 1.25cm cubes), **Bright Pickled Onions** (page 52), pitted **Kalamata olives,** cooked **farro,** and 2.5cm-long **dill fronds**. Season with **salt** and **black pepper** and toss with enough dressing to coat. Taste and adjust the seasoning, then mound the salad into individual bowls and place one or two chicken skewers atop each. Drizzle with more dressing and serve.

3 For a **White Bean, Celery, and Tuna Salad,** in a large bowl, combine 300g drained cooked gigante beans, butter beans, or other large, creamy **white beans** with 3 thinly sliced **celery** stalks, a small handful each of **parsley** and **celery** leaves, and 1 tablespoon **Preserved Meyer Lemon Paste** (page 79) or the finely grated zest of 1 lemon. Season with kosher **salt,** freshly ground **black pepper,** and 1 minced **Pickled Thai Chilli** (page 76). Add 40g **Bright Pickled Onions** (page 52) and a jar or tin of **tuna in oil** broken into large pieces. Then toss gently with dressing to coat, taste, and adjust the seasoning as needed with salt and **Chilli Vinegar** (page 76). Mound into a large, shallow bowl and top with another generous drizzle of dressing.

fava's caesar

MAKES ABOUT 360ML

75g aquafaba (see page 115)

1½ teaspoons white wine vinegar

½ teaspoon Dijon mustard

180ml neutral oil (see Note)

4 tablespoons freshly squeezed lemon juice

55g finely grated Parmesan

8 anchovy fillets, roughly chopped

3 garlic cloves, thinly sliced

¾ teaspoon Worcestershire sauce or fish sauce

½ teaspoon (2g) kosher salt

½ teaspoon coarsely ground black pepper

I named this dressing after my pup, Fava, for two reasons: First, because I don't love the sound of "Faba Caesar"—as in Aquafaba Caesar. And second, because once, when I dropped a piece of kale coated with this dressing on the floor, Fava, who'd previously rejected every vegetable I'd ever offered her, gobbled it up and begged for more.

Way back when, I learned to make Caesar dressing with a base of homemade mayonnaise. But in practice, having to start with an egg yolk discourages me from making this dressing as often as I'd like (which is basically all the time). So at some point, I wondered if I could develop an egg-free version that was just as satisfying. A little aquafaba and mustard, together with my all-time favourite kitchen tool—the immersion blender—do the trick. The dressing is as creamy and flavourful as can be, and if someone as picky as Fava loves it, I'm sure you will, too.

• • •

In a measuring jug or wide-mouth jar, combine the aquafaba, vinegar, and mustard. With an immersion blender running, add the neutral oil in a thin stream. Continue blending until all the oil is added and the aquafaba mayonnaise is thick and creamy.

In a separate measuring jug or wide-mouth jar, use the immersion blender to purée the lemon juice, Parmesan, anchovies, garlic, Worcestershire sauce, and salt.

Return the blender to the aquafaba mayonnaise. With the blender running, gradually add the anchovy mixture until it is all incorporated. Finally, add the pepper. Taste and adjust with salt, lemon juice, and vinegar as needed.

Cover and refrigerate remaining dressing for up to 1 week.

VARIATION

To make **Classic Caesar:** Substitute 1 medium **egg yolk** for the aquafaba. Reduce the neutral oil to 120ml and add 60ml **olive oil**.

THREE WAYS TO USE FAVA'S CAESAR

1 If you've ever been to Market Hall in Oakland, California, you've likely had their unforgettable **Kale and Farro Caesar Salad**. To make your own version, tear Tuscan or curly **kale** leaves into bite-sized pieces. In a large bowl, massage a little **lemon juice** and kosher **salt** into the kale to start breaking it down. Toss with cooked **farro**, torn **croutons**, a generous amount of finely grated **Parmesan**, freshly ground **black pepper,** and salt to taste.

Toss generously with dressing, taste and adjust the seasoning, and top with more Parmesan to serve. This salad is also great the next day, and it makes for a wonderful lunch with a bit of leftover roast chicken or a **Simple Chicken Thigh** (page 306).

2 The beautiful, sturdy leaves of bitter chicories such as escarole, radicchio, Treviso, endive, and Castelfranco make an ideal canvas for Caesar dressing's richness. I buy them anytime I spot them to make **Chicories Caesar with Focaccia Croutons.** In a salad bowl, combine equal parts dark- and light-coloured **chicories,** torn or cut into bite-sized pieces, focaccia **croutons**, a generous amount of finely grated **Parmesan**, freshly ground **black pepper,** and kosher **salt** to taste.

Toss generously with dressing, taste and adjust the seasoning, and top with more Parmesan to serve.

3 For a **Spicy Gem Caesar with Golden Panko,** stir **Calabrian chilli purée** into the dressing to taste. Heat 3 tablespoons of **olive oil** in a medium skillet over medium-low heat, then add 60g **panko** and toast, stirring often, until the panko is a deep golden brown. Transfer the crumbs to a plate and allow to cool.

Toss **Little Gem lettuce** with a generous amount of dressing, then taste and adjust the seasoning. Pile delicately in a mound on a serving platter, then shower with finely grated **Parmesan** and toasted panko to serve.

NOTE

Sunflower oil will make the thickest aquafaba mayonnaise, so if you can find it, use it here.

tahini sbagliato

MAKES ABOUT 240ML

- 3 tablespoons neutral oil
- 3 tablespoons well-stirred tahini
- 2 tablespoons plus 1 teaspoon freshly squeezed lemon juice
- 2 tablespoons apple cider vinegar
- 1 tablespoon water
- 2½ teaspoons white miso
- 2 teaspoons maple or agave syrup
- 2 tablespoons minced dill
- 2 teaspoons minced coriander
- 1 teaspoon minced parsley
- 1½ teaspoons onion powder
- 1 packed teaspoon finely grated lemon zest
- 1 spring onion, minced
- 1 garlic clove, thinly sliced
- ½ teaspoon (2g) kosher salt

Sbagliato means "mistaken" in Italian and though this dressing was initially a mistake, it turned out to be a good one. Shortly after I decided to develop a range of incidentally-vegan-yet-irresistibly-creamy dressings, I started working on a tahini-based ranch. But guess what—I'm no food scientist! No matter how many times I tried to combine fresh and dried herbs, fresh and powdered alliums, and multiple acids in varying combinations, the dressing didn't transport me to anyone's ranch—hidden or not! But everyone who tasted it raved about it. Eventually I admitted I'd stumbled onto something special. Even if I hadn't achieved my original goal, I couldn't deny that this savoury, tangy, herb-packed dressing is a winner.

• • •

In a measuring jug or wide-mouth jar, combine all the ingredients and whisk or purée with an immersion blender until smooth. Taste and adjust the seasoning with salt and more lemon juice as needed. Add up to 1 more tablespoon of water as needed to thin out the dressing to your desired consistency.

Cover and refrigerate remaining dressing for up to 1 week. When using leftover refrigerated dressing, you may need to whisk in a teaspoon or two of water to return it to the right consistency.

THREE WAYS TO USE TAHINI SBAGLIATO

1 Thin it out and drizzle over quartered **Little Gem lettuces** on a platter. Dot the platter with **Marinated Roast Beetroots** (page 248). Use a spoon to scoop rustic spoonfuls of **avocado** around the platter. Season each bit of avocado with **flaky salt**. Drizzle with a little more dressing, then finish with a squeeze of **lemon** and a generous handful of **Crispy Fried Shallots** (page 55). Serve immediately.

2 Use it as a marinade for **Chicken Kabob Wraps:** Season 3.8cm pieces of boneless, skinless **chicken thighs** with kosher **salt**. Place the chicken in a zip-lock plastic bag and add enough dressing to coat it generously. Seal the bag and squish the chicken around a bit. Refrigerate for 30 minutes to 2 hours, then thread onto bamboo skewers and cook in a griddle pan or on a grill over medium-high heat until browned on all sides and cooked through, 6 to 8 minutes. (Alternatively, prepare **Souvlaki-ish Chicken Thighs,** page 307, or **Joojeh Kabobs,** page 286.) Then, layer the cooked chicken into **Fluffy Pitta Pockets** (page 385) or onto lavash bread smeared with **Whipped Tahini** (page 63). Generously dress thinly sliced **cabbage or romaine** lettuce, **cucumbers,** and **tomatoes,** then pile on top of the chicken. For a little heat, add pickled **peperoncini** or fresh **jalapeño** slices. Top with more dressing, then wrap and serve.

3 Leave it thick and use it as a dip for crudités or pitta chips, or use it as a spread for sandwiches.

roquefort dressing

When I get a hankering for blue cheese dressing, it's serious. And only Roquefort will do. I'm not sure why I feel so passionate about Roquefort, but I suspect it has to do with milk. In Southern France, Roquefort is made exclusively with milk from a hardy breed of sheep called Lacaune. Exceptionally high in butterfat and protein, Lacaune milk is rich and creamy, with a subtle floral aroma (it's no coincidence that my favourite French feta-style cheese, Valbreso, is also made using this milk). As a result, Roquefort has a lush texture and just-right balance of tang, umami, and sweetness that make all the difference in this dressing, which I love slathering on thick slices of iceberg lettuce with tomatoes and bacon or in steak sandwiches.

• • •

In a medium bowl, whisk together the Roquefort, soured cream, oil, vinegar, and garlic until combined (it's fine if a few lumps remain). Taste the dressing with a leaf of lettuce, then adjust the seasoning with salt and vinegar as needed. Thin with water a tablespoon at a time to your desired consistency.

Cover and refrigerate remaining dressing for up to 1 week.

MAKES 360ML

170g Roquefort cheese, crumbled

160g soured cream

55g extra-virgin olive oil

1 tablespoon plus 1 teaspoon red wine vinegar

2 garlic cloves, finely grated

Kosher salt

1 to 3 tablespoons water

THREE WAYS TO USE ROQUEFORT DRESSING

1 Instead of a classic wedge, try an **Iceberg Slice**—it's a revelation. For one thing, it's far easier to eat—no more chasing your wedge around the plate with your fork and knife! For another, the creamy, unctuous dressing has a chance to thoroughly penetrate the sinuous crags, making every bite a delight. Place a 2.5cm-thick slice of **iceberg lettuce** on each plate, then drizzle generously with dressing. Shower with **bacon lardons,** chopped **chives,** and coarsely ground **black pepper**. Dot with halved, salted **cherry tomatoes** and serve.

2 To make a sweet and savoury **Autumn Chopped Salad,** finely dice 1 small **shallot** and macerate in 2 tablespoons **red wine vinegar** in a small bowl. In another small bowl, cover 35g **dried currants** with **warm water** and let them hydrate for 15 minutes, then drain well. To make the salad, combine 125g **pomegranate seeds,** 55g finely diced **celery,** 1 **Fuyu persimmon** (peeled and finely diced), 165g **romaine lettuce** (cut into 2cm pieces), 120g chopped **radicchio** (2cm pieces), 65g lightly toasted **pine nuts,** and 1 small **avocado** (diced). Add the drained currants, the shallots, and a teaspoon of the red wine vinegar and season with **salt**. Dress lightly with Roquefort dressing, toss to coat, and taste. Adjust the dressing with vinegar and salt, then pile the salad onto a platter and serve.

3 Left thick, this dressing also makes an excellent dip. Serve it with potato crisps, crackers, chicken wings, or crudités.

making the most of store cupboard staples

This might come as a surprise, considering my profession, but much of the time feeding myself—and anyone else for whom I'm responsible—can feel like a chore. I know I'm not alone in this. Cooking often *is* a chore—there's the labour of deciding what to make, of shopping for groceries, and, of course, the inevitable mess to clean. Yet the act of feeding ourselves lies at the heart of daily life. I've begun to wonder: If this is how so many of us spend such a large portion of our time, then couldn't we try to make it time well spent? As Annie Dillard once wrote, "Who would call a day spent reading a good day? But a life spent reading—that is a good life."

I'd argue that a life spent cooking is also a good life. Most of us spend the bulk of our time in the kitchen cooking for the everyday—feeding the kids after a long day of work and school, shovelling down a quick breakfast before heading out the door, or packing a simple lunch for a long weekend hike. While this kind of cooking is rarely glamorous, I believe it can be an important source of meaning in our lives if we shift how we approach it.

It helps that we get a chance to be creative each time we cook. In a world so focused on efficiency and productivity, every opportunity for creativity is precious. Let me be clear: In the kitchen, creativity doesn't necessarily mean innovation. Rather, it's about being present, in your body, connected to your senses and imagination. It's a sense of freedom to be curious and playful that we don't always feel when we're busy working through our to-do lists. I'm not being woo-woo here—researchers have found that everyday creative activity, including cooking, can lead to a sense of "meaning, engagement, and purpose in life." This is certainly true for me. Using my hands to cook something to satisfy my cravings is a reliable antidote to the loneliness and doubt I'm often left with after a long writing day spent in my own head.

Approaching everyday cooking as ritual helps to further sanctify and infuse it with meaning. While rinsing grains of basmati, I think of how the same musty aroma suffused the kitchens of my maternal ancestors. And though entire lifetimes and continents may divide our existences, I imagine they poured off the starchy rinsing water into their flower beds, just as I do today. Reaching for a hand-carved wooden spoon to stir salt into the pot of rice, I'm reminded of the friend who bought it for me on a trip to Denmark. I unmould the crispy, golden tahdig onto a ceramic platter made for me by a favourite artist. As I bring the rice to the table, I'm no longer aware of the mundanity of cooking such a simple dish—instead, I'm filled with a sense of gratitude for the life I've worked so hard to fill with friendship and beauty.

This chapter is a collection of everyday culinary rituals. When I look back on a month, a year, or a lifetime of cooking, these are the basic recipes that have nourished and sustained me. The ingredients you'll need to make most of these dishes are likely already in your store cupboard. A few recipes might require a quick grocery run, but none of the necessary ingredients should be too hard to find. And though I don't adhere much to the idea that there's a "wrong" time of day to eat anything, I realise it might be jarring to see a recipe for pancakes next to another for pasta or beans. So this chapter begins with a couple sweet breakfast recipes followed by a couple savoury ones that you easily can serve at any time of day, and continues with the more substantial sorts of dishes you'll likely want to pull out of your sleeve for lunch or dinner.

ricotta custard pancakes

Yes, this is a three-bowl recipe. And yes, it involves whipping egg whites. But these pancakes, made light and custardy with a generous amount of ricotta, are heavenly clouds of fluff. The only downside (besides the bowls) is that you may never settle for any other pancake again.

• • •

In a large bowl, whisk together the flour, sugar, salt, and baking powder. Set aside.

In a medium bowl, whisk together the ricotta, milk, and egg yolks until very smooth. Set aside.

Preheat a 25cm or larger cast-iron frying pan (or flat grill) over medium-low heat while you whip the egg whites.

In a small bowl, use a whisk (or handheld electric mixer on medium speed) to whip the egg whites to stiff peaks, about 3 minutes. Add the ricotta mixture to the dry ingredients and whisk gently until just barely combined. Then use a silicone spatula to stir in a small amount of the egg whites to lighten the batter. Finally, fold in the rest of the egg whites with a light touch.

Melt just enough butter in the pan to coat the surface and increase the heat to medium. Measure a 60ml ladleful of the batter into the pan. If it doesn't immediately begin to sizzle, wait until it does before pouring out more pancakes. Cook the pancakes on the first side until the bottoms are golden brown and bubbles appear around the edges, 2 to 3 minutes. Use a thin flexible metal spatula to flip—this is when they will thrillingly begin to defy gravity—and cook until golden brown on the second side, another 1 to 2 minutes. Sometimes I like to flip a second time to make sure the pancakes get completely cooked through, but the only way to be sure that they are cooked is to tear one open and check. Transfer the pancakes to individual plates or a warmed serving platter, wipe out the pan, and repeat with remaining batter.

Serve immediately, with butter or ghee; syrup, jam, or icing sugar; fresh fruit; or any other desired garnishes.

MAKES SIXTEEN TO EIGHTEEN 7.5CM PANCAKES

- 130g plain flour
- 1 tablespoon plus 1 teaspoon sugar
- 1½ teaspoons (5g) kosher salt
- 1½ teaspoons baking powder
- 232g full-fat-milk ricotta
- 183g full-fat milk
- 2 medium eggs, separated
- Unsalted butter or **Cardamom Ghee** (page 61), for cooking and serving
- Maple syrup, **Apricot and Noyau Jam** (page 433), icing sugar, and/or fresh fruit, for serving

sarit's ashura cereal

MAKES ABOUT 830G

150g neutral oil

150g soft dark brown sugar

110g honey

80g puffed wheat or Kamut

80g puffed millet

85g pecan halves

85g almonds, very roughly chopped

50g pumpkin seeds

3 tablespoons (30g) toasted sesame seeds

1 tablespoon ground cardamom

2 teaspoons (6g) kosher salt

1 teaspoon ground cinnamon

1 teaspoon ground mahlab (optional; see Note)

The first time I visited Honey & Co., the warm, tiny, Middle Eastern restaurant in central London run by pastry chef Sarit Packer and her chef-husband, Itamar Srulovich, I left with a bag of their Ashura Cereal, at Sarit's insistence. In my hotel room later that night, I couldn't resist tasting it even though I'd just brushed my teeth. The cereal looked like a cross between granola and Cracker Jack, with dark, shiny brown clusters of puffed wheat, almonds, pecans, and seeds. It smelled like burnt honey, spring flowers, and cardamom. As I bit into a piece, it burst in my mouth, somehow simultaneously light and rich, sweet and savoury, crisp and full of air. Standing there in my pyjamas, I ate nearly half the bag.

Childhood memories of sugary cereals such as Honey Smacks and Corn Pops guided Sarit as she developed this recipe. First, she made a honey syrup spiked with cinnamon, cardamom, and an almond-scented spice called mahlab. She then drizzled the syrup over a mixture of puffed wheat, nuts, and seeds and baked the whole thing into a gloriously crisp mass. Serve it as Sarit does, over yogurt with fresh berries or pomegranate seeds; or as her parents do, drowned in a bowl of milk; or simply eat it by the handful, straight from the bag, anytime you want a sweet, crunchy snack.

• • •

Adjust the oven racks to the lower-middle and upper-middle positions and preheat to 180°C. Line two baking trays with parchment paper and set aside.

In a medium saucepan, combine the oil, brown sugar, and honey and set over medium-high heat. Whisk well and bring to a boil, stirring occasionally to prevent it from scorching. Cook until the sugar dissolves completely, there is no graininess to the texture, and small bubbles are appearing uniformly across the surface of the mixture, about 5 minutes. The oil won't incorporate fully, so don't fret if the mixture appears separated.

recipe continues

NOTES

This recipe is endlessly adaptable. You can use any combination of puffed grains totalling 160g. I love a fifty-fifty mix of wheat or Kamut and millet, but quinoa and corn work well, too.

Look for mahlab, sometimes spelled mahaleb, in Middle Eastern grocery shops or online.

Meanwhile, in a large heatproof bowl, combine the puffed grains, pecans, almonds, pumpkin seeds, and sesame seeds and mix well.

Once the honey mixture is smooth and evenly bubbling, add the cardamom, salt, cinnamon, and mahlab, if using. Stir well to incorporate the spices, then carefully pour the mixture over the dry ingredients. Working quickly, use a large silicone spatula to stir, turning the contents of the bowl over until everything is coated evenly with the syrup.

Transfer the mixture to the prepared trays and use the spatula to flatten out the cereal in an even layer.

Place the trays in the oven and bake for 10 minutes. Carefully remove one tray at a time and use the spatula to stir the cereal around. Switch the trays on the racks and rotate them front to back to ensure even baking. Bake until dark golden brown and well caramelised, 7 to 9 minutes longer. Remove from the oven and allow to cool entirely on the trays before breaking up the cereal into large clusters.

Store in an airtight container at room temperature for up to 2 weeks (AS IF it will last that long!).

a small, good thing: a boiled egg

Everyone has her own thoughts about the best way to boil an egg. My friend Laurel likes to cook hers so long that sometimes all the water in the pot evaporates. For the sake of our relationship, I avert my eyes (and pinch my nose).

I prefer **7½-Minute Eggs**. I cook **medium eggs**, straight from the fridge, for 7½ minutes to get the glossy-but-firm yolks and just-set whites I prefer. I use a slotted spoon to lower them carefully into a pot of gently **boiling water** and then transfer them into a bowl of **ice water** when the timer goes off.

If the eggs are a different size or at room temperature, I'll adjust the cooking time by about 30 seconds in one direction or the other to get the texture I'm after. And if I want my yolks even more set—so I can slice cleanly through them—I'll set the timer to make **10-Minute Eggs**.

Fresh eggs can be challenging to peel. If eggs don't peel readily, I'll crack them gently against the countertop and return them to the water bowl for 10 minutes. I've found that letting water penetrate the shell membrane for a little while helps the shell slip right off.

NOW, WHAT TO DO WITH ALL THESE EGGS?

Use **10-Minute Eggs** to make **Crème Fraîche Devilled Eggs** (page 97).

•

Skip the ice bath and peel the eggs right away. Halve them lengthways, smear with cold **salted butter,** and sprinkle with **toasted sesame seeds or furikake**. Eat warm.

•

Use a fork to smash warm eggs onto buttered **toast** or a warm **tortilla**. Top with **coriander,** minced **jalapeño,** and a little grated **Monterey Jack** cheese, if you like.

•

To make **Classic Egg Salad:** Separate the yolks and whites of four **10-Minute Eggs**. In a small bowl, mash the yolks together with 2 tablespoons **mayonnaise,** 1 teaspoon Dijon or American-style **mustard,** and 1 teaspoon **white wine vinegar**. Coarsely chop the whites and place in a large bowl with 3 tablespoons finely diced **celery,** 1 tablespoon finely chopped **Bright Pickled Onions** (page 52), and 1 tablespoon finely chopped **dill**. Stir in the yolk mixture, season with **salt,** and toss to coat. Taste and adjust the seasoning with salt and vinegar as needed.

a pot of rice

I eat rice at least two or three nights a week. And sometimes for breakfast and lunch, too. Depending on the amount I'm cooking, I'll steam it in a small, enamelled cast-iron pot on the hob or a Japanese rice cooker that hums a jaunty tune when the rice is ready (and keeps it warm for two days afterwards!). To my mind, few things are as important to know as how to cook rice, which is why it always makes me so sad to hear that some folks are afraid to make it. There's no need for fear! All you've got to do is attend to a few basic steps, use the right ratio of rice to water, and cook it slowly, without stirring, until the rice absorbs all the liquid. Here's everything you need to know:

RICE VARIETIES

Long-grain varieties tend to be aromatic and cook up light and fluffy. Proper rinsing and cooking will yield distinct grains that don't stick together.

> **Basmati:** The longest-grained of all the rice, basmati boasts an earthy aroma. I like to use it for **Basic Crispy Rice** (page 155), pilaf, **Arroz Verde** (page 154), **Arroz Rojo** (page 154), and alongside dal.

> **Jasmine:** Also called Hom Mali 105, this rice from Thailand is a little plumper than basmati. I love its floral aroma and chewy texture—it's my go-to rice. I use it for **Coconut Rice** (page 154), steamed rice, fried rice, alongside Southeast Asian dishes, and in **Vanilla Bean Rice Pudding** (page 430).

Medium-grain rice cooks up fluffy like long-grain rice but becomes stickier as it cools, like short-grain varieties do.

> **Calrose:** If you're going to keep only one variety around, consider Calrose. My favourite type is Kokuho Rose from Koda Farms in California, for its sweet aroma, tender texture, and mild flavour. This is a wonderful all-purpose rice—use it for steamed rice, fried rice, **Coconut Rice** (page 154), **Basic Crispy Rice** (page 155), and **Vanilla Bean Rice Pudding** (page 430).

Brown: My preferred brown rice is a medium-grain variety from Massa Organics in California. I love it for its rich, nutty flavour and incomparably chewy texture. It's wonderful for steaming, fried rice, rice bowls, and in soups or salads.

Short-grain rice, with its chubby grains, tends to stick together as it cooks, making these varieties ideal for sushi and sticky rice.

Haiga, or semi-polished, rice: This is the only short-grain rice I keep in the store cupboard. A special milling process strips away the bran while leaving the germ intact, yielding grains that boast the nuttiness, chewiness, and much of the nutritious fibre of brown rice, as well as the short cooking time of white rice. Use haiga rice anywhere you'd use brown rice.

COOKING RICE

Rinse: To guarantee the best pot of rice, begin with a rinse—this will eliminate excess starch and prevent the rice from clumping, sticking, or ending up mushy.

Place the measured rice in a bowl and add enough cold water to cover. Swirl the rice vigorously with your fingers until the water gets cloudy, then drain the starchy water. Rinse the rice, change the water, and repeat at least five times, or until the water runs clear.

Drain: In order to prevent throwing off the rice-to-liquid ratio, make sure to drain your rice well after rinsing it. Let it sit for a few minutes in a fine-mesh sieve, then tap out as much excess water as possible.

Cook: Use a pot with a tight-fitting lid. I like to use an enamelled cast-iron pot, which keeps the temperature steady. Combine the rinsed rice, cooking liquid, and salt and bring to a boil, then reduce to a simmer. Cover and continue cooking over very low heat until the liquid is all absorbed.

recipe continues

Rest: Let the rice rest for at least 10 minutes. During this time, the grains will cool and the starches will set a bit. Then you can gently fluff the rice with a paddle or wooden spoon, stir in any last-minute add-ins, and adjust the seasoning as needed. Keep the rice covered until you're ready to eat.

WATER RATIOS

I use these water ratios, but it always helps to double-check cooking instructions on the packaging of your own rice, because the specific length of a grain can affect both the water ratio and the cooking time.

These ratios are for cooking on the hob—you may need to tweak them a bit if using an electric rice cooker (consult your manual for the recommended rice-to-liquid ratio). Feel free to replace some or all of the water with any other cooking liquid, such as stock, coconut milk, crushed tomatoes, leftover braising juices, or anything else that sounds good to you. And no matter what kind of cooking liquid you use, remember to season it generously!

FOR EACH TYPE OF RICE	USE THIS MUCH WATER
Jasmine rice: 185g	320ml
Basmati rice: 185g	360ml
Calrose rice: 190g	320ml
Medium-grain brown rice: 190g	400ml
Haiga rice: 180g	250ml plus 2½ teaspoons

These measurements will yield 3 to 4 servings. When multiplying these recipes or ratios by more than two, things may start to get a little wonky. To avoid unevenly cooked rice, try to use wide, shallow pots, rather than tall, deep ones when cooking large batches of rice. And if you do attempt to triple or quadruple the recipes, hold back about 10 per cent of the liquid to avoid mushy rice.

recipe continues

NOTES

I should confess that after publicly pooh-poohing single-use appliances, I inherited a rice cooker from a friend a few years ago and have never looked back. To say that it's improved my quality of life is a criminal understatement, because now I can wake up and eat a warm breakfast of rice with butter, good soy sauce, toasted sesame seeds, and a boiled egg without a thought. This is not to suggest that you need to run out and buy a new appliance. But if you do, I suggest seeking out a Zojirushi rice cooker that's made in Japan and touts something called Neuro Fuzzy technology.

If you've cooked rice on the hob or if your rice cooker doesn't have a "keep warm" function, immediately transfer any leftovers to the refrigerator to prevent *Bacillus cereus* spores from germinating. As long as the rice cools quickly, you'll be fine. But leave the rice to cool at room temperature and you'll tempt fate by giving toxic, food poisoning–causing bacteria the perfect environment in which to cultivate.

VARIATIONS

For a little extra kick of flavour, toast rinsed, drained **rice** until golden in 28g of **unsalted butter, ghee, or extra-virgin olive oil** and continue cooking as directed on page 151.

•

To make **Coconut Rice:** Rinse and drain 185g **jasmine rice**. Cook it with 160ml **coconut milk**, 160ml **coconut water or water**, 1 tablespoon **sugar**, and **salt** to taste.

•

To make **Arroz Verde:** Rinse and drain 275g **basmati rice**. In a blender, combine 60g coarsely chopped **onion,** 70g coarsely chopped **poblano chilli** (stalks removed and seeded), 1 de-stalked and seeded **jalapeño**, 3 **garlic** cloves, 12g **coriander** leaves, and 4g **parsley** leaves. Purée until smooth, adding a splash of **Chicken Stock** (page 314) **or water** as needed to help the blender along, then add enough stock or water to increase the total volume of the purée to 720ml. Heat 60ml **neutral oil** in a medium casserole over medium heat and toast the rice until golden, about 8 minutes. Add the purée, season generously with **salt,** and bring to a boil. Stir well, reduce the heat to low, cover, and cook until the liquid is gone, about 20 minutes. Turn off the heat and let sit, covered, for 10 minutes. Gently stir the purée back into the rice to fluff, taste and adjust the seasoning, and serve.

•

To make **Arroz Rojo:** Rinse and drain 275g **basmati rice**. In a blender, combine 180g **diced tomatoes** (tinned or fresh), 80g coarsely chopped **onion,** 3 **garlic** cloves, 3 tablespoons **tomato purée,** and 2 teaspoons **Teo's Chivi Spice** (page 348). Add enough **Chicken Stock** (page 314) **or water** to increase the total volume of the purée to 720ml. Heat 60ml **neutral oil** in a medium casserole over medium heat and toast the rice until golden, about 8 minutes. Add the purée, season generously with **salt,** and bring to a boil. Stir well, reduce the heat to low, cover, and cook until the liquid is gone, about 20 minutes. Turn off the heat and let sit, covered, for 10 minutes. Gently stir the purée back into the rice to fluff, taste and adjust the seasoning, and serve.

basic crispy rice

Wherever rice is a staple food, golden, crispy rice is a delicacy. In Korea, cooked rice spooned into unbelievably hot stone pots forms a crunchy crust that's a pleasure to eat with soft tofu soup. In Puerto Rico, families fight over the glassy pegao lining a pot of arroz con gandules. In Spain, much-treasured socarrat forms at the base of a pan of properly cooked paella. In Indonesia, crackers called intip are made out of the layer of rice that sticks to the bottom of the cooking pot. I've watched a roomful of Ghanaian, Nigerian, and Senegalese young people debate over whose version of jollof rice and its "bottom pot," as Nigerians call it, reigns supreme. This classic recipe of mine is a simplified version of tahdig, the irresistible crust that forms on a pot of Persian rice, which I gobbled up every night as a kid.

• • •

MAKES ONE 25CM TAHDIG AND RICE

370g basmati rice

Kosher salt

3 tablespoons labne or natural yogurt

3 tablespoons unsalted butter

3 tablespoons neutral oil, plus more as needed

Fill a large pot with 4 litres of water and bring to a boil.

Meanwhile, place the rice in a bowl and rinse with cold water, swirling vigorously with your fingers. Change the water at least five times, or until the water runs clear. Drain the rice well.

Once the water comes to a boil, add 75g of kosher salt. (Since the rice is going to spend only a short time in the water, it's crucial to season it heavily.) Add the rice and stir.

Set a fine-mesh sieve or colander in the sink. Cook the rice, gently stirring from time to time, until it's al dente, 5 to 7 minutes. Drain into the sieve and immediately begin rinsing with cold water to stop the rice from cooking further. Drain.

Remove 150g of the rice and combine it with the labne.

Set a very well-seasoned 25cm cast-iron frying pan or other 25cm nonstick frying pan over medium heat. Add the butter and the oil. When the butter melts, spread the yogurt-rice mixture evenly across the base of the pan. Pile the remaining rice into the pan, mounding it gently towards the centre.

recipe continues

Using the handle of a wooden spoon, gently dig five or six holes into the rice down to the bottom of the pan, which will be gently sizzling. The holes will allow steam to escape from the bottommost layer of rice so that a crisp crust can form. There should be enough oil in the pan so that you can see it bubbling up the sides. Add a little more oil if needed to see these bubbles.

Continue cooking the rice uncovered over medium heat, giving the pan a quarter-turn every 3 or 4 minutes to ensure even browning, until you start to see a golden crust begin to form at the sides of the pan, 15 to 20 minutes.

Once you see the crust turn from pale amber to gold, reduce the heat to low and continue cooking until the edges of the crust are fully golden and the rice is cooked completely through, another 15 to 20 minutes. There isn't a way to tell what tahdig will look like until you flip it, so I prefer to err on the side of overbrowning, but if that makes you uncomfortable, pull the rice after about 35 total minutes in the pan.

To unmould the rice, carefully run a silicone spatula along the edges of the pan to ensure that no part of the crust is sticking. Tip out any excess fat at the bottom of the pan into a bowl, gather your courage, and then carefully flip it onto a platter or chopping board.

And if for any reason your rice doesn't emerge in one piece, do what every Persian grandmother has done since the beginning of time: scoop out the rice, chip out the tahdig in pieces, and pretend you *meant* to do it this way.

VARIATIONS

To make **Saffron-Flecked Crispy Rice:** Carefully spoon 75g cooked **rice** out of the pan before unmoulding and set aside. In a small bowl, toss the rice with 2 tablespoons very potent **bloomed saffron** (see page 37) to tint it a marigold hue. To serve, unmould the crispy rice onto a platter and spoon the saffron rice around it.

recipe continues

To make **Persian-Style Herbed Rice:** Once you've blanched and rinsed the rice, fold 80g very finely chopped **coriander, dill, and/or parsley** and the finely chopped pale-green and white parts of 4 **spring onions** into the rice. Remove 150g of the herbed rice, combine with the labne for the tahdig, and continue as directed.

To make **Adas Polo:** Once you've blanched and rinsed the rice, fold 200g of drained cooked brown or green **lentils** (from 145g dried) into the rice. Remove 150g of the lentil rice, combine with the labne for the tahdig, and continue as directed. While the rice is cooking, sauté 110g black or golden **raisins** and 4 pitted, quartered **Medjool dates** in 28g **unsalted butter** until plump, about 2 minutes. Season with **salt** and scatter atop the plated tahdig to serve.

To make a **Sort-of Casamiento,** the Salvadoran "marriage" between red beans and crispy rice, gently heat a frying pan and add 3 tablespoons **extra-virgin olive oil**. When it shimmers, add 2 thinly sliced **garlic** cloves, half an **onion**, minced, and half a **green pepper**, minced. Cook, stirring, until fragrant and just beginning to take on colour, about 3 minutes. Remove from the heat and, if desired, stir in 2 teaspoons **chicken bouillon paste** until dissolved. Scrape this mixture into a large bowl. Blanch and rinse the rice as directed, and add to the bowl with the sautéed vegetables along with 350g cooked, drained **red beans** (black beans also work well). Taste and adjust the mixture's seasoning. Combine 150g of the rice-and-bean mixture with the labne and continue as directed.

To make **Baghali Polo:** Once you've blanched and rinsed the rice, fold 150g fresh or frozen peeled **broad beans**, 50g very finely chopped **fresh dill**, and 3 tablespoons **dried dill** into the rice. Combine 150g of the rice-and-broad-bean mixture with the labne and continue as directed.

a pot of beans

A simmering pot of beans is a promise of good things to come: soups and stews, spreads, fritters, salad, rice, and pasta. Nutritious, inexpensive, and versatile, pulses are a staple food in traditional cuisines across the world. With the help of a well-stocked spice shelf, store cupboard, and herb garden, a single pot of beans, lentils, or chickpeas can, over the course of one week, take you to Mexico, India, the Caribbean, Italy, and across the Middle East.

It's essential to soak beans and chickpeas overnight—use three parts water to one part pulse—especially if you're not sure how old they may be. Some say this is a waste of time, but I'd argue that hydrated beans cook more quickly and evenly than their parched counterparts. To the soaking pot, add salt to flavour the pulses from within and a pinch of bicarbonate of soda, which will yield the most tender beans (there's no need to soak or add bicarbonate of soda to lentils).

The next day, add whatever aromatics you have around—a bay leaf, a garlic clove, an onion end, a fresh or dried chilli—and a glug of olive oil, then simmer the beans until they're tender. Keep an eye on the pot as it fills your kitchen with its rich, starchy aroma, adding more water as needed to ensure the beans always remain submerged. Depending on the variety of beans, whether they've been soaked, and how long they've been sitting in the cupboard, a pot will require 30 minutes to 2 hours of simmering. The only surefire way to know that the beans are done is to taste five creamy, tender ones in a row. If your fourth or fifth bean isn't quite done, keep simmering. Few things are as uncomfortable to consume as undercooked pulses.

For your first meal, serve brothy beans on their own, drizzled with good olive oil and garnished with a sprinkling of herbs, finely grated lemon zest, **Crispy Fried Shallots** (page 55), or Parmesan. Or swirl a spoonful of **Calabrian Chilli Crisp** (page 56), **Basil Pesto** (page 67), **Green Sauce** (page 51), or **Garlic and Herb Labne** (page 48) into the bowl. Then turn the remainder of the pot into any of the dishes on page 161.

recipe continues

To make **Marinated Gigante Beans:** Heat 70g **extra-virgin olive oil**, 3 smashed **garlic** cloves, 1 **bay leaf**, and 1 small **dried chilli** in a small pot over medium-low heat until small bubbles appear around the garlic, about 3 minutes. Add 500g drained cooked **gigante, Spagna, or butter beans**. Cook until the beans are warm and small bubbles appear around the beans, 3 to 5 minutes. Remove from the heat and stir in 1 to 2 tablespoons **Preserved Meyer Lemon Paste** (page 79) and 1 tablespoon **red wine vinegar**. Allow to marinate for at least 1 hour, then discard the garlic and aromatics. Taste and adjust the seasoning with **salt** and vinegar. Garnish with chopped **parsley** and serve warm with **Olive Oil–Fried Bread** (page 94) for sopping up the marinade.

•

To make **Frijoles con Todo:** Cook 450g **pinto beans** with 2 teaspoons **Teo's Chivi Spice** (page 348), a few **garlic** cloves, 2 **bay leaves**, half an **onion**, **salt**, and a good glug of **extra-virgin olive oil**. Discard the aromatics when the beans are done, then taste and adjust the broth as needed. Serve with **avocado, crema or soured cream, queso Cotija**, diced **tomatoes**, chopped **coriander, jalapeño, red onion**, and some warm **corn tortillas**.

•

To make **Refried Beans:** Set a large frying pan over medium heat and add 2 tablespoons **neutral oil**. Stirring occasionally, cook ½ finely chopped **onion** and 1 **serrano chilli** (stalk removed and seeded) with a generous pinch of **salt** until tender and beginning to brown, about 8 minutes. Add 120ml **Shallot Oil** (page 55), **lard, bacon fat, or neutral oil** and 600g **pinto or black beans** plus 120ml **bean cooking liquid**. Simmer, stirring occasionally, until the liquid thickens and resembles gravy, 3 to 5 minutes. Taste and adjust the seasoning with salt. Reduce the heat to low, discard the chilli, and use a potato masher or wooden spoon to mash the beans until no whole beans remain. Add another splash of bean liquid or water to thin out the beans to your desired consistency, knowing that they'll continue to thicken as they cool. Taste and adjust the seasoning with salt and serve hot.

recipe continues

To make **Cuban-Style Black Beans:** Set a medium casserole over medium heat and add 55g **extra-virgin olive oil**. When it shimmers, add half an **onion** and half a **green pepper,** both minced, and 3 thinly sliced **garlic** cloves. Cook until fragrant and just beginning to take on colour, about 3 minutes. Add 1 teaspoon **ground cumin,** ½ teaspoon **dried oregano,** 1 **bay leaf,** and 1 **jalapeño** (stalk removed and seeded). Cook for another minute, then add 600g of drained cooked **black beans** plus 480ml of **bean cooking liquid** and bring to a boil. Add 1 teaspoon **apple cider vinegar** and season with **salt** to taste, then reduce heat and simmer, stirring occasionally, until the flavours come together, about 5 minutes. Discard the bay leaf and chilli and serve.

•

To make **Butter Beans Braised with Artichoke Hearts and Goat's Cheese:** Set a large, wide ovenproof saucepan or casserole over medium heat and add 160g **extra-virgin olive oil**. When it shimmers, add 6 smashed **garlic** cloves and cook, stirring, until fragrant but not at all browned, 1 to 2 minutes. Stir in ½ teaspoon **chilli flakes,** 2 **bay leaves,** and 3 long, wide strips of **lemon zest**. Add 340g frozen **artichoke hearts,** stir to coat with oil, and season with **salt**. Cook for 2 to 3 minutes to allow the artichokes to begin to thaw, then add 570g drained cooked **butter beans,** 180ml **bean cooking liquid,** and 1 tablespoon **white wine vinegar**. Season with salt, taste, and adjust the seasoning, then cover the pot and bake for 20 minutes. Uncover and add 115g **Marinated Goat's Cheese** (page 74) and continue baking until some of the beans are soft and others are crisp, another 15 to 20 minutes. Cool for about 5 minutes.

Meanwhile, finely grate the remaining lemon zest from the lemon into a small bowl and add 2 tablespoons finely chopped **parsley,** 20g **Crispy Fried Shallots** (page 55), and a pinch of **flaky sea salt**. Use your fingertips to combine into a uniform mixture.

Generously shower the butter beans with the shallot mixture and serve.

a garbanzo bonanza

Now that I use so much aquafaba, I often find myself awash in chickpeas (aka garbanzo beans). And since there's only so much hummus a person can eat, I've learned to get creative with my surplus. Here are some ideas for when you're facing your own chickpea glut:

Make **Chickpea Salad with Cucumbers and Dill** (below) when you're looking for a quick, filling lunch (or bring it to a picnic, since it'll only improve as it sits). Serve **Crispy Snacking Chickpeas** (page 165) as a starter or use them in salads in place of croutons. Make **Stewy Harissa Chickpeas with Winter Squash** (page 166) to warm you up from the inside out. And let **Coconut-Lemongrass Soup with Chickpeas** (page 167), inspired by the classic Indonesian chicken soup soto ayam, soothe you with its light, fragrant broth.

Familiarise yourself with the general outline of each method and then start to riff with any of your own favourite flavour combinations. For all the following suggestions, drain and reserve the aquafaba and rinse off the chickpeas if using tinned. If using chickpeas you cooked yourself, you can skip the rinse.

• • •

marinate: chickpea salad with cucumbers and dill

SERVES 4 TO 6

In a large bowl, combine 320g drained cooked **chickpeas**, 40g **Bright Pickled Onions** (page 52), and 1 tablespoon **Preserved Meyer Lemon Paste** (page 79). Toss with **Creamy Oregano Dressing** (page 125) to combine, taste, and adjust the seasoning. Cover and chill for at least 30 minutes to marinate. Just before serving add 4 roll-cut **Persian cucumbers,** 55g **feta-style cheese** in large crumbles, and 12.5g finely chopped **dill** fronds. Add more dressing as needed to coat, toss to combine, then taste and adjust the seasoning with salt. Serve immediately.

• • •

roast: crispy snacking chickpeas

MAKES ANY AMOUNT

Transfer drained cooked **chickpeas** to a salad spinner and spin to dry, then spread them out to continue drying on a baking tray lined with a clean tea towel. Remove any loose skins. If you're able to run the oven fan without turning on the oven, do so and place the pan in the oven for about 20 minutes to further dry out the chickpeas. Otherwise, leave the pan out at room temperature for 2 hours (if you're not in a hurry, you can also refrigerate the pan uncovered overnight to encourage drying). It's crucial to completely dry out the chickpeas before roasting them—otherwise they won't get crisp.

To roast the chickpeas, adjust an oven rack to the centre position and preheat to 160°C (if the fan is on, turn it off). Carefully lift the tea towel of dried-out chickpeas off the tray and set aside. Drizzle just enough **extra-virgin olive oil** onto the tray to coat it very lightly, then shake the chickpeas off the towel onto the oiled tray.

Roast for 45 minutes, then remove the tray from the oven. Transfer the chickpeas to a large bowl and toss with a couple teaspoons of olive oil, a few generous pinches of **Teo's Chivi Spice** (page 348), and a generous pinch of **salt**.

Return the chickpeas to the tray and continue roasting until crisp and golden, another 15 to 20 minutes, jiggling the tray to stir the chickpeas once or twice during this time. Turn the oven off, jiggle the tray, and return it to the oven for 15 minutes—the chickpeas will continue to crisp up.

To season the chickpeas, in a large bowl, whisk together a couple of teaspoons of olive oil and a few more generous pinches of **Teo's Chivi Spice** (page 348), then add the cooled chickpeas and toss. Taste and adjust the seasoning with salt and more spices. Serve warm or at room temperature.

Store in an airtight container at room temperature for up to 2 days. To refresh, toast in a single layer at 200°C for 3 to 4 minutes.

braise:
stewy harissa chickpeas with winter squash

SERVES 4 TO 6

NOTE

Feel free to leave out the squash here for a less wintry vibe. If you do, consider folding in 35g golden raisins instead.

In a medium casserole over medium heat, soften a finely diced **onion** and a pinch of **salt** in 3 tablespoons of **extra-virgin olive oil**, about 10 minutes. Move the onion to the edges of the pot and add 3 sliced **garlic** cloves, 2 tablespoons **tomato purée**, and 2 to 3 tablespoons **mild harissa paste** and cook until the garlic is fragrant and the oil is orangey red, about 2 minutes. Stir in 1 teaspoon **ground cumin**, ¾ teaspoon **ground ginger**, ¼ teaspoon freshly ground **black pepper**, and a pinch of **ground cinnamon** and allow to bloom until fragrant. Add 560g drained cooked **chickpeas** and stir to coat.

Add 680g peeled, seeded **Honeynut** or other winter squash cut into 2.5cm cubes, 540ml **Chicken Stock** (page 314), 110g extra-virgin olive oil, 1 **bay leaf**, 1 tablespoon **aged sherry vinegar**, and a generous pinch of salt. Bring to a boil, then reduce to a simmer. Taste and adjust the seasoning with salt. Cover and cook at a gentle simmer, stirring occasionally, until the squash and chickpeas are very soft, 35 to 40 minutes.

Garnish with a squeeze of **lemon** and a showering of chopped **coriander, parsley, or dill**.

Serve with **crusty bread** or **Fluffy Pitta Pockets** (page 385), **Marinated Feta** (page 71) or **Marinated Goat's Cheese** (page 74), and **Garlic and Herb Labne** (page 48).

• • •

simmer: coconut-lemongrass soup with chickpeas

MAKES ABOUT 3 LITRES

Use the handle of a heavy knife or a pestle to bruise 2 **lemongrass stalks,** then tie each one into a knot.

In a medium casserole, combine the lemongrass, 1 halved **onion**, 4 **makrut lime leaves**, 2 **bay leaves**, 6 smashed **garlic** cloves, 5cm thinly sliced **fresh turmeric root** (or 1 teaspoon ground turmeric), 7.5cm thinly sliced **fresh ginger**, 5cm thinly sliced **galangal**, 2 de-stalked and seeded **Thai chillies**, 1 teaspoon **black peppercorns**, 1.44 litres **Chicken Stock** (page 314) **or water**, 1 tablespoon **sugar**, and a generous pinch of **salt** and bring to a boil. Reduce the heat and simmer the broth until it's fragrant and flavourful, about 30 minutes.

Strain the broth through a fine-mesh sieve, discard the solids, rinse out the pot, and return the broth to the pot and the pot to the hob. Add 560g drained cooked **chickpeas** and, if desired, 2 or 3 **Yukon Gold (or Maris Piper) potatoes** cut into 2.5cm chunks. Taste and adjust the seasoning with salt and simmer until the potatoes are starting to fall apart, about 15 minutes.

Add 385g **coconut cream** and simmer for 3 to 4 minutes to infuse. Remove from the heat, taste and adjust the seasoning with salt, and serve with **lime wedges, coriander leaves, Crispy Fried Shallots** (page 55), and finely sliced Thai chillies.

a small, good thing: crispy open-faced quesadillas

Anytime I visit a Mexican grocer, I make sure to pick up a piece or two of queso Oaxaca. This creamy string cheese melts and crisps up beautifully, making it ideal for one of my favourite snacks—crispy open-faced quesadillas.

Set a cast-iron, carbon-steel, or nonstick frying pan over high heat. Lightly coat the pan with **nonstick cooking spray**. Tear **queso Oaxaca** into 7.5cm "strings" and lay them into the pan. If you like, sprinkle sautéed **corn kernels**, thinly sliced sautéed **summer squash**, sautéed **mushrooms**, or raw **squash blossom petals** over the cheese.

Working quickly, lay a **tortilla** over the cheese and press it down with a thin flexible metal spatula to encourage contact between the tortilla and the pan. After a minute or two, when the cheese has melted and browned into a glassy, even crust, use the spatula to flip the tortilla over. Let it brown for a minute, then transfer to a plate. Garnish with a squeeze of **lime, salsa, or hot sauce** and eat immediately.

curried carrot and coconut soup

Spicy, vibrant Thai red curries inspired this creamy soup. The multilayered flavours of curry paste, rich coconut milk, and savoury fish sauce perfectly complement the sweetness of the carrots. But it's the crunchy, umami-packed topping—a spin on miang kham, a snack full of peanuts, coconut, and chillies found throughout Thailand and Laos—that's the real standout.

• • •

Adjust an oven rack to the center position and preheat to 150°C.

To make the soup, melt the oil in a large casserole over medium-high heat. When the oil shimmers, add the shallots, ginger, pieces of lemongrass, and a generous pinch of salt. Reduce the heat to low and cook, stirring occasionally, until the shallots are tender and just starting to brown, about 18 minutes.

Increase the heat to high and add the carrots, coconut milk, curry paste, fish sauce, and 720ml of the stock. As the soup comes to a boil, partially cover the pot and reduce the heat to keep the liquid at a gentle simmer. Cook the soup until the carrots are completely tender, about 25 minutes.

Meanwhile, to make the garnish, in a medium bowl, combine the peanuts, coconut flakes, fish sauce, chillies, oil, lemongrass, sugar, and lime leaves (if using). Spread the mixture out on a baking tray in a single layer. Bake until the coconut is a deep golden brown, 18 to 20 minutes, stirring every 3 minutes after the first 10 minutes. Remove from the oven and pour the mixture immediately into a bowl to prevent overcooking. Stir to combine and set aside.

Remove the soup from the heat and discard the lemongrass. Use an immersion blender to purée the soup. (Alternatively, transfer soup in batches to a blender or food processor and purée.) Taste and adjust for salt and curry paste. Add more stock or water to thin soup to the desired consistency.

MAKES ABOUT 2 LITRES

FOR THE SOUP

60ml coconut oil

3 shallots, diced

One 5cm piece fresh ginger, peeled and thinly sliced

1 lemongrass stalk, cut into 7.5cm pieces

Kosher salt

1.4kg carrots, peeled and sliced 2cm thick

765g coconut milk

100g to 130g Thai red curry paste, or to taste

3 tablespoons fish sauce

720ml to 960ml **Chicken Stock** (page 314) or water

FOR THE GARNISH

115g salted, dry-roasted peanuts

55g dried desiccated coconut flakes

2 tablespoons fish sauce

recipe and ingredients continue

Thinly slice the Thai basil leaves and arrange on a small plate or platter, along with lime wedges and the peanut mixture. Serve the soup hot with garnishes.

VARIATION

To make a **Winter Squash and Green Curry Soup,** substitute **green curry paste** for the red and use 4 **Honeynut or 2 butternut squashes** (about 1.8kg), peeled, seeded, and cut into about 2cm cubes, instead of the carrots.

- 8 small dried red chillies, such as chiles de árbol, thinly sliced
- 1 tablespoon coconut oil, melted
- 1 tablespoon minced lemongrass
- 1 tablespoon sugar
- 10 makrut lime leaves, thinly sliced (optional)
- Handful of Thai basil leaves
- 2 to 3 limes, quartered

creamy tomato soup

MAKES 2½ LITRES

70g extra-virgin olive oil

3 celery stalks, thinly sliced

1 brown onion, thinly sliced

Kosher salt

4 x 400g tins whole tomatoes, preferably San Marzano

480ml **Chicken Stock** (page 314), vegetable stock, or water

3 tablespoons plain flour

1 tablespoon sugar

28g unsalted butter

120ml double cream

120ml full-fat milk

Olive Oil–Fried Bread (page 94), **Sky-High Focaccia** (page 372), or grilled cheese sandwiches, for serving

This is my version of a classic tomato soup—the kind that beckons for a grilled cheese sandwich to dip into it. The secret to that quintessential tomato soup flavour is a generous amount of celery. A mix of stock, roux, double cream, and milk lends this soup a rich, velvety texture that makes it a plate-cleaning pleasure to eat. And since it comes together rather quickly and without much fuss, it's also a pleasure to make.

• • •

Heat a large nonreactive soup pot or casserole over medium-high heat and add the oil. When it shimmers, add the celery, the onion, and a generous pinch of salt. Reduce the heat to medium and cook, stirring occasionally, until the vegetables are tender and translucent but have not taken on colour, about 16 minutes.

Meanwhile, pour the tinned tomatoes into a large bowl and crush very well by hand. Pour a splash of the stock into an empty tin, swirl it around, then do the same with each of the empty tins before adding to the bowl of tomatoes. Set aside.

When the vegetables are tender, use a wooden spoon to move them to the outer edges of the pot. Tilt the pot if needed to coax a little puddle of oil back into the centre and add the flour to the oil. Mix the flour into the oil and let it cook for about 30 seconds before stirring it into the vegetables. Continue to cook, stirring, for another minute or two until the roux begins to bubble, then add the remaining stock before the mixture begins to brown. Increase the heat to high, bring to a boil, and add the crushed tomatoes, the sugar, and another generous pinch of salt. Give the bottom of the pot a good scraping with the wooden spoon to release any flour that may be sticking. Bring to a simmer and cook for 20 minutes, stirring regularly and thoroughly to prevent scorching.

To finish, add the butter, cream, and milk to the soup, then purée with an immersion blender. (Alternatively, purée very carefully in batches in a countertop blender.) Taste and adjust the seasoning with salt as needed.

Serve hot, with olive oil–fried bread, focaccia, or grilled cheese sandwiches.

Cover and refrigerate leftovers for up to 5 days or freeze for up to 6 months. Return leftovers to a boil before serving.

simple soba salad

SERVES 4

Kosher salt
340g soba noodles
1 tablespoon toasted sesame oil
1 batch **Sesame-Soy Dressing** or **Peanut-Ginger Dressing** (recipes follow)
2 to 3 spring onions, thinly sliced
10g coarsely chopped coriander leaves
2 tablespoons toasted sesame seeds

Japanese buckwheat, or soba, noodles are on steady rotation at my house. Especially in the warmer months, when I use them as a base for salad. While some soba noodles are made with 100 per cent buckwheat, I always seek out those made with a combination of buckwheat and wheat flour (my go-to brand is Shirakiku). The wheat's gluten leads to pleasantly springy noodles that still have plenty of that signature buckwheat nuttiness. And, when I can, I opt for fresh soba noodles, which are the chewiest and most flavourful of all.

• • •

Bring a large pot of salted water to a boil. Prepare a large bowl of very icy water and set aside.

Add the soba noodles to the boiling water and stir to prevent sticking. Cook until just tender, 3 to 5 minutes (less if using fresh noodles). Rinse under cold water until the noodles are no longer starchy, then plunge into the ice water to chill. Drain and toss the noodles with the oil to prevent clumping. Soba noodles will degrade quickly after cooking if not dressed, so don't cook them more than 30 minutes before you plan to eat.

Meanwhile, prepare your chosen dressing (see below).

Toss the chilled noodles with your prepared dressing, the spring onions, and the coriander. Garnish with the toasted sesame seeds. Serve chilled or at room temperature.

To store, cover and refrigerate for up to 3 days.

DRESSINGS

To make **Sesame-Soy Dressing:** In a small bowl, stir together 4 tablespoons **soy sauce,** 3 tablespoons **neutral oil,** 2 tablespoons **seasoned rice vinegar,** 2 tablespoons freshly squeezed **lime juice,** 1 tablespoon **agave or maple syrup,** 1 tablespoon **Calabrian Chilli Crisp** (page 56) **or sambal oelek,** 1 teaspoon **toasted sesame oil,** 1 tablespoon finely grated **fresh ginger,**

2 finely grated **garlic** cloves, and a pinch of kosher **salt**. Taste and adjust the seasoning with salt and lime juice.

• • •

To make **Peanut-Ginger Dressing:** In a small bowl, stir together 130g **creamy peanut butter**, 4 tablespoons **soy sauce**, 3 tablespoons freshly squeezed **lime juice**, 2 tablespoons **agave or maple syrup**, 1 tablespoon **seasoned rice vinegar**, 1 tablespoon **toasted sesame oil**, 1 tablespoon **Calabrian Chilli Crisp** (page 56) **or sambal oelek**, 1 tablespoon finely grated **fresh ginger**, 2 finely grated **garlic** cloves, and a pinch of kosher **salt**. Add **water** 1 tablespoon at a time until the sauce is a smooth, pourable consistency. Taste and adjust the seasoning with salt and lime juice.

VARIATIONS

To turn the soba into a **Vegetable Extravaganza,** toss in any of the following:

- Thinly sliced **cucumbers**
- Julienned **carrots**
- Thinly sliced **peppers**
- Thinly sliced **radishes**
- Blanched **peas or edamame**
- Blanched **broccoli or tenderstem broccoli**
- Sautéed sliced **mushrooms**
- Blanched sliced **asparagus**
- Blanched sliced **sugar snap peas or mangetout**
- Blanched **sweetcorn**

•

To add some protein, add a few pieces of any of the following on top:

- **Mara's Tofu** (page 187)
- **Teriyaki-ish Chicken Thighs** (page 306)
- **Chicken Thigh Schnitzel** (page 309)
- **Slow-Cooked Salmon** (page 337)

This has been my go-to store cupboard pasta since I moved to Italy for a kitchen apprenticeship in the autumn of 2002. On one of my first evenings in Florence, I had dinner at a pizzeria near Piazza Santa Croce. In the Tuscan gloaming, I ate a pizza topped with spicy tomato sauce, flakes of oil-packed tuna, and a lightly dressed pile of rocket. That pizza—made with ingredients I'd never imagined combining—gave me my first glimpse of all the ways my time in Italy would enrich me as a cook.

For the next two years, every time I went out for pizza, I scanned the menu for spicy tuna, but I never encountered it in Italy again. So when a craving for that pizza struck, I'd make myself this simple pasta instead. The key here is using quality staples: Tinned Italian cherry tomatoes, sometimes labelled pomodorini, are sweeter than their full-sized counterparts (though you can substitute 340g whole San Marzano tomatoes in their juice if needed). Italian or Spanish olive oil–packed tuna is truly superior in flavour and texture. And of course, real Parmesan, to which all other cheeses pale in comparison.

• • •

Bring a large pot of well-salted water to a boil.

Set a large nonreactive frying pan over medium heat and add 3 tablespoons oil. When it shimmers, add the onion and a pinch of salt. Cook, stirring, until the onion is tender and just beginning to brown, about 12 minutes.

Move the onion to the edges of the pan and add 2 tablespoons oil and the garlic. Cook, stirring, until fragrant, about 1 minute. Add the anchovies, chilli paste to taste, and tomato purée and cook, gently breaking up the pastes with a wooden spoon until the oil turns uniformly orange and the anchovies dissolve, about 2 minutes.

Add the pasta to the boiling water and cook until it's nearly al dente, 7 to 12 minutes, depending on the shape. Reserve 240ml pasta water and drain the pasta.

recipe continues

spicy tuna pantry pasta

SERVES 4 TO 6

Kosher salt

Extra-virgin olive oil

1 onion, cut into 8mm chunks

4 garlic cloves, thinly sliced

2 anchovy fillets, roughly chopped

Calabrian chilli paste

1 tablespoon tomato purée

450g spaghetti, bucatini, linguine, or penne

400g tin cherry tomatoes

20g finely grated Parmesan, plus more for serving

285 to 340g canned or bottled Spanish or Italian tuna in olive oil, undrained

1 lemon

Finely chopped parsley, for garnish

Increase the heat under the frying pan to medium and add the cherry tomatoes. Ladle a little pasta water into the can, swirl it around, and add it to the pan. Bring the sauce to a simmer, using the back of the spoon to break up the tomatoes. Cook, stirring, until the tomatoes begin to appear jammy, 4 to 6 minutes.

Stir in the Parmesan, tuna, and tuna oil. Taste the sauce and, taking into consideration that you'll still be adding some salted pasta water, adjust the seasoning with salt and chilli paste as desired.

Increase the heat to medium-high and add the drained pasta to the pan, tossing with sauce until well coated. As the sauce continues to cook and thicken onto the noodles, add a few tablespoons of pasta water at a time to loosen it up as much as needed. The sauce may also need another tablespoon or so of olive oil. This last step is all about tasting, stirring, and tinkering until the sauce comes together to coat the pasta in just the right way, ideally at precisely the same moment the noodles cross over to al dente.

Grate the zest of the lemon over the pasta and add the parsley. Toss again, taste, and add lemon juice, if desired.

Serve immediately, topped with more chilli paste and Parmesan, if desired.

spaghetti cacio e pepe

**SERVES 4 TO 6
(AND MAKES ABOUT 285G PASTE)**

Kosher salt

450g spaghetti

225g finely grated Pecorino Romano

1¼ teaspoons coarsely ground black pepper, plus more for serving

4 tablespoons cold water, plus more if needed

I loved making cacio e pepe, the classic Roman pasta, in restaurant kitchens. The trick to the thick, creamy sauce lies in combining the sauce's two ingredients—pecorino cheese and black pepper—with pasta water in just the right way (this usually involves a lot of frantic stirring and sweat). A commercial hob with powerful rings, a humongous pot of starchy pasta water, and the knowledge that a cleaning crew would later wipe down the walls were all I needed to perfect the deceptively simple sauce. But at home I have a harder time getting the sauce right. Often, I'm left with a curdled mess.

I asked colleagues for advice for years. They all essentially said, "Stir harder." But no matter how hard I stirred, I couldn't get it to work. So I turned to the internet. A quick search for "cacio e pepe" yielded a three-minute video in the kitchen of Flavio de Maio, a master of cucina Romana and producer of one of Rome's most traditional bowls of cacio e pepe. I watched in a state of semi-disbelief as he used a hardly traditional immersion blender to do the work of combining the grated cheese, ground pepper, and a few spoonfuls of cold water into a thick, uniform paste. Once the task of creating a creamy emulsion was complete, all he had left to do was to vigorously toss hot, just-cooked pasta with a generous amount of the paste. He then used a little bit of pasta water to thin it out to the right consistency. It was glossy and glorious and required none of the effort I'd come to associate with the dish. I was an immediate convert, and have evangelised this foolproof method ever since.

· · ·

Bring a large pot of salted water to a boil. Add the spaghetti and cook until it's nearly al dente.

Meanwhile, in a food processor, combine the pecorino, the pepper, and the cold water and pulse until it comes together into a thick, smooth paste. If needed, add more water, 1 tablespoon at a time, to encourage blending.

When the pasta is ready, reserve 240ml of the pasta water and drain the pasta in a colander. Return the empty pot to the stove, but not over heat.

Return the pasta to the pot along with three-quarters of the pecorino paste and a splash of the pasta cooking water. Toss vigorously with tongs while shaking the pot until the cheese melts and coats the pasta with a glossy sheen. Add cooking water and more pecorino paste to taste as needed until the cacio e pepe is the right consistency—something like a thin nacho cheese sauce. If the pasta is properly seasoned but the sauce is still too thick, add warm tap water instead of salted cooking water to loosen it. Serve immediately.

Cover and refrigerate any remaining paste for up to 1 month.

USES AND VARIATIONS

Make **Cacio e Pepe Farro** by tossing warm, just-boiled **farro** with cacio e pepe paste.

•

Whip together room-temperature cacio e pepe paste and **unsalted butter** in a 2:1 ratio to make **Cacio e Pepe Butter** to spread on grilled corn, toast, bagels, pitta, focaccia, or savoury scones.

•

Add thinly sliced **asparagus,** sliced **sugar snap peas,** peeled **broad beans,** or freshly shucked or frozen **peas** into the pasta pot for the last 30 to 60 seconds of the pasta cooking time.

creamy one-pot pasta with ricotta and peas

SERVES 4 TO 6

Kosher salt

450g dried pasta (any shape is fine)

225g shelled peas (fresh or frozen)

450g full-fat-milk ricotta, drained or **Whipped Ricotta** (page 66)

85g finely grated Parmesan, plus more for serving

Freshly ground black pepper

Large handful of basil leaves

Think of this pasta as the elegantly understated aunt to a box of mac and cheese. In the same amount of time it takes to make a box of Annie's, combining ricotta, Parmesan, and a little bit of pasta cooking water makes a rich, creamy sauce that is far greater than the sum of its parts. I can't imagine a more infallible argument for always having ricotta around.

...

Bring a large pot of well-salted water to a boil. Add the pasta and cook until it's nearly al dente. One to three minutes before the pasta is done cooking, add the peas to the water and cook until the pasta is al dente and the peas are barely cooked. Reserving 240ml of the cooking water, drain the pasta and peas into a colander.

To finish, return the empty pot to the hob. Add the ricotta and Parmesan. Stir to combine, then add the pasta and peas and stir vigorously to coat. Over low heat, add the cooking water, a little at a time to thin the sauce as needed. Taste and adjust the seasoning with salt and pepper, then tear the basil leaves into the pasta and stir to bring everything together.

Serve immediately with more Parmesan.

VARIATIONS

This recipe is endlessly adaptable—substitute any of these vegetables for the peas:

- 675g **broccoli or tenderstem broccoli**, trimmed and cut into bite-sized pieces
- 450g **asparagus**, snapped and cut into 5cm pieces on a sharp angle
- 225g peeled **broad beans** (fresh or frozen)
- 150g sliced **sugar snap peas or mangetout**
- 225g **corn kernels** (fresh or frozen)

stewed clams with tomatoes and saffron

No seafood dish has a better effort-to-flavour payoff ratio than stewed clams. If you've never cooked clams before, this is a perfect starter recipe. And if you're already an expert, let the classic flavourings of saffron, garlic, and white wine transport you to the Mediterranean. Either way, make sure to purge your clams of grit before you start (see Note for instructions). And don't skimp on either the fat or the crusty bread. A last-second addition of butter transforms the stew into a sauce so rich and heady, you'll want to sop up every drop.

• • •

Pour the tomatoes into a large bowl and crush them very well by hand.

Set a large wide saucepan or casserole over medium-high heat and add the oil. When it shimmers, add the garlic and chilli paste and cook until the garlic is fragrant but hasn't taken on any colour. Add the tomatoes and bloomed saffron. Season with salt and cook, stirring, until the tomatoes reduce a bit and start to become jammy, 10 to 12 minutes.

Add the clams and the wine, increase the heat to high, and cover the pot. Let the clams steam until they open, 3 to 4 minutes. Use tongs to transfer clams to a bowl as they open. Discard any clams that refuse to open after 5 minutes (sometimes, a little tap with the tongs will encourage a stubborn one to open).

Taste and adjust the seasoning of the sauce with salt, chilli paste, oil, and wine, all while continuing to simmer. When the sauce is just right, remove the pan from the heat and stir in the butter. Return the clams to the pot and shower with the parsley.

Serve with crusty bread to sop up the sauce, which everyone knows is the best part.

SERVES 4

2 x 400g tins whole tomatoes, preferably San Marzano

3 tablespoons extra-virgin olive oil

4 garlic cloves, thinly sliced

½ teaspoon Calabrian chilli paste or pinch of chilli flakes

¼ teaspoon saffron threads, ground and bloomed (see page 37)

Kosher salt

1.4kg littleneck clams, washed and purged of grit (see Note)

240ml dry white wine

2 tablespoons unsalted butter

2 tablespoons coarsely chopped parsley

Crusty bread, for serving

recipe continues

NOTE

To purge clams before cooking, scrub and rinse them well in cold water. In a large bowl, whisk 3 tablespoons plus 2 teaspoons (33g) of kosher salt into 960ml very cold water until dissolved. Place the clams in the water and refrigerate. They should start to open slightly and stick their siphons out. After 1½ to 2 hours, carefully lift them out of the bowl to leave the sand and grit behind. If the water is very gritty, you may want to repeat with another round of salt water for a couple more hours. Rinse the clams and store on a tray under a damp towel in the refrigerator until ready to use.

VARIATIONS

For a **Saffron and Tomato Fish Stew,** substitute 450g of **cod, rockfish, or halibut,** cut into 55g pieces, for the clams. Season the fish with **salt,** add it to the pan along with the wine once the tomatoes are jammy, then cover and simmer until tender and flaky, 3 to 8 minutes (halibut will be done in closer to 3 minutes, while cod and rockfish will seize up and then relax, taking closer to 8 minutes). Shower with **parsley** or torn **basil**.

•

To use **fresh tomatoes** instead of tinned, halve and coarsely grate about 6 tomatoes, discarding the skin, until you have 500g of pulp. Cook as described on page 185, until jammy, about 5 minutes.

•

To add a little summer flourish to the stew, add 150g of packed coarsely grated **summer squash** to the tomatoes.

•

To make **White Bean Stew with Tomatoes and Saffron,** skip the seafood altogether and stir 375g of **cooked white beans** into the tomato base. Finish with **butter, Parmesan,** and **parsley, oregano leaves,** or torn **basil**.

mara's tofu

With only a few steps and three ingredients, this dish barely requires a recipe, yet the results are both nourishing and deeply satisfying. I learned the method from my friend Mara Greenaway, who based the recipe on the memory of her favourite marinated tofu from the grocery co-op where her mom shopped in Kona, Hawaii. Steeped in aminos (soy sauce's unfermented cousin), the semisoft tofu melts away with each bite, leaving behind steamy contrails of salt and umami. The coconut oil lends a trace of its sweet, tropical aroma, and it yields a crisp, lacy crust. To complete the meal, serve it with steamed rice or **Simple Soba Salad** (page 174) and boiled green vegetables.

SERVES 4 TO 6

- 800g medium-firm tofu, drained
- 6 tablespoons Bragg liquid aminos
- 4 to 6 tablespoons coconut oil

• • •

Line a baking tray or large plate with kitchen paper. Set aside.

Pat the tofu dry, then halve lengthways. Cut crossways into 1.25cm-thick slices. Drizzle 2 tablespoons of the aminos onto the bottom of a large, shallow glass or ceramic baking dish, then set a layer of tofu in it. Drizzle with another 2 tablespoons aminos, then layer in the remaining tofu. Drizzle with the remaining 2 tablespoons aminos. Marinate for 5 minutes, then rotate and flip the tofu slices, and tilt the dish to coat them evenly. Marinate for 5 more minutes, then drain away excess aminos.

Set a 25cm cast-iron or nonstick frying pan over high heat. When the pan is hot, add 2 tablespoons of the oil. Just as the oil begins to smoke, carefully add pieces of tofu in a single layer, leaving room between the pieces.

Reduce the heat to medium-high, do not touch the tofu, and cook it until golden brown, 6 to 7 minutes. Use a thin metal spatula to carefully flip the pieces and cook until golden brown on the second side, another 6 to 7 minutes. Cook the rest the same way, adding more oil as needed.

Blot the cooked tofu on the kitchen paper to drain excess fat, then serve hot.

good things come to those who wait

seasonal produce

Produce—especially produce at the peak of its season—has always been at the heart of my cooking. I build most of my meals around vegetables, fruit, flowers, and seeds. And after decades of cooking this way, anticipating the arrival of each season and its produce feels like a sacred ritual. In the spring I look forward to the arrival of asparagus like a kid counting down the days until Christmas. Making my first BLT of the summer is such a momentous occasion that I usually end up throwing a little party to celebrate it. And each winter, as I peel and roast my first squash, I think of the thousands of ravioli di zucca I've filled and folded over the years.

I've organised this chapter by season to reflect how I generally shop for and cook vegetables (since autumn produce continues to be available throughout the winter, I've combined the two seasons into a single section). Once I bring produce home, I rarely have a concrete plan for how to use it. Instead, a handful of variables—including available time and energy, cravings and preferences, and the other ingredients in a dish or meal—guides my decisions each time I cook. To reflect this, instead of offering recipes that are set in stone, I've included instructional guides for each type of produce. Think of each one as a playbook—with shopping tips, suggested cooking methods, winning flavour combinations, and the occasional precise recipe—for each vegetable.

More often than not, you'll rely on one of three methods—boiling, roasting, or sautéing—for cooking produce, so this chapter begins with a thorough primer on each. Here, you'll find general cooking times and temperatures, how and when to add salt to a dish, and other details to support you if cooking without a written recipe makes you feel uneasy. And if you're already a confident, intuitive cook, let the primers refresh your memory as needed.

Since I'm loath to write about produce in any way that might limit, rather than expand, your imagination, I've also included a handful of matrices, complete with photo collages, to inspire and guide you. I've designed them to help you combine simply prepared vegetables with dressings, condiments, and toppings to create stunning side dishes and composed salads.

After a calendar year of using these guides and charts, you'll discover a new level of confidence with produce. You'll learn to look at, say, broccoli and see a creamy, comforting pasta with ricotta and silky broccoli purée. You'll learn to think of a glut of summer tomatoes not as a cause for overwhelm but as a doorway to endless possibility. And as you get to know your preferences and notice which vegetables you await most eagerly, you just might create some seasonal rituals of your own.

vegetable cooking basics

I often feel my path as a cook has been a bit backwards. I went from my mother's kitchen, where I learned to make a few basics, such as scrambled eggs and tuna salad, to college. There I excelled at combining cheese with carbohydrates to make macaroni and cheese, grilled cheese, quesadillas, English muffin pizzas, and tuna melts. Most people—whether home cooks or professionals—tend to start out cooking simply, like I did, in young adulthood. And as their interest, skill level, and resources increase gradually over time, so does the relative complexity of their cooking.

But that's not how it went for me. Towards the end of college, I got a job bussing tables at Chez Panisse restaurant in Berkeley. Within a few months, I began volunteering in the kitchen, and eventually I was hired as a cook. World-class chefs taught me to boil an egg, roast a chicken, make a salad dressing, and bake a cake. In just a few short years, I could tend a wood-fired oven, make a demi-glace, and perfectly crimp a pastry case. Along the way, I adopted my mentors' rules as my own and believed that the way I'd been taught was the only right way to do things.

Twelve years later, I left restaurants and began spending my days at my desk, writing. I had to learn how to cook all over again—this time without daily produce deliveries, an always-stocked cupboard, or full-time dishwashers. Without that essential infrastructure at my fingertips, I began to see that the stratospheric standards I'd always held myself to in professional kitchens didn't necessarily make sense at home.

I realised that home cooking is a practice distinct from—not lesser than—its professional counterpart, each with very different goals. Over time, I've identified and filtered out the restaurant techniques that felt overly fussy and time-consuming. Now I only do what is absolutely essential for cooking great food.

This trend towards simplicity is perhaps most evident in how I approach cooking vegetables. I tend to default to one of three methods: boiling, roasting, or sautéing. Then—if the occasion calls for it—I'll garnish the vegetables with a dressing, sauce, or condiment. Simple doesn't have to mean boring. In fact, you'll find that mastering these three basic methods and knowing when to employ each one will open the door to an infinite bounty of vegetable dishes for you.

boil

M. F. K. Fisher wrote that "the natural progression from boiling water to boiling water with something in it can hardly be avoided, and in most cases is heartily to be wished for." I've often found myself wanting to write, much less eloquently, "Trust me—just boil it in generously salted water until it's barely tender."

I've cooked nearly every vegetable that's entered my kitchen this way. Kids and adults alike gobble up salty boiled potatoes dressed with melted ghee. Sometimes, a pile of boiled tenderstem broccoli topped with toasted sesame oil constitutes my entire dinner—a deeply satisfying one, too. I don't know of a better way to cook baby turnips and their greens than to boil them separately, reunite them on the plate, and drizzle them with good olive oil. Peas, whether fresh or frozen, take mere moments to cook in a salted, roiling bath. Toss them immediately upon their emergence from the pot with the fat of your choice—I like salted cultured butter or a fruity olive oil.

I should state that, due to its overwhelming simplicity, boiling won't transform inferior, overly fibrous, or starchy vegetables or produce that's otherwise past its prime into something that's a joy to eat. We're cooking, not performing magic, after all.

• • •

so for the best results, remember:

- If it tastes good raw, it'll taste even better cooked.

- Use a larger pot than you think you need so that the water can return to a boil as quickly as possible.

- Add vegetables to generously salted water at a rowdy boil—except for potatoes, which should start in cold water and cook at a gentle simmer.

- Cut produce into similar-sized pieces so it all cooks evenly. And take a look at **Eating with Your Eyes** (page 32) for a few of my favourite ways to cut vegetables.

- If cooking more than one kind of vegetable, boil each type separately to ensure they all cook properly. You can use the same pot of water, but save anything bitter or sulfurous—that means broccoli, cauliflower, cabbage, or their kin—for last to prevent passing unwanted flavours onto milder vegetables.

- Cook produce until it's barely tender and account for a little more cooking once it's out of the water. Have a colander ready in the sink, or use a spider strainer to pluck vegetables from the pot as soon as they're done. If they're not headed straight to

- the table, spread hot vegetables out in a single layer to prevent them from overcooking as they cool.

- To prevent the shrivelling that tends to occur as boiled vegetables cool, toss them with a little bit of oil as soon as they're drained.

- And finally, taste your vegetables while they're in the water and after they emerge. You can always add salt to the pot while they're still cooking to ensure they're properly seasoned from within. Once they're on the platter, add a sprinkling of flaky salt and a squeeze of lemon if you like.

vegetables to boil

- Artichokes
- Asparagus
- Broad beans
- Broccoli and tenderstem broccoli
- Cabbage
- Carrots
- Cauliflower and Romanesco
- Chard
- Corn
- Fennel
- Hardy leafy greens
- Parsnips
- Peas
- Potatoes
- Rapini
- Spinach
- String beans
- Sugar snap peas and mangetout
- Summer squash
- Sweet potatoes
- Turnips and their greens

roast

Roasting yields vegetables unmatched in tenderness and sweetness, especially when you dare to toe the line of darkness. My general experience is that most home cooks don't roast their vegetables long or dark enough. In fact, I like to call my vegetables "dark roasted" or "nearly burnt" rather than simply "roasted" to properly convey how far I cook them. The magic happens during that last little stretch of time in the oven: Sugars concentrate and caramelise. The Maillard reaction produces a broad range of browning across the pan of vegetables. So let me bestow upon you the courage to take your carrots and cauliflower further than you otherwise might—you'll be rewarded for your bravery.

When cooking for just one or two, you can use a toaster oven (if you have one!) to cook a bunch of carrots, a small head of cauliflower, some potatoes, or a couple small winter squashes. For larger amounts—or when cooking multiple types of vegetables at once—use a full-sized oven. The heat source doesn't matter nearly as much as the way you attend to your vegetables.

. . .

how to roast any vegetable

Preheat the oven to 220°C. Adjust a rack to the centre position (if using two baking trays, adjust the racks to the upper-middle and lower-middle positions). Line one or more baking trays with parchment paper and set aside.

Cut the vegetables into even-sized pieces that aren't too thick or too thin—for most vegetables, a one-and-a-half-bite-sized piece is perfect. (Consult **Eating with Your Eyes,** page 32, for a primer on my favourite ways to cut various vegetables.)

Place the vegetables in a large bowl. Toss with enough oil or melted fat to coat and enough salt to season generously. Add any desired spices.

Spread the pieces onto the prepared tray(s), making sure to scrape out any oil and spices that might remain in the bowl. Bake on the prepared rack(s) for 25 to 45 minutes (most vegetables will be done around the 30-minute mark), using tongs or a thin metal spatula to flip the vegetables and move them around the pan every 10 minutes. Rotate the tray(s) front to back and, if using more than one tray, swap racks after 15 minutes.

Cook until the edges/sides/tips are very dark brown and a paring knife easily slides in and out.

Serve hot, warm, or at room temperature.

and remember:

- Unlike boiling, roasting can coax out all the sweetness a vegetable has to offer by browning and crisping its surface to create textural contrast. Opt to roast any produce that's been sitting in your crisper drawer for a little too long.

- Use any fat that feels right for the dish—olive oil, neutral oil, lard, schmaltz, ghee, butter, or coconut oil will all work.

- To ensure even browning, allow time for the oven to preheat and use a baking tray instead of a roasting dish. Cut produce into similar-sized pieces and spread them out in a single layer, leaving room between them for steam to escape.

- You can combine similar types of produce on a single tray with great success—potatoes and sweet potatoes, broccoli and cauliflower, carrots and turnips. But avoid combining vegetables that have dissimilar amounts of sugar, starch, or water—they won't cook at the same rate. Instead, use a separate tray for each, or use half of the tray for one type and the other half for another, and remove each as it's done cooking.

- For the most even browning, carefully tend to your vegetables as they roast. Stir them, turn or flip them, rotate the trays front to back, and swap racks.

- And finally, salt watery produce—including aubergines, summer squash, and tomatoes—in advance. This will encourage browning and prevent the vegetables from cooking in a puddle of their own juices. Season these ingredients 30 to 60 minutes before cooking, then drain or blot off excess water and proceed as directed on page 196. If you're in a hurry, skip the salt before cooking, then season the tray only once the vegetables have begun to brown.

vegetables to roast

- Aubergines
- Beetroot
- Broccoli and tenderstem broccoli
- Cabbage wedges
- Carrots
- Cauliflower and Romanesco
- Fennel
- Onions
- Parsnips
- Potatoes (simmer until tender first for maximum creaminess)
- Summer and winter squashes
- Sweet potatoes
- Tomatoes
- Turnips

sauté

The term *sauté* refers to the "jump" or flip of a wrist that tosses food in a pan while cooking over high heat. Keeping the food in motion will prevent burnt spots.

To best manage the high heat involved in sautéing, use a high-quality stainless or carbon-steel pan and make sure not to overcrowd it. If you can, choose a pan with curved sides, which will discourage jumping vegetables from landing on the floor (you can also use a carbon-steel wok, if you have one). And use a sturdy pair of stainless steel kitchen tongs to keep food moving as it cooks.

• • •

how to sauté any vegetable

Have everything ready before you begin—sautéing moves fast. This includes your cooking fat, prepped vegetables, aromatics (including minced garlic and ginger), salt and other seasonings, and any garnishes. Trim produce into small pieces to ensure they'll cook quickly.

If your smoke alarm is hypersensitive, ventilate your kitchen before you begin. Open kitchen windows and set your ventilation hood to high.

Next, set your pan over high heat. When you think it's ready, test it by adding a drop of water. If it immediately vaporises, you're good to go. Now, add just enough olive oil, neutral oil, ghee, or coconut oil to coat the bottom of the pan. When it shimmers, add your vegetables and cook them over high heat. To prevent vegetables from steaming, cook them in batches of no larger than 225g.

If you're after a little browning, let the vegetables cook undisturbed until they start to take on colour, then season them with salt and start to move them around the pan. To prevent browning, add salt early and keep vegetables constantly moving in the pan. Depending on the type of vegetable and the size of the pieces, it'll take anywhere between 3 and 10 minutes to cook them through.

If your vegetables are browning more quickly than they're growing tender, turn down the heat a bit, add a small splash of water, and cover the pan with a lid. This will give them the opportunity to cook through before they burn. Once they are tender, remove the lid, tip out any remaining water, and increase the heat to crisp them up.

Taste and adjust the seasoning, transfer to a serving platter, and serve immediately.

and remember:

- Sliced and chopped garlic is prone to burning, so wait until vegetables are tender to add it. Then move the vegetables to the outer edges of the pan. Add another tablespoon of cooking fat into the centre of the pan, then add the garlic. Let it sizzle until it's fragrant, then toss it into the vegetables before it has a chance to take on any colour.

- Treat fresh ginger—minced or cut into matchsticks—and fresh or dried chillies the same as garlic to prevent burning.

vegetables to sauté

- Asparagus
- Aubergines
- Broccoli and tenderstem broccoli (blanch first)
- Cabbage
- Cauliflower and Romanesco (blanch first)
- Chard
- Corn
- Fennel
- Hardy leafy greens (blanch first)
- Onions
- Peppers
- Sugar snap peas and mangetout
- Spinach
- String beans (blanch first)
- Summer squash
- Turnips

to prepare vegetables for sautéing:

- Cut **asparagus** on a very sharp angle (about 30 degrees) into slices that are 6mm thick and about 5cm long.

- Use a Japanese mandoline to thinly slice small **turnips** before sautéing them.

- Blanch bite-sized pieces of **string beans, broccoli, tenderstem broccoli, cauliflower, or Romanesco** until barely tender, drain well on a towel-lined baking tray, and proceed as directed on page 198.

- Trim **sugar snap peas or mangetout,** then cut them in half on a gentle bias.

- Strip **chard** off the stalk and cut the leaves into 1.25cm-wide ribbons. Cook **baby spinach** whole and cut **larger spinach** in half. Thinly slice **cabbage** or dice it into bite-sized pieces.

- Shuck ears of fresh **corn**, remove the silk, then strip kernels from the cob.

- Thinly slice **onions, fennel, or peppers,** or cut them into bite-sized pieces.

- Thinly slice **aubergines or summer squash,** or cut them into bite-sized pieces. Do not season either until they've begun to brown—otherwise they'll end up mushy after steaming in a puddle of their own juices.

- Lightly blanch the leaves of **kale, spring greens, or mustard greens**. Then squeeze out any excess water and cut the greens into ribbons before sautéing.

- Trim away the woody ends from **rapini** stalks, then cut the rest into 5cm pieces on a bias. Lightly blanch the stalks and florets together, then squeeze out any excess water before sautéing.

asparagus

SPRING

Somewhat counterintuitively, thicker asparagus spears are more tender—and more nutritious—than their skinnier counterparts. For this reason, when given the option I opt for spears thicker than my forefinger. Look for firm spears with tight green buds. Avoid wrinkled stems or ends that are splitting or excessively dry—all signs that they were picked ages ago and have likely lost much of their sweetness.

A 450g bunch of asparagus will serve two or three people. To prepare asparagus stalks for cooking, snap off their tough ends. A stalk will snap in the middle if that's where you put pressure, so keep your hands near the bottom to avoid waste. Use a sharp vegetable peeler to gently peel the skin of any spears thicker than your pinky finger.

• • •

Asparagus lends itself well to stewing and sautéing, but I usually cook it in the simplest possible way—by boiling it briefly in heavily salted water.

blanched asparagus

Blanch prepped asparagus in **salted water** until very al dente and still shockingly bright green, 2 to 4 minutes depending on thickness. Pull out a spear and take a bite to check its doneness, keeping in mind that the asparagus will cook a bit more after it emerges from the water. In other words, it should be a little firmer than you'd like. Use a spider or other large strainer to carefully lift the spears out of the water and spread them out on a parchment-lined tray in a single layer, then drizzle and toss them with a bit of good **olive oil** to prevent them from shrivelling. Since the short amount of time asparagus spends in the blanching pot is rarely long enough to season it through, you may want to sprinkle a bit of **flaky salt** over the spears as you transfer them to a platter. Serve as is, or:

Drizzle warm asparagus with **extra-virgin olive oil**, melted **butter, House Dressing** (page 117), or **Creamy Lemon-Miso Dressing** (page 122). Or, chill blanched asparagus and serve it with a dollop of **mayonnaise** seasoned with a bit of finely grated **garlic**.

warm asparagus vinaigrette

For this bistro staple, dress still-warm blanched asparagus with **House Dressing** (page 117), **flaky salt,** and a few grinds of **black pepper**. Arrange on a warm serving platter. Season 3 halved **7½-Minute Eggs** (page 149) with flaky salt, pepper, and a little of the dressing and nestle them among the spears. Serve immediately.

broad beans

SPRING

I named my pup Fava Bean (a type of broad bean in the USA) because this harbinger of spring braids together the three strands of my culinary heritage. All throughout my childhood my mom enlisted me to pop and then peel broad beans for **Baghali Polo** (page 158), an Iranian dish of crispy rice with broad beans and dill. In Italy, raw young broad beans are served as a starter with sheep's milk cheese—usually ricotta or a mild pecorino. And at Chez Panisse, where I learned to cook like a Californian, a paste of lightly cooked broad beans seasoned with mint, garlic, and an abundance of olive oil makes a mouthwatering topping for grilled bread.

Preparing broad beans requires a fair bit of work. And since 450g of broad beans in the pod will yield only about 75g shelled beans, enlist friends and family to help out.

First, broad beans must be popped from their pods. To do this efficiently, loosely wrap the fingers of your nondominant hand around a pod. Locate a bean and press on it with both thumb pads to pop it out, then continue along the length of the pod. Do this over a large bowl to catch all of the beans. The skin on broad beans larger than a thumbnail is tough and unpleasant to eat. To peel it off, blanch the beans in salted, boiling water until their skins are loose, about 1 minute. Immediately transfer to a bowl of ice water. Allow to cool completely, then pinch and peel away the skins.

・・・

Besides lightly blanching broad beans for salad, I suggest cooking in one of two ways: stewed gently on their own or with other spring vegetables for a verdant side dish, or boiled until completely soft and mashed into a purée. From there you can make:

pasta with broad beans and mint

Toss stewed broad beans or broad bean purée with just-cooked **pasta**, **Whipped Ricotta** (page 66), **mint**, and **Parmesan**.

broad bean and preserved meyer lemon dip

Stir a little **Preserved Meyer Lemon Paste** (page 79) into broad bean purée, then season with chopped **dill** and finely grated **garlic**. Place in a bowl, top with a dollop of **Garlic and Herb Labne** (page 48) and serve with **pitta chips** or warm **Fluffy Pitta Pockets** (page 385).

broad bean crostini

Liberally smear **Marinated Goat's Cheese** (page 74) onto **Olive Oil–Fried Bread** (page 94), then pile on stewed broad beans. Garnish with chopped **parsley, mint, dill, chives, or basil**.

spring salad with broad beans

Add blanched, peeled broad beans to a salad of **Little Gems, sugar snap peas,** thinly sliced **radishes, dill** fronds, and 2.5cm lengths of **chives**. Toss with **Creamy Lemon-Miso Dressing** (page 122) and top with **croutons or Golden Panko** (page 131).

peas and sugar snaps

SPRING

While peas in the pod need shelling, sugar snap peas and mangetout need to be strung before cooking or eating. Use a paring knife or your thumbnail to cut into the stalk end and pull the string away towards the blossom end. Then turn and remove the string from the other side, too.

About 450g of English peas in the pod will yield 150g shelled, enough for two generous portions. About 450g of sugar snap peas or mangetout will serve four.

For most preparations, you can keep sugar snap peas and mangetout whole or halve at a sharp angle. To sauté or use them in salads where you might want them in smaller bits, slice them into 1.25cm pieces on a gentle bias.

Peas in the pod, sugar snap peas, and mangetout are sweetest the moment they're picked. The longer they sit in the fridge, the starchier they become, so use them up as soon as you can once you bring them home. A quick dip in a pot of salted, boiling water or a minute or two of sautéing will help perk up peas of any kind that are no longer at their peak. (And, when you're jonesing for peas but can't find any decent fresh ones, don't forget about the freezer aisle. Since frozen peas are picked and processed when perfectly ripe, they're reliably sweet.)

• • •

sugar snap pea chopped salad

To make a chopped salad you won't want to stop eating, string and slice 450g of the sweetest sugar snap peas into 1.25cm pieces on a gentle bias. Halve a small **fennel bulb** and use a mandoline or sharp knife to slice it thinly. Use the tip of a table knife to chip 85g of **aged Gouda** into pea-sized crumbles. Toss the peas, fennel, and cheese in a large bowl with 4 chopped, pitted **Medjool dates**, 100g lightly toasted **pine nuts**, and a large handful each of **basil** and **mint** torn into pieces. Toss with **Creamy Lemon-Miso Dressing** (page 122), taste and adjust the seasoning with **salt** and **lemon juice** as needed, then mound onto a platter and serve.

pea purée

Combine 450g of shelled, lightly blanched peas in a food processor with 3 tablespoons **extra-virgin olive oil**, 1 packed teaspoon finely grated **lemon zest**, 1 tablespoon **lemon juice**, 1 finely grated **garlic** clove, **salt**, and 4 tablespoons coarsely chopped **soft herbs** of your choice. Pulse into a coarse paste, then taste and adjust seasoning with salt and lemon juice. Serve as a dip, spread onto **Olive Oil-Fried Bread** (page 94), or smear liberally onto a platter, top with large crumbles of **Marinated Feta** (page 71) or **Marinated Goat's Cheese** (page 74), and serve with **crusty bread**.

a small, good thing: stewed spring vegetables

This is my go-to dish when I've got a little bit of this and a little bit of that. It's inspired by vignarola, a classic Roman spring vegetable and herb stew. Start with a base of alliums—green garlic and spring onions are ideal, but if you can't get your hands on them, an onion and a few garlic cloves, all thinly sliced, will work just fine. You can use any amount of broad beans, asparagus, sugar snap peas or mangetout, and tender leafy greens in any combination here.

Set a large nonreactive frying pan or casserole over medium heat and add enough **extra-virgin olive oil** to generously coat the bottom. Add the thinly sliced bulbs and first 7.5cm pale green part of 1 or 2 **salad onions** and 1 or 2 stalks of **green garlic**. Add a pinch of **salt** and cook, stirring regularly to prevent browning, until the onions and garlic are tender, about 10 minutes.

Add a generous splash of **water** and peeled **broad beans** (fresh or frozen), and cook, stirring, until nearly tender, 2 to 4 minutes.

Then add **asparagus** (sliced into 1.25cm-thick pieces on a sharp bias) and **sugar snap peas or mangetout** (strings removed and cut in half on a sharp bias). If most of the water has evaporated, add another splash to reach a stewy consistency. Add another generous splash of olive oil, season with salt, and cook until nearly tender, about 2 minutes.

Finally, add shucked **peas** (fresh or frozen) and delicate spring greens such as **pea shoots, broad bean leaves, or spinach**. Season with salt and cook until all the vegetables are warmed through and the final additions are tender but still bright, 2 to 3 minutes.

Season with finely grated **lemon zest** and freshly squeezed **lemon juice**. Shower with finely chopped **soft herbs**. Serve warm as a side dish or alongside **crusty bread, rice, or buttered noodles**.

boiled spring vegetable matrix

Spring vegetables are all about sweetness and crunch, so cook them with an aim to preserve— and even heighten—those qualities. In ample salted boiling water, cook:

- thick asparagus spears for 3 to 4 minutes
- thin asparagus spears for 90 seconds to 3 minutes
- asparagus cut into pieces for 1 to 2 minutes
- sugar snap peas and mangetout for 1 to 2 minutes
- peas for 1 to 2 minutes
- broad beans for 2 to 3 minutes until tender

Once you pull them from the water, dab them on a baking tray lined with a clean tea towel. Then, while still warm, toss with just enough olive oil to coat to prevent shrivelling.

Serve tossed with:

- finely grated lemon zest
- Bright Pickled Onions
- Golden Panko, pitta chips, or torn croutons
- Pickled Thai Chillies
- Creamy Lemon-Miso Dressing, Creamy Oregano Dressing, or House Dressing
- a little flaky salt

and/or

- basil, chervil, chives, mint, parsley, shiso, or tarragon

or

For something a little more substantial, combine the crunch with something creamy. Pile the warm vegetables atop a platter smeared liberally with:

- Garlic and Herb Labne
- Whipped Tahini
- Whipped Ricotta
- feta, crumbled (not smeared)

or

- burrata, torn (not smeared)

And then top with:

- Green Sauce
- Crispy Fried Shallots
- Preserved Meyer Lemon Paste
- Calabrian Chilli Crisp

Broad bean fattoush with **Bright Pickled Onions** (page 52), feta-style cheese, dill, **Creamy Lemon-Miso Dressing** (page 122), and **Preserved Meyer Lemon Paste** (page 79)

Asparagus with torn burrata, lemon zest, and extra-virgin olive oil

Sugar snap peas and peas with **Creamy Sesame-Ginger Dressing** (page 119), **Pickled Thai Chillies** (page 76), and shiso

corn

SUMMER

The fresher the corn, the sweeter, so use it as soon as possible after bringing it home. Look for ears with bright green husks that aren't yet brittle. Peel back the tips of the husks to check for plump kernels and pale green or yellow silks that haven't begun to brown.

The simplest way to strip kernels from an ear of corn is to lay it horizontally on a chopping board. Use a serrated knife or sharp chef's knife to remove two or three rows of kernels at a time by sliding the knife along the cob. Get as close to the cob as you can and resist the temptation to cut off too many rows at once—that'll leave behind lots of precious corn.

Whether boiling or grilling whole ears, or sautéing kernels, cook corn quickly over high heat to preserve its sweetness and prevent it from drying out.

. . .

corn on the cob

Boil whole or halved shucked ears of corn in abundant **salted water** just until the kernels change in colour, 2 to 4 minutes. Or grill them over high heat until charred, 12 to 15 minutes. Slather with **salted butter, Cacio e Pepe Butter** (page 181), or **Marinated Goat's Cheese** (page 74) and drizzle with **Green Sauce** (page 51) or **Calabrian Chilli Crisp** (page 56).

sautéed corn

Shave kernels from raw ears of corn, then sauté them in **extra-virgin olive oil or unsalted butter** and season simply with **salt**.

For a **Creamy Corn and Squash Sauté,** combine corn kernels with an equal amount of **summer squash** diced into kernel-sized pieces and sauté together in **extra-virgin olive oil**. Transfer to a large serving bowl and fold in torn **basil or coriander,** crumbled **feta-style or goat's cheese,** a generous spoonful of **crème fraîche or soured cream,** and a drizzle of **Green Sauce** (page 51). Taste and adjust the seasoning and serve warm.

corn salad

For salad, shave kernels raw from the freshest, sweetest ears. Or strip grilled or boiled corn.

To make an **Elote-Style Salad,** char 4 to 6 ears of corn on a grill or in a dry cast-iron frying pan set over high heat, about 15 minutes. Strip the kernels, then transfer to a large bowl. In a medium bowl, whisk together 4 tablespoons **mayonnaise,** 4 tablespoons **Mexican crema or soured cream,** 4 tablespoons finely grated **queso Cotija,** 1 teaspoon **mild chilli powder,** 1 finely grated **garlic** clove, and 2 tablespoons finely chopped **coriander**. Toss the corn with the dressing, then taste and adjust the seasoning with **salt** and freshly squeezed **lime juice**. Garnish with more Cotija, coriander, and chilli powder to serve.

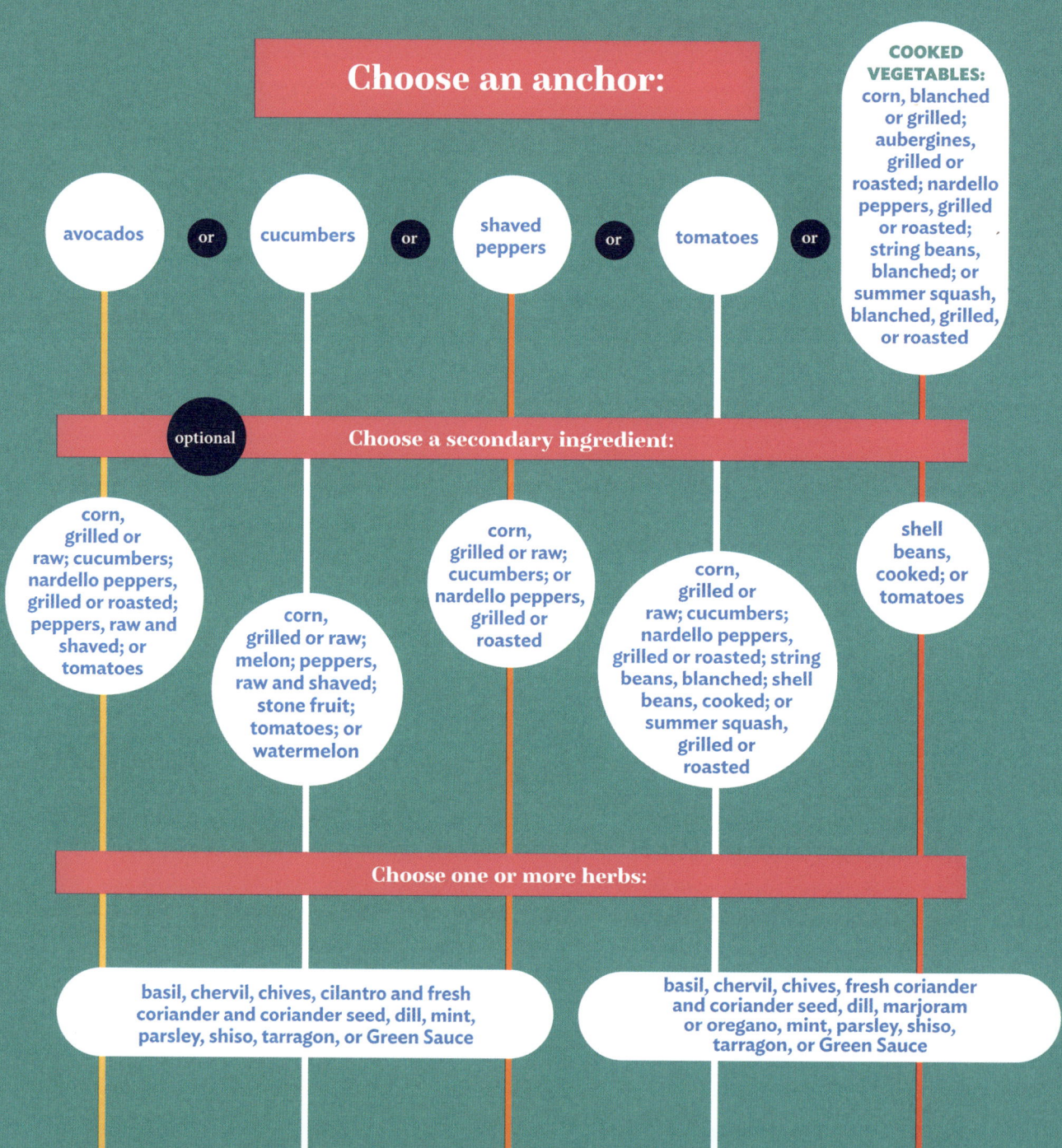

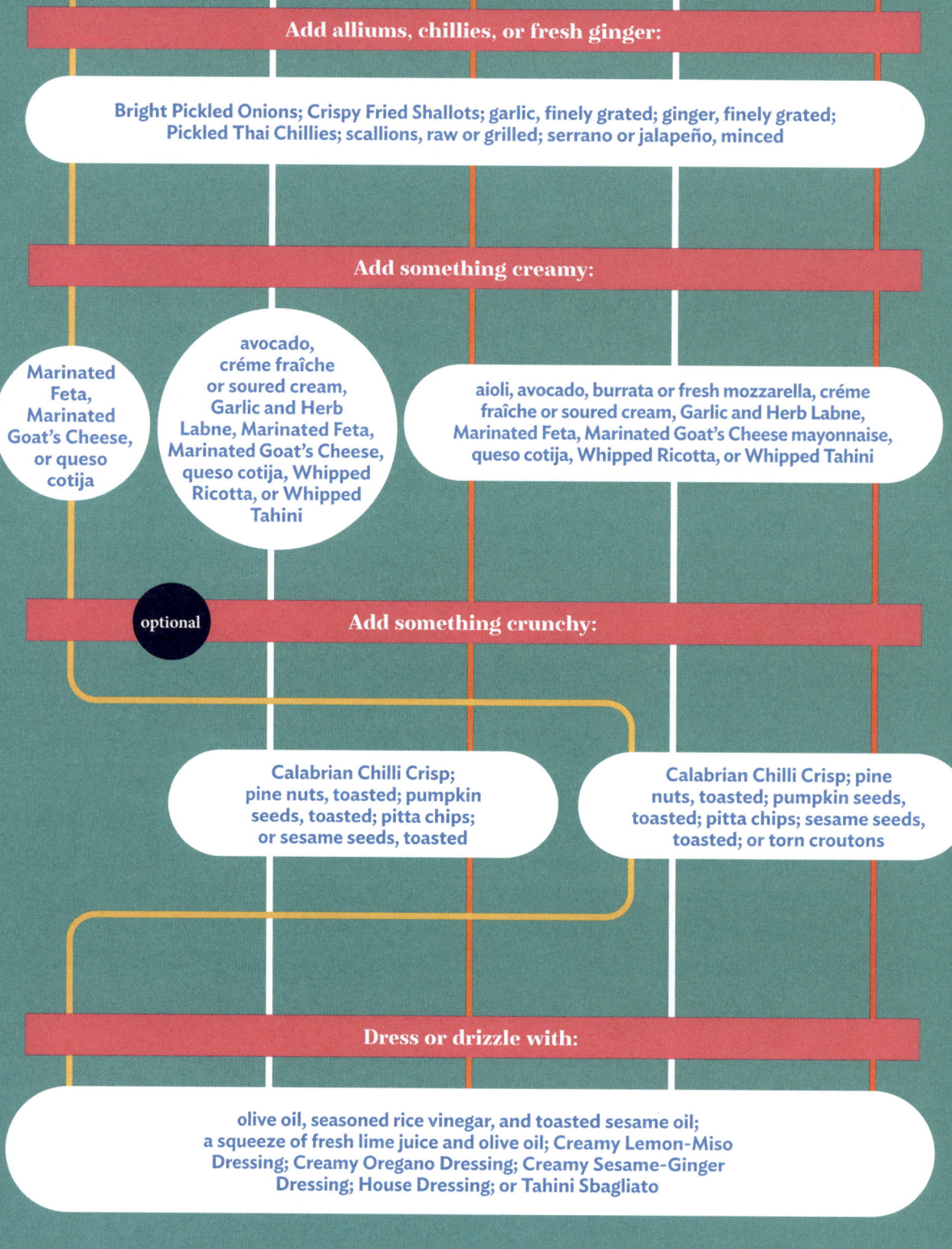

Shaved peppers with **Creamy Sesame-Ginger Dressing** (page 119), **Crispy Fried Shallots** (page 55), spring onions, and coriander

Blanched runner beans and yellow wax beans and cannellini beans with **Creamy Oregano Dressing** (page 125) and basil

Blanched corn and summer squash with soured cream, crumbled feta-style cheese, coriander, **Green Sauce** (page 51), and a squeeze of lime

Grilled corn and Nardello peppers with tomatoes, avocado, cucumbers, dill, extra-virgin olive oil, and a squeeze of lime

Avocado and cucumbers with **Tahini Sbagliato** (page 132) and **Bright Pickled Onions** (page 52)

a small, good thing: herb salad

Or just herbs in your salad. Soft herbs work best here (you don't want to have to pick woody bits of rosemary out of your teeth as you eat). Little **dill or chervil** fronds, torn **mint or basil,** thinly sliced **shiso leaves,** 2.5cm pieces of **chives,** or **coriander, parsley, or tarragon** leaves will each add a special touch to any leafy salad. Or, combine a few of them for a luxurious little side salad. Herb salad also makes a great garnish for sandwiches and tacos. Dress it with a touch of good **olive oil,** a squeeze of **lemon,** and a pinch of **flaky salt,** or use a restrained amount of **House Dressing** (page 117), but either way, avoid overdressing.

cucumbers

SUMMER

The ghosts of my ancestors will rise to smite me if I dare profess allegiance to any variety of cucumber besides Persian. The love of cucumbers runs deep in our culture—and in me, too. In fact, cucumbers are one of the few types of seasonal produce I happily eat year-round. I can never get enough of the freshness and crunch they offer. But cukes really stand out in the summer. It's when I'll venture beyond my beloved Persians and buy Japanese, Armenian, Painted Serpent, and any other thin-skinned, small-seeded variety I encounter.

At the market, look for slender, firm cucumbers with thin, bright skin. Bigger does not equal better when it comes to cukes—the wider and older they get, the bigger and tougher their seeds will be. Refrigerate them in a sealed zip-lock bag and use them within a few days.

Thin-skinned cucumbers need not be peeled, though they certainly can be—I usually stripey-peel them. Remove all of the peel from English or other thick-skinned cucumbers, and if their seeds are large, slice the cukes lengthways and use a teaspoon to scrape away and discard the seeds.

I love to roll-cut slender cucumbers so they can pick up as much dressing and adornment as possible. The irregular shapes are also pleasing to look at, fun to crunch on, and don't get slimy as quickly as thin slices do. Cut bigger cucumbers whose seeds have been removed on the bias to get long C-shaped slices.

• • •

quick cucumber salad

I make one form or another of cucumber salad practically every day throughout the summer. Often, it's as simple as peeling and roll-cutting a couple cukes straight from the garden, tossing them with **salt, seasoned rice vinegar,** a little **olive oil,** and some chopped **dill, mint, or coriander**.

smashed cucumber salad

Trim the ends from 450g (about 7) Persian cucumbers, then place them in an extra-large zip-lock bag and seal. Use a rolling pin or small frying pan to gently smash the cucumbers until flattened and splitting lengthways. Split the cucumbers along the seams with your hands, tear into 4cm pieces, and transfer to a large bowl. In a small bowl, whisk together 3 tablespoons **seasoned rice vinegar,** 1 teaspoon **toasted sesame oil,** 1 tablespoon **sugar,** 1 teaspoon (3g) kosher **salt,** 1 finely grated **garlic** clove, and 1 teaspoon finely grated **fresh ginger** to dissolve the salt and sugar. Add to the cucumbers and toss to coat. Refrigerate for 30 minutes, then use a slotted spoon to transfer the cucumbers to a serving dish.

recipe continues

Top with chopped **roasted peanuts**, coarsely chopped **coriander**, and **Calabrian Chilli Crisp** (page 56).

cucumber-chia agua fresca

For a refreshingly tart summer drink, purée 6 sliced, skin-on Persian cucumbers in a blender with 180ml **lime juice,** 65g **sugar or 110g agave syrup**, a handful of **ice,** and a generous pinch of **salt**. I like the bits of cucumber, but strain the purée if you prefer. Stir in 3 tablespoons of **chia seeds** and refrigerate for 20 minutes. Once the chia seeds are hydrated, dilute the cucumber mixture with 480ml to 720ml of **water** to taste, and adjust the flavour with more sugar and lime juice as needed. Serve over ice.

aubergine

SUMMER

Aubergine is a chameleon, able to absorb the flavours of accompanying ingredients and present them as its own. Its unique capacity for shape-shifting allows it to transition seamlessly from sauce to starter to side dish to main course all summer long.

When shopping, look for a slightly firm aubergine that's heavy for its size. Lustrous skin and a bright green stalk indicate freshness. And when choosing between sizes, opt for smaller aubergines—they'll have smaller seeds and will be less likely to be bitter.

Aubergine skin is generally tender enough to eat, so the choice to peel it is usually an aesthetic one. White, magenta, and striated aubergine varieties tend to have tougher skin than their darker kin, so I usually peel them. When cutting an aubergine into rounds, I'll usually split the difference and stripey-peel the skin, leaving just enough behind to provide structure.

If you have the time, it's worth it to salt sliced aubergine before roasting or grilling to draw out excess moisture and encourage browning. Simply trim the ends and leaves from the aubergines. Use a vegetable peeler to peel the aubergines in wide, alternating stripes, then slice them crossways into 2cm rounds. Layer the aubergine pieces into a colander and sprinkle lightly with salt. Leave for at least 30 minutes and up to 90 minutes (if you're in a hurry, you can skip this step and season the aubergine with salt at the end of the cooking process). When it's time to cook, blot away the water with kitchen paper before proceeding.

Raw aubergine soaks up oil like a sponge, so it's important to be generous with cooking fat in order to keep pieces from sticking to the grill or the pan and to ensure even browning. This is not a place to skimp on olive oil!

• • •

grilled aubergine

Grill generously oiled aubergine wedges or slices over hot coals or a gas grill set to medium-high. Cook until well browned on both sides and completely tender throughout, about 6 minutes per side. See **Whipped Baba Ganoush** (page 100) for instructions for charring whole aubergine.

roasted aubergine

Roast aubergine slices or wedges at 230°C. Generously brush both sides of each piece with **extra-virgin olive oil** and set onto a greased baking tray in a single layer, allowing space between slices (use a second tray if needed to prevent touching). Roast until completely tender and brown in spots, 40 to 45 minutes; about halfway through, use a thin metal spatula to flip the slices to encourage even browning. Taste and adjust the seasoning with **salt** as needed.

good things come to those who wait

italian-style marinated aubergine

In a small screw-top jar, make a **Simple Vegetable Marinade** with 80ml **red wine vinegar**, 70g **extra-virgin olive oil**, 2 finely grated **garlic** cloves, 1 tablespoon (9g) kosher **salt**, 1 tablespoon **sugar**, 2 teaspoons **dried oregano**, and ½ teaspoon **chilli flakes**. Cover and shake vigorously to combine.

Layer grilled or roasted aubergine into a baking dish with thinly sliced garlic, chilli flakes, torn **basil** or crumbled **dried oregano**, and generous drizzles of the marinade. (You can also marinate cooked aubergine, courgettes, and peppers together in a single dish.) Let it sit at room temperature for at least 30 minutes, then serve as an antipasto, with big slices of **crusty bread**.

roasted aubergine parmesan

Salt, slice, and roast 2 or 3 Italian or globe aubergines (see **Roasted Aubergine,** page 223). Assemble 750g of **Simple Tomato Sauce** (page 359), a large handful of **basil** leaves, 350g coarsely grated **low-moisture mozzarella,** 340g sliced **fresh mozzarella,** and 125g finely grated **Parmesan**. Ladle 240ml of the sauce into a 23 × 33cm baking dish, then arrange one-third of the aubergine on top. Tear one-third of the basil leaves over the aubergine, then evenly scatter one-third of the grated mozzarella, fresh mozzarella slices, and Parmesan on top. Repeat the sauce, aubergine, basil, and cheese layers twice more, ending with Parmesan. In a small bowl, toss 100g **panko** with 2 finely grated **garlic** cloves, 3 tablespoons finely chopped basil, and 70g **extra-virgin olive oil**. Sprinkle the mixture evenly over the aubergine. Place the baking dish on a baking sheet and bake on the centre rack at 220°C until bubbling and golden brown, about 45 minutes. Let stand for 10 minutes before serving.

a small, good thing: chilled melon with mint

Throughout my childhood, my brothers and I visited our grandparents every Saturday for lunch. We'd play in their back garden while our grandmother prepared the meal. The pungent smell of garlic wafting from a neighbour's kitchen always tickled my nose while I drew hopscotch squares under the shade of the orange trees.

No matter the time of year, at some point our grandmother would come out to the garden with a platter of watermelon slices. We'd usually demur, saying we weren't hungry yet. "But that's precisely why you *need* to eat some," she'd respond in Farsi. "*Eshtehatoon baz mikoneh.* It'll whet your appetites." Though the idea of eating something to inspire hunger felt suspicious, I'd usually relent and take a piece of fruit. And regardless of whether my grandma's old-country claims hold any truth, I've clung fast to the idea that cold melon makes for a perfectly appropriate starter.

I love tasting many different melons at peak season to find the varieties with the perfect hit of sweetness and the crispest or most melt-in-your-mouth texture. These days, my favourite watermelon is the Japanese black-skinned variety Densuke, which is grown and sold in the United States under the brand name Yumi. It's crisp, incredibly sweet, and nearly seedless. I love white-fleshed Gaya and canary melons, which are creamy at the centre when ripe and a little crisper toward the rind. Both varieties are downright ambrosial. Working in restaurants, I fell in love with orange honeydew, a cross between cantaloupe and honeydew with salmon-coloured skin and dense, succulent flesh. When I can find them (and justify having three whole melons around), I'll buy one of each so I can create a mélange (mélonge?) of varied colours, flavours, and textures.

Once I've chosen my **melons,** I'll chill, halve, and seed them, then fish the rarely used melon baller out of the utensil drawer. I'll pile a mixture of melon balls into a bowl and then dress them with a little **lime juice** and torn **mint**. Then I'll set out a dish of toothpicks so that everyone can experience the appetite-whetting thrill of predinner melon for themselves.

peppers

SUMMER

I believe there's a pepper out there for everyone, even the most staunchly bell pepper–averse among us. While I pretty much love them all, the Jimmy Nardello stands out. This candy-apple-red frying pepper travelled to the East Coast in 1887 with the Nardello family, who emigrated there from Basilicata, in southern Italy. With thin skins, delicate seeds, and a perfect balance of sweetness and a rich pepper flavour, Nardellos are hard to beat. After grilling or roasting Nardellos in a hot oven until they're soft and charred, I'll serve them whole as a starter, a side dish, or mixed into a salad. If anyone at the table hesitates at the sight of a whole pepper, I'll pick one up and slip it into my mouth, biting off only the stalk end to discard. That's usually enough to get everyone going.

. . .

flame-roasted peppers

Roast larger peppers over a flame to make them more flavourful than anything you can get from a jar. If you've got a gas hob or grill, then just click it on. If you're already planning to barbecue over wood or charcoal, add peppers to the shopping list to take greater advantage of your already-burning fuel. (And if you don't have any flames available to you, grill or roast the peppers in an oven set to 240°C until the skins are charred.)

Use tongs to place fleshy sweet peppers such as bell peppers, corno di toro, or sheepnose pimento directly over a high gas flame (or alternatively, live coals). You can also use this method to roast poblano or Anaheim chillies for use in Mexican dishes, including **Teo's Brisket Chivis** (page 346). Cook, turning as the peppers begin to blacken, until all of the skins are charred, about 10 minutes. And don't forget the stalk ends!

Place the peppers on a plate or baking tray to cool, then halve them lengthways and remove the stalks. Scrape away the seeds and skins with a paring knife—you don't need to remove every bit of char; a little left behind will recount a gentle hint of the flame.

sweet pepper antipasto

Slice flame-roasted peppers into 1.25cm-wide strips and layer them into a baking dish with generous drizzles of **Simple Vegetable Marinade** (page 225) and torn **basil** or crumbled **dried oregano**. Serve with **Olive Oil–Fried Bread** (page 94) or **Sky-High Focaccia** (page 372).

grilled summer salad

For a juicy peak-summer salad, toss 3 ears of **corn** and 340g of Nardello or shishito peppers in a large bowl with **olive oil** to coat. Season with **salt** and grill until the peppers are charred and soft and the corn is blistered in places. Set aside to cool, then strip the kernels from the cobs and toss in a large salad bowl with the whole peppers,

450g halved **cherry tomatoes,** 3 roll-cut **Persian cucumbers,** 1 ripe **avocado** in rustic spoonfuls, 40g **Bright Pickled Onions** (page 52), and a large handful of **coriander** leaves. Taste and adjust salt, then dress with **lime juice** and **extra-virgin olive oil or Creamy Lemon-Miso Dressing** (page 122).

crunchy shaved pepper salad

Halve Cubanelle or bell peppers, remove the stalk and any white membranes, then use a mandoline or a very sharp knife to slice them lengthways into generous 4mm-thick pieces. Toss with **Bright Pickled Onions** (page 52), torn **basil, Creamy Oregano Dressing** (page 125), and if you like, big crumbles of **Marinated Goat's Cheese** (page 74) or **Marinated Feta** (page 71).

peperonata

Finally, when you find yourself up to your neck in peppers, stew up a batch of velvety Tuscan-style peppers and onions to eat and serve over the coming days. This dish works equally well as both a side and a sauce for grilled sausages, chicken, pork, steak, or fish. You can also serve peperonata warm alongside white beans or chickpeas drizzled with good olive oil and showered with fresh basil. Or, use it to top **Olive Oil–Fried Bread** (page 94) smeared with **Whipped Ricotta** (page 66) or **Marinated Goat's Cheese** (page 74).

Set a large casserole over medium heat and add 3 tablespoons of **extra-virgin olive oil**. When it shimmers, add 2 thinly sliced **red onions** and a generous pinch of **salt**. Cook, stirring regularly, until the onions are tender and just beginning to brown, about 12 minutes.

Move the onions to the edges of the pot and add another tablespoon of oil and 4 thinly sliced **garlic** cloves into the center. Cook the garlic, stirring, until fragrant, about 2 minutes. Stir the garlic into the onions and add 1.4kg of bell or Cubanelle peppers sliced into 1cm-wide strips. Season with salt, increase the heat to medium-high, and cook, stirring regularly, until the peppers begin to wilt, about 8 minutes.

Tear in a large handful of **basil** leaves and add a splash of **water**. Reduce the heat to medium-low and continue cooking for 45 minutes, stirring and scraping the bottom of the pot regularly to prevent sticking. If at any point all of the liquid evaporates from the pot, add another small splash of water.

Once the peppers are completely tender and their skins are curling, add 225g of **tomatoes** cut into chunks. Keep cooking, stirring, and scraping attentively to prevent scorching. Once the tomatoes have cooked down into a silky sauce, turn off the heat, tear in another palmful of basil leaves, season with salt, and stir in 1 teaspoon **red wine vinegar**. Allow the flavours to settle for a few minutes, then taste and adjust for salt and acid.

Serve hot, warm, at room temperature, or cold.

a small, good thing: green coriander seed

I love to grow ingredients I can't readily find at the shops or market. And while I geek out on rare varieties as much as the next horticultural nerd, my favourite garden flavour is neither delicate nor esoteric. Green coriander seed—the fresh seed of the coriander plant—is the most special thing I grow. It's also something many others view as a mistake. Gardeners typically dread letting plants go to seed, but when it comes to coriander, I look forward to it because nothing is as welcome in my kitchen as the intensely aromatic, slightly citrusy, mild flavour of the plant's fresh seeds.

I like to pound green coriander seeds gently in a mortar, then incorporate them anywhere I'd use coriander leaves: for marinades and dressings; in stews, soups, or braises; in herbed rice; with soba or rice noodles; or mixed with oil and drizzled atop poached eggs.

If it were possible, I'd use fresh green coriander seeds year-round. Since it's not, I like steeping them in vinegar to use in vinaigrettes and marinades throughout the year. To make **Green Coriander Vinegar,** gently pound 55g **green coriander seeds** in a mortar with a pestle to break them down a bit, then proceed with the recipe for **Pickled Thai Chillies** (page 76), substituting the coriander for the chillies. Add it to **Whipped Baba Ghanoush** (page 100), **Whipped Tahini** (page 63), **Green Sauce** (page 51), **Tahini Sbagliato** (page 132), or anywhere else you'd like to add a hint of green coriander seed flavour.

shell beans

SUMMER

Fresh shelling beans are a wonder, bearing little resemblance to their dried kin. For one thing, they cook far more quickly—usually in 20 to 30 minutes. Not having yet lost their inherent moisture to the drying process, shelling beans are creamier and more tender than dried beans, too. Taste fresh butter beans once and you'll immediately understand how they got their name.

I'm a maximalist when it comes to fresh shell beans. The plumper the bean, the more of that creamy interior you get with each bite. Two of my favourite varieties are the shockingly pink Tongue of Fire borlotti and jumbo-sized white Spagna beans.

When harvesting or shopping for shell beans, choose firm, plump pods that feel heavy for their size. Avoid spotted, browning, or shrivelled pods. When shaken, the beans inside a pod shouldn't rattle. If in doubt, slit a pod open and look for shiny, smooth beans that fit cosily inside.

Raw shelled beans will start to oxidise after a day or two in the fridge, so keep them in their shells until cooking when possible. Or, cook and then store them. About 900g of shelling beans will yield about 450g cooked, enough for about 4 servings.

• • •

pot of fresh shell beans

Place shelled beans in a pot with just enough **water** to cover them, a clove or two of **garlic**, a **dried chilli**, a splash of **extra-virgin olive oil**, and plenty of **salt**. Bring to a boil, then reduce to a simmer. Start tasting smaller beans around the 20-minute mark for doneness—larger beans will take closer to 30 minutes. Cook until all trace of crunch has disappeared and you're left with nothing but creamy, succulent beans. Serve warm, garnished with **fresh herbs** and **lemon zest**, **Garlic and Herb Labne** (page 48), **Calabrian Chilli Crisp** (page 56), **Crispy Fried Shallots** (page 55), or a drizzle of **Green Sauce** (page 51).

•

For more shell bean preparations, take a look at **A Pot of Beans** (page 159)—any recipe for dried beans will work beautifully for fresh beans. Simply skip the soaking step, and simmer just until tender.

marinated shell bean salad

Gently warm and dress 450g drained cooked white beans—cannellini or gigantes are nice options—with **Simple Vegetable Marinade** (page 225). Add the finely grated zest of 1 **lemon**, 2 tablespoons finely chopped **parsley**, and 40g **Bright Pickled Onions** (page 52), then taste and adjust the seasoning with **extra-virgin olive oil**, **salt**, and **red wine vinegar**. If you like, fold in some halved **cherry tomatoes** or torn **basil**. Large crumbles of **feta-style or goat's cheese** also make nice additions.

string beans

SUMMER

String beans—including green beans, haricots verts, wax beans, runner beans, and long beans—are immature seed pods, picked and eaten whole. Depending on the variety and the point at which they are picked, they'll be more or less tender. When shopping for or harvesting string beans, choose small, uniform pods. Avoid lumpy pods or pods containing beans with bulging outlines. Both are signs of adolescent beans, meaning their pods will be too fibrous to enjoy. If you're unsure, just take a bite—if you find yourself still chewing after an uncomfortably long time, the beans are too mature. To further avoid excess fibre, trim the stalk ends—and if they're tough, the tails—of the beans with a paring knife before cooking. About 675g of string beans will yield 4 to 6 servings.

Mixing a few different varieties of string beans in a single dish can be a lovely way to play with colour and texture on the plate, but make sure to cook each type separately to avoid overcooking some and undercooking others. Combine the cooked or parcooked beans as you dress them for a salad or toss them together in the pan one final time for a quick sauté.

· · ·

blanched string beans

Boil string beans whole or sliced into pieces on a bias. The tiniest, most tender haricots verts will cook in about 2 minutes, while more mature Blue Lake beans and runner or wax beans can take up to 5 minutes. Pull them from the pot as soon as they begin to relax but still crunch satisfyingly when bitten into. To avoid slimy, overcooked beans, stand over the pot, tasting, waiting, and tasting again, until the moment they're ready.

Serve string beans straight from the pot, drizzled with good **olive oil** and a sprinkle of **flaky salt**. Or, spread them out in a single layer, toss with a little oil to coat, and let them cool.

runner beans with tomatoes and aioli

Lay slices of **heirloom tomatoes** onto a platter. Season them with **salt** and and drizzle lightly with **House Dressing** (page 117). Halve blanched runner beans at a sharp angle, toss them in a bowl with a little more dressing, then spread them out over the tomatoes. Use the same bowl to toss halved **cherry tomatoes** or bite-sized chunks of **larger tomatoes** with salt, torn **basil**, and more dressing. Scatter the tomatoes over the beans. To make **Aioli,** stir 1 finely grated **garlic** clove and a squeeze of **lemon juice** into 55g **mayonnaise** and finish the salad with a generous dollop.

three-bean salad

Halve blanched green beans and yellow wax or runner beans on a sharp angle, then toss them in a bowl with **Creamy Oregano Dressing** (page 125). Spread the beans out on a platter. Use the same bowl to toss drained cooked fresh shell beans with more dressing. Scatter the shell beans over the string beans and shower generously with torn **green** and **purple basil**.

sautéed string beans

First, blanch string beans in **salted water**. Pull them from the pot when they're still very crisp and let them drain and cool in a single layer. Sauté the beans in a hot pan in **extra-virgin olive oil, unsalted butter, or ghee** with a little bit of minced **garlic** and some **chilli flakes**, if you like.

string beans with ginger and shallots

Sauté parcooked beans (or a mix of beans and **sugar snap peas**) in neutral oil or **Shallot Oil** (page 55) with a bit of minced **ginger** and **garlic**, then top with a few drops of **toasted sesame oil** and **Crispy Fried Shallots** (page 55).

summer squash

SUMMER

The large summer squash family includes courgette, which are long, cylindrical green or golden squashes. Whether long or round, crookneck or scalloped, white, green, yellow, or bicoloured, all summer squash is harvested before maturity, when its skin is still glossy, its flesh is still buttery, and its seeds are barely formed. Any type of summer squash can be used in just about any recipe calling for courgettes, and vice versa, even if the terms aren't interchangeable.

I usually grow two or three varieties of summer squash and look forward to buying others throughout the summer. My favourites include the mild-tasting, ribbed Costata Romanesco, classic green Black Beauty, and two-toned Zephyr, which looks like a yellow squash dipped in pistachio paste.

. . .

boiled summer squash

To fully appreciate the sweetness and flavour of fresh squash, pick or buy baby courgette no longer than 10cm. Trim the ends, then boil them whole in **salted water** until barely tender (it's better to undercook than overcook here, if you're not sure). Remove the squash from the pot with a slotted spoon and blot them dry on a clean tea towel. Transfer to a platter, shower with good **olive oil**, finely grated **lemon zest**, a squeeze of **lemon juice**, and an abundance of shaved **Parmesan**. Serve immediately.

grilled summer squash

My favourite way to grill courgette—or any summer squash—yields charred, smoky skin and juicy, toothsome flesh. Prepare to grill over medium-high heat. Halve 4 to 6 courgettes (about 900g) lengthways, leaving the stalks intact. Toss in a large bowl with 3 tablespoons **extra-virgin olive oil**. Grill, turning and rotating the pieces once they begin to brown, until steamy and tender within and charred all over, 12 to 16 minutes. Transfer to a baking tray, season liberally with **salt**, and allow to cool a bit.

charred courgette with labne

Pile charred courgettes onto a platter smeared liberally with **Garlic and Herb Labne** (page 48). Drizzle with **Calabrian Chilli Crisp** (page 56) and shower with **green coriander seeds**.

torn charred courgette with chillies and mint

Combine 2 tablespoons **red wine vinegar**, 1 to 2 tablespoons **Calabrian chilli paste**, 1 tablespoon **sugar**, and a generous pinch of **salt** in a large bowl. Tear cooled charred courgettes into 4cm pieces and add to the bowl along with a large handful of torn **mint** leaves and a palmful of **Bright Pickled Onions** (page 52). Toss to combine, then let sit for 5 minutes for the flavours to come together, then taste and adjust the seasoning with salt

good things come to those who wait

and vinegar. Use a slotted spoon to transfer the courgettes to a platter and top with a few more mint leaves.

roasted summer squash

Roast roll-cut or thick-sliced summer squash tossed with **extra-virgin olive oil** at 220°C until completely tender and browned in spots, 25 to 30 minutes, using a thin metal spatula to flip the pieces halfway to encourage even browning. Season with **salt** immediately upon removal from the oven.

summer squash au gratin

Top roasted squash with **Golden Panko** (page 131) and finely grated **Parmesan** a few minutes before it's done, then continue roasting until the crumbs are golden brown.

sweet and spicy courgette with meyer lemon

Toss roasted courgettes with a dressing of 2 tablespoons **extra-virgin olive oil**, 1 tablespoon **Preserved Meyer Lemon Paste** (page 79), 1 minced **Pickled Thai Chilli** (page 76), and 2 teaspoons **agave or maple syrup**. Shower with chopped **coriander, parsley, dill, shiso, or basil**.

courgette antipasto

Toss grilled or roasted courgettes with **Simple Vegetable Marinade** (page 225), torn **basil**, and **salt** as it comes out of the oven or off the barbecue. Marinate for at least 30 minutes before serving with **Sky-High Focaccia** (page 372) or **crusty bread.**

tomatoes

SUMMER

In the summer, "the tomato invades the kitchen," to quote Pablo Neruda. And since I can't bring myself to eat mealy, flavourless supermarket tomatoes during the rest of the year, I eagerly anticipate the invasion.

While I grow some cherry tomatoes in our garden, I avail myself of the many varieties of heirlooms, plum tomatoes, and intensely flavourful Early Girls available at the farmers' market. I take immense pleasure in considering their varied sizes, flavours, textures, and colours as I decide how to use each.

Heirloom tomato varieties are available in a rainbow of hues—each with its own distinct flavour. Use them to make eye-catching salads, pastas, and salsas. The dry flesh of plum-style tomatoes, including San Marzano and Roma, makes them ideal for sauce. And I consider small, flavourful tomatoes, such as Early Girls and cherry tomatoes, to be all-purpose—perfect for roasting, confiting, or using in salad.

When shopping, choose moderately firm, deeply coloured tomatoes. And since refrigeration will invariably destroy a tomato's delicate flavour compounds, store tomatoes in a single layer at room temperature, away from direct sunlight.

...

confit of little tomatoes

Use the sweetest cherry or ping-pong-ball-sized tomatoes you can find and you'll be rewarded with explosions of umami and sugar with every bite of this confit.

Place 900g of stemmed cherry tomatoes or 900g of little tomatoes in a single layer in a shallow roasting dish over a bed of **basil** leaves and a handful of peeled **garlic** cloves. Add about 430g of **extra-virgin olive oil**—the tomatoes don't have to be submerged, but they should all be in contact with oil. Season them liberally with **salt**, give them a stir, and cook at 150°C for about 35 minutes. At no time should the dish ever boil—a simmer, at most, is fine. You'll know the tomatoes are done when they're tender all the way through and the first skins start to split. Pull them from the oven and let them cool a bit.

Serve warm, or at room temperature. Keep tomatoes refrigerated, in their oil, for up to 5 days. Toss the still-warm tomatoes and a bit of their oil with just-cooked **pasta**, torn **basil**, and **Marinated Goat's Cheese** (page 74) or **Parmesan** for a simple pasta dish. Spoon confit and oil over rice or eggs, or serve as a saucy vegetable with fish, chicken, meat, or tofu. Strain, save, and reuse the oil for a second round of confit, a vinaigrette, or a truly amazing pan of **Refried Beans** (page 161; try it with white beans!).

roasted tomato sauce

To take the most straightforward path from tomato to sauce, preheat the oven to 220°C. Halve any whole tomatoes and cut very large ones into quarters or eighths. Place in a single-ish layer in a nonreactive roasting tin or large ovenproof frying pan over a bed of **basil** stalks or leaves and a head or two of **garlic**, halved horizontally. Drizzle very generously with **extra-virgin olive oil or confit oil** and season with **salt**. Roast, uncovered, for 40 to 45 minutes, stirring occasionally, until the tomatoes have broken down and reduced a bit, and there's a little browning happening around the edges of the pan. The garlic should be nice and soft at this point, too.

Allow to cool a bit, then pass everything through a food mill. Taste and adjust the seasoning with salt.

creamy tomato and goat's cheese pasta

Add a tiny splash of **fish sauce** to a pan of **Roasted Tomato Sauce** (above) and reduce it over medium-high heat, stirring regularly, until it's a bit thicker than you'd like. Turn off the heat and stir in a generous amount of **goat's cheese** and a little **unsalted butter**. Taste and adjust the seasoning as needed, then toss with just-cooked **pasta** and finish with torn **basil**.

shakshuka

Bring a 2cm depth of **Roasted Tomato Sauce** (at left) to a simmer in a shallow nonreactive frying pan over medium-low heat. Season with **ground cumin** and **harissa paste** to taste. You can stir in a little **Peperonata** (page 230), too, if you like. Crack an **egg** into a coffee cup. Use a large spoon to make a divot in the sauce and carefully tip the egg into the sauce. Repeat with 2 more eggs and 3 **egg yolks**. Cover the pan and gently simmer until the egg whites are set, 6 to 9 minutes. Serve hot, with chopped **coriander, Fluffy Pitta Pockets** (page 385), **Garlic and Herb Labne** (page 48), or **Marinated Feta** (page 71) and more harissa paste.

tomato-poached fish

Portion and season **cod, halibut, or rockfish**. Set a shallow nonreactive frying pan over medium heat. Add a splash of **neutral oil** and a thinly sliced **shallot**. Just as it starts to brown, add a few thinly sliced **garlic** cloves. As soon as they're fragrant, add a 1.25cm depth of **Roasted Tomato Sauce** (at left), a minced **Pickled Thai Chilli** (page 76), and a tiny splash of **fish sauce**. Bring to a simmer, taste and adjust the seasoning as needed, then add the fish and cover the pan. Cook until the fish is opaque and just starting to flake, about 6 minutes (slightly longer for a thicker piece of fish, such as halibut). Serve with steamed **jasmine rice, Crispy Fried Shallots** (page 55), **Calabrian Chilli Crisp** (page 56), **Garlic and Herb Labne** (page 48), and a shower of coarsely chopped **coriander** and **mint**.

tomato salad

When I look at a pile of ripe tomatoes, I'm overcome by a wonderful sense of possibility (and something like the **Tomato Salad Matrix** on page 246 flashes through my mind). I hope you'll come to feel as excited as I am by the countless possible ways to combine tomatoes with herbs, dressings, and other ingredients to create the ideal salad for each moment. When you've got ripe tomatoes around, salad should never be too far behind. So, instead of feeling pressure to adhere to any particular recipe, simply consider **presentation, seasoning,** and **assembly**.

Presentation: First, use a small, sharp knife to remove the core. Hold the knife at an angle, pierce the tomato just outside its core, then cut around the core and lift it out. Use the same technique to remove any visibly mushy or bruised bits. Now decide how to cut your tomatoes—and don't be afraid to play with a mix of shapes and sizes.

> **Slice:** Cut large, colourful tomatoes crossways into 6mm-thick slices. Slices work best for Caprese salad, for shingling onto crostini, and for creating an ombré effect on the platter. Use slices for salads you plan to serve on flat platters.
>
> **Chunk:** Cut smaller tomatoes into wedges or irregularly shaped chunks. Chunky tomato pieces work well for salads that incorporate other chunks, including corn, cucumbers, or peppers. They are also ideal for panzanella (Tuscan tomato and bread salad) or fattoush (Lebanese tomato salad with pitta chips). Use chunky tomatoes for salads you plan to toss and serve in a bowl—or strew some chunks atop a foundation of slices.
>
> **Halve:** Cut little tomatoes and cherry tomatoes in half through the stalk end. Halves function like chunks, and I will often combine halved cherry tomatoes with chunks of larger tomatoes to incorporate a variety of shapes into a dish.

Seasoning: Sprinkle all cut tomatoes with salt and let them sit while you prepare everything else. Your salad will be immeasurably better for it—a few minutes is all it'll take for salt to coax out every bit of flavour bound within the tomato.

To season slices, lay them out on a plate or parchment-lined baking tray and sprinkle lightly with salt. Tip the plate so any released juices run off to the side. Season chunks, wedges, and halves in a bowl, tossing to coat. Use a slotted spoon when assembling the salad in order to leave behind excess juices.

Assembly: To build your salad, shingle slices on the platter as a foundation, drizzling them with good olive oil or a little bit of dressing as you go. Then add other ingredients and tomato shapes as you continue to build. Or toss halves and chunks in a bowl with dressing and other ingredients, then use a slotted spoon to transfer them to the final serving dish.

tomato salad matrix

Cherry tomato fattoush on a bed of **Garlic and Herb Labne** (page 48) with **Bright Pickled Onions** (page 52), coriander, and **House Dressing** (page 121)

Panzanella with torn croutons (page 37), halved cherry tomatoes and heirloom tomato chunks, torn basil, **Bright Pickled Onions** (page 52), and **House Dressing** (page 117)

Shirazi salad with cucumbers, tomato chunks, **Bright Pickled Onions** (page 52), dill, olive oil, and freshly squeezed lime juice

Torn burrata on **Olive Oil–Fried Bread** (page 94) with **Confit of Little Tomatoes** (page 242), basil, and olive oil

Sliced heirloom tomatoes with blanched runner beans, olive oil, and aioli

beetroot

AUTUMN AND WINTER

The poor, belittled beetroot. Even British food writer and documented vegetable lover Jane Grigson besmirches its name in her *Vegetable Book,* an ode to produce. In the span of three sentences, she maligns it repeatedly, declaring, "It is not an inspiring vegetable." Then, it is "far too bossy a vegetable. I have never heard anyone claim it as their favourite."

I wonder if Jane had such a hairy relationship with beetroot because her preferred cooking method involved leaving them in the oven for 3 to 4 hours? If I cooked them that long, I'd probably detest them, too.

• • •

marinated roast beetroot

Whether served on their own, over a dollop of labne, or in a salad with cucumbers, avocado, or citrus slices—I'm certain this preparation would've converted even Ms. Grigson from resister to beetroot enthusiast.

To roast, place a single layer of scrubbed, trimmed beetroot in a baking dish and add a 6mm depth of **water** (if cooking more than one colour of beetroot, use separate dishes to avoid staining them all red). Lay a piece of parchment over the beetroot and cover the dish tightly with foil. Roast at 230°C until completely tender when pierced with a knife, about 1 hour.

When the beetroot are cool enough to handle, rub them with kitchen paper to slip off the skins. Cut into wedges or slices as you like and dress with **seasoned rice vinegar or red wine vinegar,** a splash of **extra-virgin olive oil,** and **salt.** Or, dress with olive oil and a bit of **Preserved Meyer Lemon Paste** (page 79). Taste and adjust the seasoning—the acid and salt should amplify the beetroot's natural sweetness. Let the beetroot marinate for 15 minutes, then adjust the salt and acid as needed, and serve. Keep marinated beetroot in the fridge for up to 1 week.

Tangy, sweet marinated beetroot make a lovely addition to any salad, but they pair especially well with creamy components including **Whipped Ricotta** (page 66), **Marinated Goat's Cheese** (page 74), **Marinated Feta** (page 71), **Whipped Tahini** (page 63), **Garlic and Herb Labne** (page 48), and **7½-Minute Eggs** (page 149).

vibrant beetroot labne

Coarsely grate 3 or 4 roasted beetroot, then stir them into a full quantity of **Garlic and Herb Labne** (page 48), along with 2 teaspoons **red wine vinegar** and 1 teaspoon finely chopped **tarragon.** Taste and adjust **salt** and acid as needed. Serve as a dip with **Fluffy Pitta Pockets** (page 385) or crudités, or alongside **Basic Crispy Rice** (page 155), **Joojeh Kabob Roast Chicken** (page 284), or **Slow-Cooked Salmon** (page 337).

broccoli and cauliflower

AUTUMN AND WINTER

Broccoli, tenderstem broccoli, cauliflower, and broccoli Romanesco are my safety vegetables—I start to worry if I don't have any of them on hand. And since cauliflower and Romanesco hold up particularly well in a crisper drawer, I keep them in the fridge as a kind of vegetable insurance.

When shopping for broccoli and cauliflower, let the leaves, the florets, and the ends of stalks and stems guide you. Leaves should be perky and vibrant. Florets should be green and tightly formed. And a glance at the cut ends will reveal just how long it's been since the produce left the field. The greener and fresher the cut end, the more recently the vegetables were harvested and the sweeter they will taste.

My favourite cruciferous discovery of the last few years is something my grocer calls "broccoli niños." At first I thought these large, single florets on thick, sweet stalks were an entirely new varietal. But a bit of research revealed that they're simply prunings, removed early in the season from the broccoli plant to encourage growth. I love niños because they're so unbelievably sweet and tender. They also have my ideal ratio of stalk to floret, which is about 3 to 1.

Speaking of stalks—they're often the sweetest part of the broccoli, so please take care not to waste them! Use a vegetable peeler or paring knife to remove the fibrous skin from mature broccoli stalks, then slice and add them to the rest of the pot.

• • •

dark-roasted broccoli

Toss broccoli (cut into two-bite florets) or tenderstem broccoli (whole, with the woody ends trimmed) with **extra-virgin olive oil**, season with **salt**, and roast at 220°C for 25 to 30 minutes, flipping the pieces halfway (if using more than one baking tray, switch racks and rotate the trays front to back). Straight from the oven, shower the broccoli with finely grated **lemon zest**, and as soon as it's cool enough to handle, massage the zest into the florets a bit to release the fragrant oils. Garnish with a squeeze of **lemon** and serve.

dark-roasted cauliflower

Lightly trim the root end of a head of cauliflower or Romanesco, then slice it through the core into 1.25cm-thick slabs. Brush on both sides with **extra-virgin olive oil**, season with **salt**, and roast at 220°C for 25 to 30 minutes, flipping the cauliflower halfway (if using more than one tray, switch racks and rotate the pans front to back). Roasted cauliflower is so sweet that I usually serve it on its own. But it's also an ideal base for a **Roasted Vegetable Salad** (page 272).

long-cooked broccoli

Gentle heat and extended cooking time encourage broccoli's bitter and sulfurous aromatic compounds to dissipate, leaving only sweetness behind in this silky purée.

Set a large casserole over low heat and add 110g **extra-virgin olive oil**, 6 thinly sliced **garlic** cloves, and a big pinch of **chilli flakes**. When the garlic is aromatic and gently sizzling, stir it around a bit, then add 900g of broccoli, cut into 2.5cm pieces (don't forget to peel, slice, and add the stalks!), and 360ml **water**. Season generously with **salt**, increase the heat to medium, and stir to combine. When the water boils, cover the pot and reduce the heat to keep it at a simmer.

Cook until the broccoli florets and stalks are completely tender when pressed with the back of a wooden spoon, 30 to 35 minutes. If at any point the pot runs dry, add a splash of water. If there's still water in the pot when the broccoli is done, remove the lid and increase the heat to high to boil off the excess.

Once you're satisfied with the texture of the broccoli and the amount of liquid, reduce the heat to low and mash the broccoli. Season the purée with 40g finely grated **Parmesan** and ¼ packed teaspoon finely grated **lemon zest**. If the purée still seems to lack body, drizzle in a few more tablespoons of oil and let it simmer for another minute. Remove from the heat, then taste and tinker with the seasoning as needed with more salt, chilli flakes, lemon zest, Parmesan, and freshly squeezed **lemon juice**.

Serve this silky purée as a warm side dish, or smear a generous amount onto **Olive Oil–Fried Bread** (page 94) lightly swiped with a cut **garlic** clove. Or, for a light lunch, top a bowl of long-cooked broccoli with a few **anchovy fillets** or torn **burrata** and a drizzle of good **olive oil**. Serve with warm **crusty bread**.

pasta with long-cooked broccoli

Mix broccoli purée with **Whipped Ricotta** (page 66) to make a creamy, comforting sauce. Toss with hot, just-cooked **pasta**. Shower everything generously with more grated **Parmesan** before serving.

carrots

AUTUMN AND WINTER

I'll grab a bunch or two of Nantes carrots anytime I encounter them while grocery shopping. Wrapped properly, they'll last for weeks in the crisper drawer, which is a boon for someone as disorganised as I am. Even when they're not labelled, Nantes carrots are easy to spot—deep orange in colour and evenly cylindrical rather than tapered, they're also a bit shorter than Imperator carrots, the variety you'd typically find bagged or piled in a grocery store display. Most American farmers grow Imperators because they store better and peel more easily, but I prefer Nantes because they're sweeter and more tender.

. . .

shaved carrot salad

Thinly slice 450g of carrots on a mandoline or use a peeler to shave them into thin, wide ribbons. In a large bowl, combine the carrots with 3 pitted and chopped **Medjool dates**, 2 teaspoons finely grated **fresh ginger**, 2 teaspoons **ground cumin**, 1 finely grated **garlic** clove, 20g coarsely chopped **coriander**, and 1 or 2 minced **Pickled Thai Chillies** (page 76). Make a simple dressing by whisking together 3 tablespoons **extra-virgin olive oil**, 1 tablespoon freshly squeezed **lime juice**, 1 tablespoon **Chilli Vinegar** (page 76), and **salt** to taste. Season the carrots with salt and toss with enough dressing to lightly coat. Let sit for at least 30 minutes before serving.

dark-roasted carrots

Toss roll-cut carrots with **extra-virgin olive oil** (or another cooking fat) and **salt**, then spread them out on a baking tray in a single layer. Roast at 220°C until they're tender throughout and their tips get so dark that they pick up a little edge, just this side of bitter—perfect for balancing with an acidic condiment or a creamy bit of cheese or labne. Or place still-warm dark-roasted carrots on a platter and drizzle with **Creamy Lemon-Miso Dressing** (page 122), **House Dressing** (page 117), or **Creamy Oregano Dressing** (page 125).

For a little flavour variation, season carrots for roasting with **ground cumin** and **chilli flakes** along with salt and toss with melted **Cardamom Ghee** (page 61) instead of olive oil to coat.

hardy leafy greens   AUTUMN AND WINTER

A bit of time spent in a pot of salted boiling water will only improve any hardy leafy greens you plan to sauté—including rapini, cabbage, chard, spring greens, kale, and mustard greens. While the water tenderises the greens and draws out some of their bitterness, the salt will season them from within.

The quickest way to strip leafy greens is to grip the base of the stalk with one hand, then gently pinch the base of the leaf with the other hand and pull upwards. Either discard the stalks or blanch them until tender, slice thinly, and reunite them with their cooked leaves. (I particularly love the flavour of chard stalks and refuse to let anyone scrap them in my presence.) With rapini, first trim away the woody ends of the stalks, then cut the rest into 5cm pieces on a bias—these stalks and florets can be blanched at the same time. In general, one bunch of greens will serve one as a main dish, two as a side dish, or four to six as an antipasto.

• • •

blanched greens

Bring a large pot of generously **salted water** to a boil, add the greens, and cook until tender. For chard, this may take 2 minutes or fewer, while for spring greens with very fibrous leaves, this could take upward of 15 minutes. You'll know they're done when the leaves tear easily with no resistance. Use tongs to spread out the blanched greens in a single layer on a parchment-lined baking tray. When they are cool enough to handle, squeeze out the excess water, and then very coarsely chop the greens.

sautéed greens

Blanch, squeeze dry, and chop the greens as directed. Set a large frying pan over medium-high heat. When it's hot, add enough cooking fat of your choice—**extra-virgin olive oil**, **Shallot Oil** (page 55), and **Ghee** (page 62) are all good options—to lightly coat the bottom. If you like, add a smashed clove or two of **garlic** and **Calabrian chilli purée or flakes** and cook, stirring, until fragrant, about 90 seconds. Now add the chopped blanched greens and toss. It'll take only a few minutes for the other flavours in the pan to infuse the greens, since they're already seasoned and tender. Keep everything moving in the pan to avoid burnt or crispy bits, then taste and adjust the seasoning as needed. Discard the garlic, transfer to a plate or shallow bowl, and serve hot.

To gussy up sautéed greens, try any of the following:

- Use **neutral oil** and minced **ginger** and **garlic** instead of whole garlic cloves.

- For a Sicilian spin, start with a base of diced **onion**. Cook in **extra-virgin olive oil** with a pinch of **salt** and some **bloomed saffron** (see page 37) until tender. Add the greens to sauté, then fold in a handful each of **currants** and lightly toasted

pine nuts. Top with finely grated **lemon zest** and a good squeeze of **lemon juice**.

- For a little smokiness, start with a base of diced **shallots** and **bacon**. Cook in **extra-virgin olive oil** until tender, with a pinch of **salt** and a generous pinch of **smoked paprika**. Add **mustard greens, kale, or spring greens** and cook, stirring. Finish with a drop or two of **apple cider vinegar**.

- For a classic southern Italian flavour combination, gently warm a splash of **extra-virgin olive oil** in the pan, then add a couple whole **garlic** cloves and an **anchovy fillet** or two. Cook until the anchovy begins to disintegrate, then stir in some **Calabrian chilli paste** and add your greens. Finish with a squeeze of **lemon**.

rapini pesto

Parmesan, toasted pecans, and garlic balance out rapini's inherent bitterness in this pesto. Of course it's a wonderful sauce for pasta, but slathered on **Olive Oil–Fried Bread** (page 94) or toast, it also makes a glorious savoury landing pad for a fried egg. And it can add welcome complexity to a one-note sandwich—I love pairing it with **fresh tomatoes, turkey,** or **Whipped Tahini** (page 63).

In a food processor, combine 80g cooled lightly toasted **pecans,** 2 cloves sliced **garlic,** ¼ teaspoon **chilli flakes,** and 80g finely grated **Parmesan** and pulse until the nuts break down into a fine meal, about 10 seconds. Add 1 bunch of blanched rapini, squeezed dry and coarsely chopped, and pulse a few more times. Then, with the machine running, stream in 70g **extra-virgin olive oil** and add another 45g finely grated Parmesan. Once the mixture comes together, stop the machine and taste the pesto. Adjust the seasoning with **salt** and chilli flakes as needed. Continue blending to purée into a creamy, smooth sauce.

braised kale with chillies and marinated feta

Set a large casserole over medium heat and add 55g **extra-virgin olive oil**. When it shimmers, add 1 thinly sliced **onion** and a pinch of **salt**. Cook, stirring occasionally, until translucent and just beginning to brown, about 12 minutes. Add 6 cloves thinly sliced **garlic** and cook, stirring, until fragrant and soft, about 2 minutes.

In batches, add 3 bunches of kale, stalks removed and torn into pieces, tossing to wilt before adding more. Stir in 1 or 2 sliced **Pickled Thai Chillies** (page 76) and season with salt. Add 180ml **water** and bring to a gentle simmer. Reduce the heat and cook, partially covered, until the greens are very tender, 35 to 45 minutes. If at any point the pot starts to run dry, add a little more water.

Finely grate the **zest** of 1 lemon onto the greens and squeeze in **lemon juice** to taste. Taste and adjust the seasoning with salt. Use tongs to transfer the greens to a serving dish, then drizzle with a little braising liquid. Dot with large crumbles of **Marinated Feta** (page 71) and drizzle with **Calabrian Chilli Crisp** (page 56), and serve hot.

gingery roasted cabbage wedges

While the dry heat of the oven won't do most hardy greens justice, it's a boon for slices or wedges of cabbage. Using a sharp knife, cut a head of **cabbage** through the core into 8 wedges.

Lightly coat a baking tray with **neutral oil,** then lay out the cabbage wedges, cut-side down. Drizzle generously with more oil and season with **salt**. Roast at 230°C, flipping the cabbage and rotating the tray front to back after 20 minutes. Cook until the cores are tender and the leaves are golden and crisp, another 10 to 15 minutes. When the cabbage is done, transfer it to a platter.

In a small bowl, combine 3 tablespoons **seasoned rice vinegar,** 2 teaspoons **toasted sesame oil,** 1 tablespoon finely grated **fresh ginger,** 1 finely grated **garlic** clove, and a pinch of kosher **salt**. Spoon the dressing over the cabbage, sprinkle with 1 thinly sliced **spring onion,** and serve hot or at room temperature, alongside **rice** and **tofu, chicken, or fish.**

parsnips

AUTUMN AND WINTER

The prospect of nutty, sticky-sweet roast parsnips is reason enough to look forward to the colder months. If you remain unconvinced, perhaps thinking of them as "vegetable toffee," like Nigel Slater does, will change your mind about this tragically underrated root.

. . .

roasted parsnips

To get the most out of roasted parsnips, peel and roll-cut them into bite-sized pieces. As you cut towards the stalk end, you'll encounter a fibrous core. When you do, halve or quarter the parsnip lengthways to remove the core, which is tough and chewy, before continuing.

Blanch the cut parsnips in boiling **salted water** for 5 minutes, then drain and dry them well. Toss with melted **coconut oil** and a little more **salt**, then roast at 230°C until caramelised on the surface, creamy within, and mildly redolent of a tropical breeze.

Alternatively, lay a bed of roll-cut parsnips in a baking pan, then place a **spatchcocked chicken or a Sunday roast** on top. Skip the blanching step here since the parsnips will absorb the drippings, transforming into meaty bites coated in caramel.

silky parsnip purée

Peel and slice parsnips into 1.25cm slices, discarding the fibrous core. Boil in generously **salted water** until tender, then drain and purée in a food processor until as smooth as can be. Taste and adjust the seasoning with salt and then, with the machine still running, add as much cold **unsalted butter** as Julia Child would, which is to say, a lot more than you think you need. Transfer to a serving bowl and, if you are so inclined, grind some **black pepper** over the top. Serve alongside **grilled or roasted meats,** or as an elegant holiday side dish.

potatoes

AUTUMN AND WINTER

Once I began spending time on farms as a young cook I learned that certain crops—including potatoes, onions, and garlic—are dug from the ground only once a year, in summer or early autumn, even though they're available in the market year-round. The rest of the time, they're carefully stored. Understanding how potatoes transform over the course of their months in storage will help you determine which potato to use when.

Potatoes are sweetest—which is to say highest in sugar content—when they're first harvested, typically in the summer or early fall. The moment a potato is dug, its innate sugars begin transforming into starches. And while some potato varieties are naturally starchier and others waxier, all potatoes undergo this process over the course of their time in storage.

This means that new potatoes, which are exactly what they sound like—freshly dug young potatoes of any size—are the sweetest of all. Not quite mature, they tend to emerge from the ground with more tender skins than their full-grown counterparts. In order to prevent damaging their fragile skins, farmers often leave them unwashed, with dirt caked on. So give these sweet spuds a scrub, but don't bother with peeling before boiling or roasting them.

Take a potato's age and sugar and starch content into account when deciding what to cook. A February potato will behave much differently in the pan than a September potato, even if they're the same variety. The higher a potato's sugar content, the more quickly it'll brown—or even burn. For this reason, avoid using new potatoes in high-heat preparations such as chips or fries. Months after harvest, a potato will be rife with starch, which is why it's essential to rinse sliced or cut potatoes until the water runs clear, then dry them well, for the crispiest, most evenly cooked fries.

• • •

warm potato salad

Toss just-boiled, still-warm new potatoes with **House Dressing** (page 117), thinly sliced **celery** and **spring onions**, and abundant coarsely chopped **dill** and serve alongside grilled or pan-fried **meat or fish**, including **Chicken Thigh Schnitzel** (page 309).

pan-fried potato gratin

Preheat the oven to 200°C. In a well-seasoned 25cm cast-iron or other ovenproof frying pan, combine 210ml each **full-fat milk** and **single cream**, 1 clove finely grated **garlic**, 2 **bay leaves**, 2 tablespoons **unsalted butter**, 1 tablespoon (9g) kosher **salt**, and a few grinds of **black pepper**. Bring to a simmer over medium heat, then turn off the heat and allow to steep.

good things come to those who wait

Use a mandoline to very thinly slice 1.2kg of russet (or King Edward) potatoes. Remove the bay leaves from the cream and discard. Add the potatoes and use a silicone spatula to spread them out in a somewhat even layer. The cream should barely cover the potatoes. If it doesn't, add up to 60ml more until it does. Taste and adjust the cream mixture as needed—it should be lightly redolent of garlic and generously salted.

Cover the pan and cook the potatoes over medium heat until they begin to soften, about 10 minutes. Thoroughly scrape the bottom of the pan every 2 minutes or so with the spatula to prevent scorching. When the potatoes begin to soften and the cream has begun to thicken, ensure the potatoes are somewhat evenly spread out, then scatter 85g finely grated **Parmesan** atop and dot the surface with 2 tablespoons unsalted butter. Bake the gratin on the top rack, uncovered, until it's golden brown and tender when pierced with a knife, about 25 minutes. Rest for 10 minutes before serving.

crisp hash browns

To make extraordinarily crisp hash browns, simmer whole, unpeeled russets (or King Edward) of any age in **salted water** until tender, about 50 minutes, then refrigerate overnight. Peel and coarsely grate them before frying with a generous amount of **extra-virgin olive oil, neutral oil, or ghee** over medium-high heat. Cook until browned, 5 to 7 minutes. Use a thin flexible metal spatula to gently break apart and flip the potatoes in chunks. Add more fat if the pan seems dry, and cook for another 8 minutes, flipping once or twice more until well browned and crisp in some parts, tender in others. Season with **salt** and serve hot.

shaken roast potatoes

Cut 1.2kg of Yukon Gold or other waxy potatoes into 4cm chunks and place in a large pot. Cover with **water,** season generously with **salt,** and bring to a moderate simmer. Cook the potatoes until a paring knife meets very little resistance when inserted, 12 to 15 minutes.

When the potatoes are cooked, gently drain them into a colander, then return them to the pot and season with salt to taste. Add 3 tablespoons of melted **ghee, schmaltz, or extra-virgin olive oil,** then cover and gently shake the pot until the potatoes break down a bit and a pasty, shaggy outer layer forms.

Drizzle a baking tray with 3 more tablespoons of fat, then evenly spread out the potatoes. Roast at 220°C for 20 minutes. Use a thin flexible metal spatula to release any stuck potatoes, shake the pan, and turn the potatoes. Continue turning, shaking, and roasting until all the potatoes are golden brown and crisp all over, 15 to 20 minutes longer. Transfer to a serving dish, season with salt to taste, and serve immediately.

roast chicken and potato dinner

For a simple, two-in-one dinner, shingle 4 or 5 layers of thinly sliced, rinsed, and dried Yukon Gold (or Maris Piper) potatoes into a 25- or 30cm ovenproof frying pan, seasoning each layer with **salt** and a light drizzle of melted **ghee** as you go. Place a seasoned, **spatchcocked chicken** atop the potatoes, breast-side up. Drizzle with a bit more ghee and roast at 220°C until done, about 50 minutes. The potatoes will absorb the chicken drippings and emerge from the pan gloriously flavourful, creamy, and golden brown.

fluffiest mashed potatoes

Use a fifty-fifty mix of Yukon Golds and russets (or Maris Piper and King Edward)—but cook them in separate pots since they'll cook at different rates. Peel and cut potatoes into 5cm pieces, and rinse them well to get rid of excess starch. Simmer the potatoes in **salted water**. When they're tender, drain them, spread them out in a single layer on a baking tray, and dry them out for a few minutes in an oven set to 400°C. Pass the potatoes through a ricer or food mill while they are still hot. Add generous amounts of **unsalted butter** and **soured cream** as you pile potatoes into the food mill—milling the potatoes with the fat helps incorporate it evenly, so you won't have to stir them as much later. The less you stir, the less you risk ending up with gummy potatoes. Taste and adjust the potatoes with more **salt** and soured cream as needed, stirring as little as possible. Serve immediately, or place the potatoes in a heatproof bowl and keep them warm in a simmering water bath for up to an hour before serving.

a small, good thing: winter citrus salad

In the depths of winter, nothing is more life-affirming than a salad of citrus fruit, bright in both colour and flavour. In recent years, I've become obsessed with mild Oro Blanco grapefruit. The pale yellow flesh is astonishingly low in acidity and bitterness, letting its inner "grapefruit-ness" shine with each bite. And while the perfect balance of sweet and tart in a Valencia orange is hard to beat, I also love pink pomelos and blood oranges.

Think of a citrus salad as winter's response to a plate of sliced, ripe summer tomatoes—which is to say, when it comes to garnishing, less is more. For a vibrant first course, arrange one or more varieties of sliced or segmented **citrus** on a platter, season with **flaky salt**, and drizzle with good **olive oil**. That's all you need.

To prepare any citrus fruit for salad, use a sharp knife to cut off its top and bottom so that it sits flat. Place it on a chopping board and cut along the sides of the fruit to remove the peel and pith in strips—narrower strips will waste less fruit and yield rounder slices. Fruit with tender membranes, including oranges, blood oranges, and mandarins, can now be cut into slices—just remove the seeds as you encounter them.

Cut larger fruit with tougher membranes, such as grapefruits and pomelos, into segments rather than slices. Holding the peeled fruit in one hand over a large bowl, use a knife with a sharp, thin blade to cut along the membrane down towards the centre. Continue cutting along both sides of the membrane to release each segment, removing the seeds as you encounter them. (Alternatively, you can use your fingers to pull the flesh from the membrane instead of using a knife, though this method will yield more rustic-looking pieces of fruit.) Once you've removed the fruit, squeeze the juice from the flesh remaining on the membranes into a small bowl or jug to use in a dressing or drink.

For a **Sicilian Citrus Salad**, add **Bright Pickled Onions** (page 52) and torn, pitted **olives**.

For a classic **California Citrus Salad**, add **Bright Pickled Onions** (page 52) and rustic spoonfuls of ripe **avocado**.

And for a dish inspired by the classic **Thai Pomelo Salad** called yum som-o, start with a base of **pomelo** and **grapefruit** segments. In a small bowl, whisk together 2 tablespoons **lime juice**, 1 tablespoon **fish sauce**, 1 tablespoon **soft brown sugar**, 1 tablespoon minced **lemongrass**, and 1 or 2 minced **Pickled Thai Chillies** (page 76). Drizzle the mixture over the fruit and top with toasted **coconut chips**, salted **roasted peanuts**, **coriander**, and **mint**.

sweet potatoes

AUTUMN AND WINTER

I love all sweet potatoes, but my favourite kind is the purple-skinned Japanese variety. Its white flesh is denser, starchier, and less fibrous than its orange-fleshed kin. And if only for aesthetic reasons, I prefer smaller sweet potatoes—about the size of my fist—to huge ones.

• • •

roasted sweet potatoes

Wash, dry, and trim the ends from however many sweet potatoes you'd like to cook. Halve small sweet potatoes lengthways. Slice larger ones into 2cm-thick coins.

Generously brush a parchment-lined baking tray with melted **coconut oil**. Lay the potatoes down (skin-side down if cut lengthways), coat the top of each with more oil, season with **salt**, then roast at 220°C. Cook, flipping after about 15 minutes, until the potatoes are completely tender when pierced with a knife, and dangerously dark, with bits of char appearing around the edges.

fluffy steamed sweet potatoes

Place a metal steamer basket inside a large casserole. Add **water** until it's just below the bottom of the basket and bring to a boil over medium-high heat.

Line the steamer with whole small sweet potatoes (or larger ones halved crossways)—in a single layer if possible. Cover and reduce the heat to medium. After 15 minutes, turn and rotate the potatoes and add more hot water to the steamer if needed. Cook until the potatoes are completely tender when pricked with a paring knife, about 40 minutes total, depending on their size.

Think of steamed sweet potatoes as a blank slate for flavour. Tear them open and garnish with toppings such as **labne, bacon bits, spring onions,** and **Green Sauce** (page 51). Try slathering them with **Whipped Tahini** (page 63) or **Cacio e Pepe Butter** (page 181). Or, smear a platter with **Whipped Ricotta** (page 66) and **Rapini Pesto** (page 258), then pile torn steamed sweet potatoes on top and shower with finely grated **lemon zest**.

charred sweet potatoes

For a little something different, char whole steamed or roasted sweet potatoes by using tongs to place the potatoes directly over a gas ring set to high (alternatively, barbecue over medium-high heat or set the potatoes directly atop live coals). Turn and cook until all the skin is charred, 5 to 7 minutes. Tear into large pieces, arrange on a platter, and drizzle with **honey**. Dot with dollops of **Garlic and Herb Labne** (page 48) and drizzle with **Calabrian Chilli Crisp** (page 56).

winter squash

AUTUMN AND WINTER

Honeynut (sometimes called Honeypatch or 898 squash) is tops in my book when it comes to winter squash. The variety was born when a chef asked a vegetable breeder for a butternut with less water weight and more concentrated flavour. The resulting squash, which looks like a miniature butternut, is spectacular. Even though it's a relatively new hybrid, it's so popular that farmers in the USA are already growing it. Like butternut, Honeynut is ideal for dark-roasting and simmering in stews and soups, such as **Stewy Harissa Chickpeas with Winter Squash** (page 166) and **Winter Squash and Green Curry Soup** (page 171). The Honeynut's intense flavour and sweetness also make it the ideal squash for "pumpkin" pie: Halve and lightly oil 3 squashes, then roast them until their skins are brown and their flesh is tender. Scoop out the flesh and purée or pass it through a food mill, then proceed with your favourite pie recipe.

The dry, starchy flesh of the kabocha squash makes it ideal for steaming and adding to soups and stews. I prefer red kabocha to green for its sweeter flavour, but you can use the two interchangeably.

Delicata is the rare winter squash with skin tender enough to eat. Stripey-peel then halve a delicata squash lengthways before scooping out its seeds. Slice into half-moons and dark-roast or steam until tender.

No matter the variety, choose winter squashes that are firm, heavy for their size, and free of blemishes, soft spots, and cracks. Store in a dark, cool, dry space for up to a month.

• • •

dark-roasted winter squash

Toss chunky slices or wedges of squash (approximately 2 to 2.5cm thick) with **extra-virgin olive oil** (or another cooking fat) and **salt**, then spread out in a single layer and roast at 220°C, until the squash is tender throughout and dangerously dark at the edges, about 35 minutes. Serve on its own, or turn it into a room-temperature salad by enhancing it with sweet and sour flavours and crunchy and creamy textures.

sweet and spicy winter squash

To make my favourite winter side dish, slather **Whipped Ricotta** (page 66) on a platter, then pile dark-roasted squash on top. Drizzle with a little runny **honey or maple syrup**, then top with **Calabrian Chilli Crisp** (page 56) and chopped **parsley**.

steamed kabocha with sesame-ginger dressing

Peel, seed, and slice kabocha squash into 1.25cm-thick wedges, then steam until tender, about 15 minutes. Season with **salt** and **toasted sesame oil** and drizzle with **Creamy Sesame-Ginger Dressing** (page 119).

roasted vegetable salad matrix

Turn any one or two of these roasted vegetables into a composed salad layered with a multitude of colours, flavours, and textures. But resist the urge to include every optional element—thoughtfulness and restraint will keep your salad from becoming a "kitchen sink" dish. Instead, let classic flavour combinations and memories of favourite meals inspire you as you make your choices here.

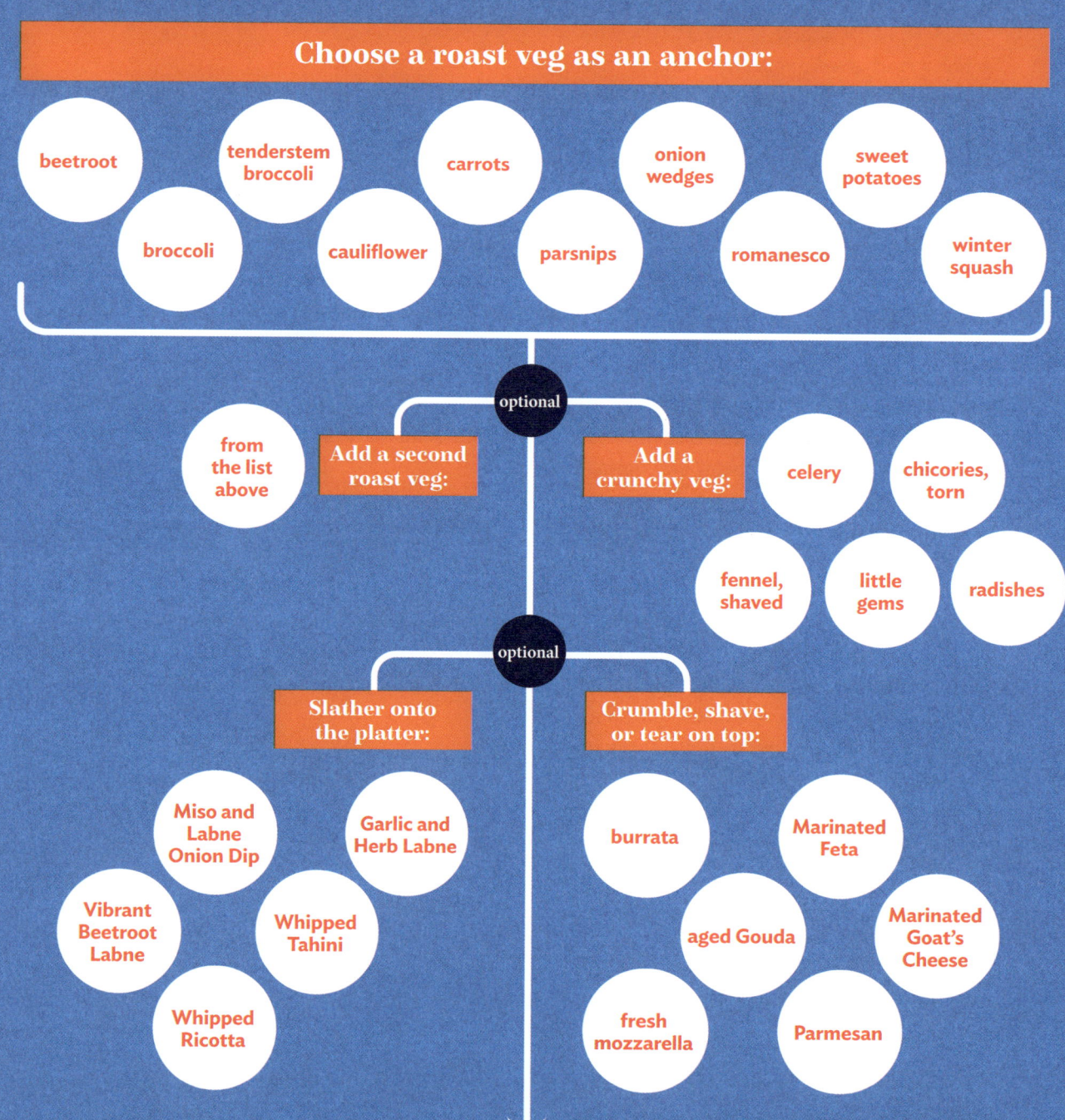

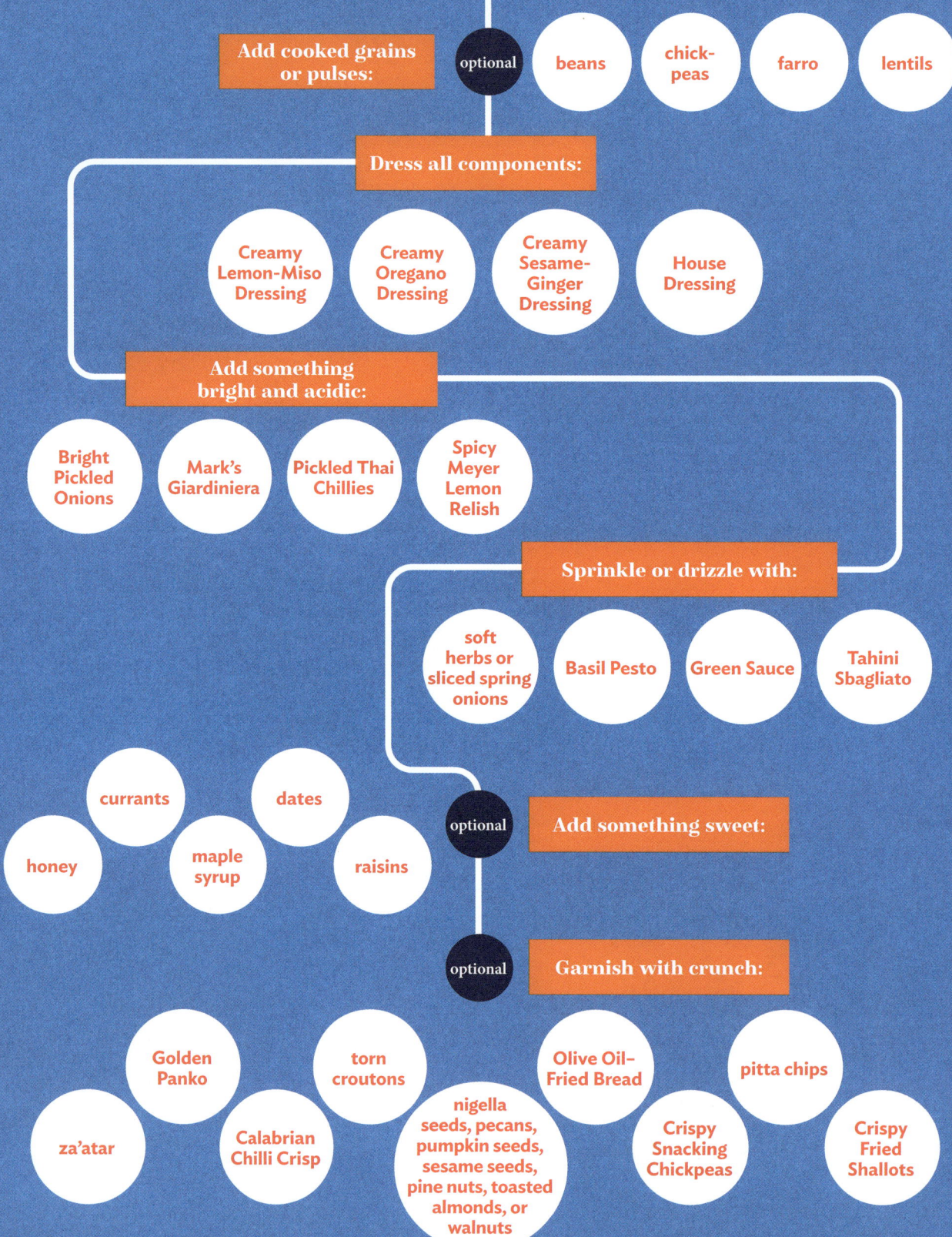

Cauliflower and onion wedges with saffron, currants, toasted pine nuts, parsley, and **House Dressing** (page 117)

Winter squash on a bed of **Whipped Ricotta** (page 66) with honey, parsley, and **Calabrian Chilli Crisp** (page 56)

Tenderstem broccoli with corona beans, **Marinated Feta** (page 71), **Preserved Meyer Lemon Paste** (page 79), and **Pickled Thai Chillies** (page 76)

Carrots on a bed of **Whipped Tahini** (page 63) with coriander and **Green Sauce** (page 51)

Marinated chioggia and red beetroot on a bed of **Vibrant Beetroot Labne** (page 248) with nigella seeds and dill

finger-licking good things

chicken, chicken, and more chicken

Emily Su-Bowden, a founding member of my Culinary Brain Trust, once told me about a meal she'd just had at a restaurant in Los Angeles where the bread and butter plate cost thirteen dollars. Which, at first, seemed insane. But then, the crusty house-made baguette and salted cultured butter from Normandy arrived, and were so exquisitely satisfying that, after one bite, she flagged down a waiter. "In for a penny, in for a pound," she figured, and ordered the pan drippings, which cost another eight bucks, to spread onto her bread.

"Twenty-one bucks well spent," she said. "And I don't regret it one bit. But it did sort of feel like I was paying for a cook snack."

"Nah," I responded with a laugh. "If they really wanted to sell you a cook snack, they'd roll out a massive trash can to your table, have you crouch over it, and hand you a chicken carcass."

Professional cooks all have our own names for cook snacks, the special little bites we make for ourselves with kitchen odds and ends while we're cooking for others. Usually, they're far more interesting and exciting than anything on the menu. Some cook snacks are elaborate, like the extraordinary flatbreads Emily used to make for us when we worked in restaurants. She'd grill spent pizza dough into pittas, then layer on slices of the unservable ends of lamb roasts and top everything with yogurt, harissa, and herb salad. Other times, cook snacks are as simple as a crumble of three-year-old Parmesan topped with a drop of aged balsamic.

As hinted above, my own ultimate cook snack involves a small ritual: stealthily crouching out of sight of our guests with one or two of my colleagues over an industrial-sized rubbish bin, as we each pick the best bits from a rotisserie chicken carcass. I always go for the salty, golden "pope's nose" from the tail end first. Then, I check for any thigh "oysters" and white meat that might be left behind. Finally, I'll pick off any remaining bits of burnished, crispy skin and use a crust of bread to sop up the pan drippings.

"The sound of a chicken roasting," writes Nigel Slater, "is a message that says all is well." It's true. Across the world, people who eat chicken associate it with comfort and safety. I'm no different. I just draw my comfort not from the sound, smell, or even taste of a roasting chicken, but rather from the knowledge that once I deliver a platter of carved white and dark meat to the table and encourage everyone to serve themselves, I'll return to the kitchen. There, I'll pick at the carcass and let one perfect, golden bite melt on my tongue. When I'm cooking I often forget to connect with my own body, my own tastes and desires, because I'm so focused on everyone else. But, somehow, roasting a chicken always shows me the way back to myself.

It feels right for me to share an entire chapter of chicken recipes—not only for roasting but also for grilling, simmering, braising, and frying—in the hope that they'll be a source of ease and comfort for you, too.

a few important notes before we dive in

Recipes: The recipes in this chapter are **organised like chicken in a butcher's case**—the whole bird, bone-in pieces, boneless meat, and bones—so you can decide what to make based on what you've got.

Shopping: I recommend choosing an **organic**—and **preferably free-range**—chicken. It might be a little harder to source (and certainly more expensive), but to quote Laurie Colwin, "Not only is it tastier . . . but you also do not have to worry about feeding anabolic steroids to friends and loved ones," or eating them yourself, for that matter.

Salting: When possible, **season chicken in advance of cooking** so that salt has time to penetrate, enhance flavour, and—if done early enough—tenderise. In terms of timing, any time is better than none, and more is better than some, up to about 48 hours, after which a chicken will begin to cure. The true sweet spot—when you can manage it—is the night before you plan to cook. But seasoning in the morning, or even the afternoon, will yield a better chicken than no time at all. I like to do it as soon as I get home from the supermarket, so I don't have to think about it again. And if you're monitoring your salt intake, remember: **Seasoning with a smaller amount of salt in advance will make a larger impact than a larger amount applied just before cooking or serving.**

WHOLE CHICKEN
simple spatchcocked chicken

SERVES 4

1 whole chicken (1.6 to 1.8kg)
Kosher salt
Extra-virgin olive oil

These days, I rarely roast a chicken without spatchcocking it first. Removing the backbone and pressing the chicken flat does two wonderful things—it decreases the cooking time by almost half while maximising the surface area for crispy, brown skin. In an ideal world, you'll spatchcock and season the chicken a day in advance of cooking, but even when that's something you can't manage, simply flattening the bird will allow seasoning to penetrate more quickly and evenly.

• • •

To spatchcock, use heavy-duty kitchen scissors to remove the backbone (on the underside of the bird) by snipping down along both sides of it. You can start from the tail or neck end, whichever you prefer. Next, clip off the wingtips. Reserve the backbone and wingtips for stock.

Lay the chicken, breast-side up, on the chopping board. Use your hands to push down on the breastbone until the bird flattens and you hear the cartilage pop. Generously season the bird with salt on both sides. Place in a shallow roasting dish, breast-side up, and refrigerate, uncovered, overnight. (The air circulating in the fridge will dry out the chicken skin so it cooks up glassy and crisp.) If you're planning on cooking the chicken right away, skip the fridge and leave the bird out at room temperature.

Pull the bird out of the fridge an hour before you plan to cook it. Adjust an oven rack to the upper-middle of the oven and preheat to 220°C.

Heat a 25- or 30cm cast-iron frying pan or other ovenproof frying pan over medium-high heat. Add just enough oil to coat the bottom of the pan. As soon as the oil shimmers, place the chicken in the pan, breast-side down, and brown for 6 to 8 minutes, until golden. It's fine if the bird doesn't lie completely flat as long as the breast is in contact with the pan. Flip the bird over (again, it's fine if it doesn't lie entirely flat) and slide the entire pan into the oven. Push the pan all the way to the very back of the oven, with the handle of the pan facing left.

After about 20 minutes, carefully use an oven glove to rotate the pan 180 degrees so the handle faces right, and return it to the very back of the rack.

Cook until the chicken is browned all over and the juices run clear when you cut between the leg and the thigh, another 20 to 25 minutes.

Let rest for 10 minutes before carving. Serve warm or at room temperature.

WHOLE CHICKEN

joojeh kabob roast chicken

SERVES 4

Requires overnight marinating

- 1 whole chicken (1.6 to 1.8kg)
- Kosher salt
- ½ teaspoon saffron threads, ground and bloomed (see page 37)
- 1 tablespoon tomato purée
- 4 tablespoons freshly squeezed lime or lemon juice
- 365g natural yogurt or buttermilk
- 1 brown onion, thinly sliced
- 2 garlic cloves, finely grated
- ½ teaspoon coarsely ground black pepper
- **Basic Crispy Rice** (page 155), for serving
- **Garlic and Herb Labne** (page 48), for serving
- **Shirazi Salad** (page 247), for serving

Growing up, my family didn't eat out very often. But when we did, it was almost always at a Persian chelo kababi, where we'd each order a humongous platter of buttery saffron rice topped with two skewers of grilled meat and a grilled tomato. We each had our favourites, and mine was invariably joojeh kabob—tender, tangy pieces of saffron-and-yogurt-marinated chicken. Joojeh kabob was so deeply ingrained into my food memories that years later it was a primary source of inspiration when I developed my recipe for Buttermilk-Brined Roast Chicken.

And because it's just about the best roast chicken I've ever tasted, I used that recipe as the starting point for this one. The chicken still brines overnight in a flavourful, well-seasoned marinade of yogurt or buttermilk, but this time, saffron, onions, lime, garlic, and a little tomato purée are layered in to deliver the precise combination of acidity, sweetness, and umami that makes joojeh kabob so irresistible.

• • •

The day before you plan to cook, spatchcock the chicken (see page 282) and generously season it with salt on both sides. Let the chicken sit at room temperature while you prepare the marinade.

In an extra-large zip-lock plastic bag, whisk together the bloomed saffron, tomato purée, and lime juice until evenly combined. Add 2 tablespoons (18g) kosher salt and the yogurt, onion, garlic, and pepper. Add the chicken, seal the bag, and squish the yogurt all over the chicken. Place it on a rimmed plate and refrigerate. If you're so inclined, over the next 24 hours you can turn the bag so every part of the chicken gets marinated, but it's not essential.

An hour before cooking, remove the chicken from the yogurt and scrape off any aromatics. Bring the chicken to room temperature.

Adjust an oven rack to the centre position and preheat to 220°C.

recipe continues

Arrange the chicken, breast-side up, on a wire rack set over a baking tray (line the tray with parchment to make cleanup easier). Cook until the chicken is a dark golden brown and the juices run clear when you cut between the leg and the thigh, about 45 minutes. (Loosely cover the chicken with a piece of foil for the last 10 minutes if the skin is getting too dark.)

Let the chicken rest for 5 minutes before serving with crispy rice, garlic and herb labne, and Shirazi salad.

VARIATION

To barbecue **Joojeh Kabobs,** marinate 900g to 1.4kg of seasoned boneless, skinless **chicken thighs** cut into 4cm pieces overnight. Remove from the marinade and thread onto metal or bamboo skewers. Grill over medium-high heat until cooked through and gloriously charred and golden on the surface, about 5 minutes per side.

Not so long ago, I sat at a long outdoor table with old friends and new, alongside a tiny East London canal. As the sun set on that first balmy night of summer, I felt grateful to be alive. I'll never forget that evening because I hadn't felt such lightness in a very, very long time. But it didn't hurt that the piri piri chicken was such a spicy, tangy, charbroiled pleasure to eat. This recipe is my attempt to channel that evening's meal—prepared by Sam and Sam Clark of Moro restaurant, who were in turn inspired by their own Portuguese and Brazilian cooks.

• • •

Preheat the oven to 180°C.

Spread out all the chillies on a baking tray in a single layer. Roast until browned and tender, 10 to 12 minutes. Transfer to a plate and allow to cool.

Wearing disposable gloves, remove the stalks and roughly chop the chillies. In a small saucepan, combine the chopped chillies, garlic, bay leaves, smoked paprika, oil, vinegar, sugar, and 1½ teaspoons (5g) kosher salt. Bring to a simmer over medium heat and cook for 3 minutes to infuse, then set aside to cool to room temperature.

Transfer the mixture to a blender and purée until completely smooth, then taste and adjust the seasoning with salt, sugar, and vinegar as needed. Transfer to a sterile glass jar (see **Sterilizing Jars,** page 38) and refrigerate for up to 3 months. Stir well before using.

The night before you plan to cook, use poultry scissors to spatchcock the chicken (see page 282) and then halve it through the breastbone. Flatten each breast as much as possible by bearing down with the heel of your palm, then generously season all sides of the chicken with salt. Use a pastry brush to marinate the chicken in about 180ml of the piri piri sauce, taking care to brush it all over. Cover with parchment and refrigerate overnight.

recipe continues

WHOLE CHICKEN
piri piri chicken

**SERVES 4
(AND MAKES ABOUT 360ML SAUCE)**

Requires overnight marinating

- 10 red Thai chillies
- 8 green Thai chillies
- 8 Fresno chillies
- 4 garlic cloves, sliced
- 3 bay leaves, crumbled
- 1½ teaspoons smoked paprika
- 110g extra-virgin olive oil
- 80ml white wine vinegar
- 2 teaspoons sugar
- Kosher salt
- 1 whole chicken (1.6 to 1.8kg)
- **Shaken Roast Potatoes** (optional; page 264), for serving

Let the chicken sit at room temperature for at least an hour before cooking.

When ready to cook, prepare a barbecue. If using charcoal, light a fire, let the flames die down, and wait until the coals ash over. Push the coals over to one side of the grill to create a medium-high zone and an indirect-heat zone. If using a gas grill, set up a medium-high-heat zone and an indirect-heat zone. The total cooking time for a 1.8kg chicken will be about 45 minutes, most of which will happen over indirect heat.

Scrub the grill grates clean, then lay the chicken, breast-side down, over the indirect heat. Cook until the skin starts to brown nicely, 8 to 10 minutes, rotating once or twice after 4 or 5 minutes. Flip the halves over and cook the chicken, skin-side up, for 15 to 20 minutes.

At this point, the inner part of the breast may need some heat, so you can prop the halves up on their sides for a few minutes. Finally, brush the skin side with a few tablespoons of piri piri sauce and place the pieces over medium heat one last time, skin-side down, to crisp up the skin. If, at any point, you feel like the chicken needs to take on a little more colour, stoke the fire or move the chicken over direct heat for a few minutes to brown and crisp, but take care—the sugars in the peppers and sauce will hasten burning!

Allow to rest for 8 to 10 minutes before carving, then serve immediately with the remaining piri piri sauce and roast potatoes if desired.

NOTE

To roast the chicken rather than grill it, set it skin-side up on a baking tray and cook at 220°C, brushing once with the sauce at the onset of cooking and a second time after about 30 minutes. Roast until the skin is burnished and crisp and the thigh and breast meat are cooked through, 45 to 50 minutes.

WHOLE CHICKEN

one-pot chicken with giant couscous and preserved lemon

SERVES 4 TO 6

- 4 tablespoons extra-virgin olive oil
- 375g giant couscous
- 1 whole chicken (1.6 to 1.8kg), salted in advance (see page 281)
- 6 garlic cloves, peeled and left whole
- 1 large onion, diced
- 2 tablespoons ground cumin
- 480ml water
- 6 tablespoons **Preserved Meyer Lemon Paste** (page 79)
- 12 Medjool dates, pitted and torn in half
- Kosher salt
- Finely grated zest and juice of 1 lemon
- Finely chopped coriander or parsley, for garnish

Nigella Lawson has mastered the art of creating recipes that balance comfort and appeal—especially when chicken is involved. This is a play on her essential one-pot chicken with orzo. It's a do-it-all dish that'll make you feel both satisfied and cared for, whether you prefer dark or white meat; the sweetness of Medjool dates or the funk, salt, and acid of preserved lemon; an abundance of braising juices or the playful chewiness of giant couscous.

• • •

Set a large casserole over medium-high heat and add 2 tablespoons of the oil. When it shimmers, add the couscous. Cook, stirring constantly, until toasted and golden brown, about 6 minutes. Transfer the couscous to a bowl and set aside.

Return the pot to the heat and add the remaining 2 tablespoons oil. When it shimmers, carefully lay in the chicken, breast-side down, and cook until golden brown, 4 to 6 minutes. Use tongs to carefully remove the chicken to a plate.

Reduce the heat to medium and add the garlic, onion, and cumin and cook, stirring occasionally, until the onions are just starting to grow tender, about 6 minutes.

Return the chicken to the pot, breast-side up. Add the water and preserved lemon paste and stir to combine. Bring the mixture to a boil, then reduce to a simmer and cover tightly with a lid. Cook until the chicken thigh is tender at the bone, 45 minutes to 1 hour.

Uncover the pot and stir in the couscous and dates. Taste the broth—it should be flavourful and highly seasoned. If needed, adjust the seasoning with salt (I've never needed to add more salt at this point, but your preserved lemon paste may not be as salty as mine). Cover and cook at a simmer, stirring occasionally, until the couscous is al dente, about 15 minutes. Leave the pot covered off the heat for another 10 to

15 minutes—the couscous will continue absorbing the broth and finish cooking, and the chicken will rest during this time.

Remove the chicken to carve it. Stir the lemon zest and juice into the couscous, and adjust the seasoning with salt as needed. Return the carved chicken to the pot and garnish with coriander. Serve hot.

Cover and refrigerate leftovers for up to 3 days. Add a little water and, stirring, gently return to a boil to reheat.

WHOLE CHICKEN
golden chicken soup

I started working on this recipe a few years ago in the dreary depths of winter. Flooded with grief and struggling with a bout of severe depression, I wasn't particularly inspired to cook. But something kept drawing me to the idea of a chicken in a pot. So back I went.

Let me be clear—it wasn't nostalgia calling. Chicken soup doesn't warmly transport me to my childhood. Simply put, it wasn't an arrow in my mom's vast quiver of cold remedies. And on the rare occasion when she did make a soup with chicken, it was so dense with barley and tart with lemon that I found it more of a burden than a comfort to eat.

As I tinkered with the soup, I kept returning to saffron, lemon, turmeric, and black pepper. At some point, I spooned a little cooked rice into my bowl and drizzled it with warm cardamom ghee. Sitting and sipping, childhood memories of my mom's poached chicken with saffron and lemon flooded into my head. My brothers and I always fought over the broth, which we used to douse our tahdig so that it'd soften a bit. So while my childhood chicken soup may not have inspired this one, a warm memory found its way into the pot.

• • •

To make the broth, cut the chicken into 6 pieces (leg quarters, breasts, and wings) and place them in a stockpot along with the carcass, onions, celery, carrots, parsley, bay leaves, garlic, ginger, lemon halves, and salt. Add the water and bring to a boil over high heat.

Reduce the heat to a simmer. Use a fine-mesh skimmer or slotted spoon to skim any scum from the surface and discard. Add the bloomed saffron, then swirl a little hot broth in the mortar to coax every bit of saffron into the soup. Stir in the cardamom, peppercorns, turmeric, and cayenne and continue simmering the soup until the breasts are cooked, 15 to 20 minutes.

MAKES ABOUT 6 LITRES

FOR THE BROTH

- 1 whole chicken (1.6 to 1.8kg), salted in advance (see page 281)
- 2 brown onions, unpeeled and quartered
- 2 celery stalks, cut into 7.5cm pieces
- 2 carrots, peeled and cut into 7.5cm pieces
- Small handful of parsley sprigs or stalks
- 2 bay leaves
- 1 head garlic, halved horizontally
- 7.5cm piece fresh ginger, sliced into thick coins
- 1 lemon, halved
- 2 tablespoons (18g) kosher salt
- 4.3 litres water
- ¼ teaspoon saffron threads, ground and bloomed (see page 37)
- 5 cardamom pods, cracked
- 1 tablespoon black peppercorns

recipe and ingredients continue

2 teaspoons ground turmeric

¼ teaspoon cayenne pepper

FOR THE SOUP

Kosher salt

Freshly squeezed juice of 1 to 2 lemons

3 celery stalks, very thinly sliced

4 carrots, very thinly sliced

1 large bunch Tuscan (lacinato) or curly kale, tough stalks removed and thinly sliced (optional)

FOR SERVING

Lemon wedges, for squeezing

Cardamom Ghee (optional; page 61)

Remove the breasts from the pot and set aside to cool. (Pierce through to the centre of the breast with a paring knife to check doneness; return meat with any sign of pink to the pot to keep cooking for a few minutes longer.)

When the legs are cooked and the meat is falling off the bone, 25 to 30 minutes longer, remove them from the pot, strip the meat from the bones, and return the bones to the pot. Continue simmering the stock for an additional 30 minutes, for a total cooking time of 1½ hours.

When the meat is cool enough to handle, shred it into a bowl and set aside, discarding any gristle or cartilage you encounter. If you like chicken skin, you can chop it into tiny bits and add it into the pile of shredded meat to add back into the soup. Otherwise, discard the skin along with the gristle. (I've found that using all of the meat from chickens larger than 1.6kg can overwhelm this soup, so if you prefer a brothier soup, hold back at least a breast's worth of meat—use it to make **Chilli Crisp Chicken Salad,** page 313!)

To finish the soup, strain the broth through a fine-mesh sieve into a very large bowl or container. Rinse out the pot, then return the broth to the pot along with the shredded meat. Bring to a simmer, then taste and adjust the seasoning with salt and lemon juice. Add the thinly sliced celery, carrot, and kale (if using). Simmer until the vegetables are tender, about 20 minutes, then taste and adjust the seasoning again.

Serve with lemon wedges and cardamom ghee for everyone to add as they like.

Cover and refrigerate chilled soup for up to 1 week or freeze for up to 6 months. Bring to a boil before serving.

This soup is a loving ode to the version at Tacubaya, a gem of a taqueria around the corner from Eccolo, the Berkeley, California, restaurant whose kitchen I ran for several years. Sometimes, in the middle of a long day, I'd sneak over to Tacubaya for a moment to myself. I ate many, many bowls of this soup in blissful solitude and never tired of it. I'm expert at gauging the precise moment when the hot broth melts the Oaxacan cheese just enough to produce a dramatic pull. And I always feel a small thrill when I get to slurp up a best bite—a warm and lightly spiced spoonful rich with bits of shredded chicken and broth, and packed with the contrasting textures of melted cheese, crunchy tortilla chips, and creamy avocado.

• • •

To make the broth, heat a cast-iron frying pan over medium heat. Add the ancho chillies and toast them evenly on all sides, turning occasionally, until they soften, darken, and puff slightly, 2 to 3 minutes. Remove from the heat, then discard the seeds, ribs, and stalks.

In a blender, combine the toasted anchos, chipotle peppers, and tomatoes and purée until smooth. Set the tomato-chilli purée aside.

Cut the chicken into 6 pieces (leg quarters, breasts, and wings) and place in a 10- or 12-litre soup pot along with the carcass, tomato-chilli purée, onion, garlic, coriander, bay leaves, peppercorns, and salt. Add the water. (If your pot is too small to add the full amount of water, add what will fit—you can add the remaining water after shredding the chicken.)

Bring to a boil, then reduce to a simmer and cook until the breasts are cooked, 15 to 20 minutes. Remove the breasts from the pot and set aside to cool. (Pierce through to the centre of each breast with a paring knife to check doneness; return meat with any sign of pink to the pot to keep cooking for a few minutes longer.)

WHOLE CHICKEN
tortilla soup

MAKES ABOUT 6 LITRES

FOR THE BROTH

- 3 large ancho chillies
- 2 to 3 chipotle peppers in adobo sauce
- 2 x 400g tins whole tomatoes, preferably San Marzano
- 1 whole chicken (1.6 to 1.8kg), salted in advance (see page 281)
- 1 brown onion, cut into eighths
- 1 head garlic, halved horizontally
- Small handful of coriander sprigs or stalks
- 2 bay leaves
- 1 teaspoon black peppercorns
- 2 tablespoons (18g) kosher salt
- 5.3 litres water

FOR THE SOUP

- 4 tablespoons extra-virgin olive oil
- 2 brown onions, cut into 1cm dice

recipe and ingredients continue

Kosher salt

6 garlic cloves, very thinly sliced

FOR SERVING

Tortilla chips

Soured cream

Coriander leaves and tender stems, roughly chopped

Red onion, finely diced

Lime wedges, for squeezing

Oaxacan cheese, cubed

Baby spinach leaves

When the legs are cooked and the meat is falling off the bone, 25 to 30 minutes longer, remove them from the pot, strip the meat from the bones, and return the bones to the pot. Continue simmering the stock for an additional 30 minutes, for a total cooking time of 1½ hours.

When the meat is cool enough to handle, shred it into a bowl and set aside, discarding any gristle or cartilage you encounter. If you like chicken skin, you can chop it into tiny bits and add it into the pile of shredded meat to add back into the soup. Otherwise, discard the skin along with the gristle. (I've found that all of the meat from chickens larger than 1.6kg can be too much for this soup, so if you prefer a brothier soup, hold back at least a breast's worth of meat—you can use it to make **Chilli Crisp Chicken Salad,** page 313!)

To make the soup, strain the broth through a fine-mesh sieve into a very large bowl or container. Rinse out the pot and return it to the hob over medium heat. Add 3 tablespoons of the oil. When it shimmers, add the onions and a generous pinch of salt. Reduce the heat to medium-low and cook, stirring occasionally, until the onion is translucent and tender, about 15 minutes.

Move the onions to the edge of the pot, clearing a spot in the center. Add the remaining 1 tablespoon oil and the garlic. Cook until aromatic, but not at all beginning to colour, about 1 minute. Return the broth to the pot along with the shredded meat. Bring to a simmer, then taste and adjust the seasoning with salt. Simmer for 20 minutes, then taste and adjust the seasoning again.

To serve, prepare bowls of tortilla chips, soured cream, coriander, red onion, and lime wedges and bring to the table. Place Oaxacan cheese and spinach into individual bowls and ladle hot soup over to wilt. Bring to the table and let diners use remaining garnishes as desired.

Cover and refrigerate chilled soup for up to 1 week or freeze for up to 6 months. Bring to a boil before serving.

BONE-IN CHICKEN

chivi spice chicken thighs

MAKES 8 THIGHS, OR ABOUT 1KG SHREDDED MEAT

- 8 bone-in, skin-on chicken thighs (about 1.4kg)
- Kosher salt
- 3 tablespoons **Teo's Chivi Spice** (page 348)
- Extra-virgin olive oil
- 2 red onions, thinly sliced
- 1 head garlic, halved horizontally
- 1 to 2 chipotle peppers in adobo sauce
- 2 bay leaves
- Small handful of coriander stalks
- 240ml **Chicken Stock** (page 314) or water
- 500g crushed tomatoes (tinned or fresh)
- Coarsely chopped coriander leaves, for garnish
- Lime wedges, for serving
- Tortillas, **Arroz Rojo** (page 154), or **Arroz Verde** (page 154), for serving

This braise is so flavourful that even when you don't get around to seasoning the chicken in advance (gasp!), it'll still win over everyone at the table. You can serve the thighs on the bone alongside rice and pinto or black beans for a well-rounded meal. Or, to use the chicken as a filling for tacos, burritos, or enchiladas, shred the thigh meat, discard the bones and gristle, and chop the skin finely. Bring the skin and meat to a simmer in a medium saucepan with enough braising liquid to make the mixture unctuous, then taste and adjust the seasoning as needed.

• • •

Season the chicken in advance (overnight if possible) with salt and 2 tablespoons of the chivi spice. Cover and refrigerate, then bring to room temperature before cooking.

Adjust an oven rack to the centre position and preheat to 190°C.

Set a large frying pan over medium-high heat and add 2 tablespoons oil. When it shimmers, add the onions and a generous pinch of salt. Reduce the heat to medium and cook, stirring occasionally with a wooden spoon, until the onions are wilted and lightly browned, 10 to 12 minutes.

Meanwhile, lay the garlic, chipotles, bay leaves, and coriander stalks over the bottom of a 23 × 33cm baking dish or similar size nonreactive roasting tin.

Scrape the cooked onions over the bed of aromatics. Return the frying pan to medium heat and add the stock, tomatoes, and remaining 1 tablespoon chivi spice. Scraping the pan with a wooden spoon to release any browned bits, bring the liquid to a boil, then add it to the baking dish. Nestle the chicken thighs into the dish, skin-side down. The braising liquid should come about halfway up the sides of the chicken, so if you're at all short, add a splash of water or stock to make up the difference. Cover with a piece of parchment and then tightly wrap the dish with foil.

Cook until the chicken is completely tender and shows no resistance when pierced with a sharp knife, about 1½ hours.

Adjust the oven rack to the highest position and increase the oven temperature to 220°C. Remove the foil and parchment from the dish and flip the chicken thighs over so that they sit skin-side up. Return the dish to the top rack to brown the chicken skin and reduce the braising liquid, 15 to 20 minutes longer.

To serve, use tongs to gently arrange the chicken in a rimmed serving dish or shallow bowl. Discard the bay leaves, garlic skins, and chillies and pass the remaining aromatics and braising liquid through a food mill or use an immersion blender to purée. Skim any excess fat from the surface, then adjust the seasoning of the liquid as needed with salt. Pour 480 to 720ml of braising juice back into the serving dish, then garnish with coriander leaves. Serve with lime wedges and tortillas or rice.

Refrigerate leftover meat and liquid together in a covered container for up to 1 week or freeze for up to 3 months. Bring to a boil before serving.

BONE-IN CHICKEN
shoyu chicken

MAKES 8 THIGHS

- 8 bone-in, skin-on chicken thighs (about 1.4kg)
- Kosher salt
- 180ml soy sauce
- 360ml water
- 50g soft dark brown sugar
- 85g honey
- 4 tablespoons mirin
- 6 garlic cloves, smashed and peeled
- 2 tablespoons finely grated fresh ginger
- 1 tablespoon toasted sesame oil
- 1 onion, cut into 1.25cm wedges through the root
- 2 tablespoons cornflour
- Steamed rice, for serving
- Coarsely chopped coriander leaves, for garnish
- Toasted sesame seeds, for garnish

During a visit to the Big Island of Hawaii a few years ago, I cooked my way through Alana Kysar's wonderful cookbook, *Aloha Kitchen*. Every recipe I tried was a winner—especially the chewy butter mochi. But this is the dish, with a few minor tweaks, that's made it into my regular rotation.

Even the pickiest eaters I know gobble up this take on Hawaiian-style shoyu chicken with gusto. With crisp skin and fork-tender meat in a sea of glossy, gingery braising juices, it's one of those dishes that gets everyone so focused on eating that all conversation comes to a halt.

• • •

Very lightly season the chicken in advance (overnight if possible) with salt.

In a large casserole, mix together the soy sauce, water, brown sugar, honey, mirin, garlic, ginger, and oil. Lay in the onion wedges, then nestle in the chicken, skin-side down. The braising liquid should come about halfway up the sides of the chicken, so if you're at all short, add a splash of water or stock to make up the difference.

Cover the pot and simmer for 30 minutes. Using tongs, gently turn the chicken to face skin-side up, then cover and continue simmering until the meat falls off the bone, about 30 minutes longer. Turn off the heat and use tongs to remove the chicken to a plate.

Preheat the grill.

Place the cornflour in a small bowl and whisk in 120ml of the braising liquid until no lumps remain, then whisk the cornstarch mixture back into the pot. Cook over medium heat for 5 minutes, until the sauce visibly thickens. Return the thighs to the pot, skin-side up.

Place the pot under the grill 5 to 10cm from the heat source and grill until the skin is crisp and lightly browned, about 2 minutes (or longer, depending on your grill). Tend to them closely to ensure that the skin does not burn—with all of that sugar and soy sauce in the marinade, they will brown quickly!

Serve chicken with the sauce and steamed rice, garnished with coriander and toasted sesame seeds.

VARIATION

To make **Shoyu Chicken Wings,** substitute 1.8kg of wings for the thighs.

BONE-IN CHICKEN

chicken braised with apricots and harissa

MAKES 8 THIGHS

Requires overnight marinating

FOR THE TEBIL

- 2 tablespoons ground coriander
- 1¼ teaspoons turmeric
- ½ teaspoon caraway seeds, ground
- ¼ teaspoon freshly ground black pepper

recipe and ingredients continue

I thought I knew my harissa after nearly two decades of making it from scratch. Then I tasted a spoonful of rich, wine-dark paste from an unmarked jar that arrived on my doorstep from brothers Mansour and Karim Arem. They were on the verge of launching Zwïta, a company focused on celebrating their Tunisian heritage. Whereas Western cooks and food writers are somewhat familiar with many of the food traditions of nearby Morocco, we've largely neglected to learn anything about Tunisia or its culinary history. And judging by the Arem brothers' harissa, that's entirely to our detriment.

Made with mild, sun-dried chillies, the traditional Tunisian pepper paste is layered with garlic, caraway, and coriander. Multidimensional in flavour and distinctly thick, this harissa will be a revelation to anyone who has only encountered it squeezed from a tube (or any other version similarly doctored up with tomato products, hydrated chilli powder, or fresh peppers).

Once I tasted their harissa, I began to incorporate it into my everyday cooking, stirring it into **Garlic and Herb Labne** (page 48) and drizzling it over roasted vegetables. But one of my favourite ways to use it is as a rub or marinade for chicken. When I asked Mansour what other spices I should add to this braise he told me about tebil (pronounced *tah*-bill), a Tunisian coriander-based spice blend that varies from family to family. In some households, it consists entirely of coriander! He also said that cumin is used sparingly in Tunisia, and always added at the end of cooking to keep it from overwhelming the dish. With Mansour's guidance, I tinkered with the spices to develop my own tebil for this dish.

Every time I've made this for friends, there hasn't been a morsel left. Since I use mild harissa, even the most spice-averse kids lap up every sip of braising juice and eat every bite of chicken off the bone. It's a winner, if there ever was one. I highly recommend serving this chicken with steamed couscous because it absorbs the braising juices on your plate as you eat—ensuring that you'll get to enjoy every last drop.

• • •

FOR THE CHICKEN

- 8 bone-in, skin-on chicken thighs (about 1.4kg)
- Kosher salt
- 2 tablespoons mild harissa paste
- 3 tablespoons **Cardamom Ghee** (page 61), **Ghee** (page 62), or extra-virgin olive oil
- 1 brown onion, thinly sliced
- 2 carrots, peeled and roll-cut (see page 32) into 2cm pieces
- 8 garlic cloves, peeled and left whole
- 245g crushed tomatoes (tinned or fresh)
- 240ml **Chicken Stock** (page 314) or water
- 2 bay leaves
- Small handful of coriander stalks (reserve leaves for serving)
- 160g dried apricots, halved
- 1 teaspoon ground cumin

FOR SERVING

- Coriander leaves and tender stalks
- Steamed couscous, giant couscous, or rice
- **Garlic and Herb Labne** (page 48)
- **Green Sauce** (page 51)

To make the tebil, in a small bowl, stir together the coriander, turmeric, caraway, and pepper.

The day before you plan to cook, season the chicken generously on both sides with kosher salt. In a medium bowl, mash together the harissa paste and about half of the tebil. Add the chicken and use your hands to evenly coat it all with the spiced harissa paste. Cover and refrigerate overnight, then bring to room temperature before cooking.

Adjust an oven rack to the centre position and preheat to 190°C.

Set a large nonreactive frying pan over medium-high heat and add the cardamom ghee. When the fat shimmers, add the onion, carrots, and garlic. Season lightly with salt and sprinkle in the remaining tebil, then reduce the heat to medium and cook, stirring occasionally, until the onions are tender, translucent, and just beginning to take on colour, about 12 minutes.

Add the tomatoes and chicken stock and stir to deglaze, then let the mixture return to a boil.

Transfer the vegetable and tomato mixture into a 23 × 33cm baking dish and layer in the bay leaves and coriander stalks. Arrange the chicken thighs, skin-side down, atop the bed of aromatics, then nestle the apricots around the chicken. The braising liquid should come about halfway up the sides of the chicken, so if you're at all short, add a splash of water or stock to make up the difference. Lay a piece of parchment atop the chicken, then seal the pan tightly with aluminium foil.

Transfer to the oven and cook until the chicken is completely tender and shows no resistance when pierced with a sharp knife, about 1½ hours.

When the chicken is completely tender, adjust the oven rack to the highest position and increase the oven temperature to 220°C. Remove the foil and parchment from the dish and flip the chicken thighs over so that they sit skin-side up. Sprinkle the cumin into the braising liquid as you flip the thighs.

Return the baking dish to the oven and cook the chicken until the liquid is nicely reduced and the skins are crisp and golden brown, 18 to 20 minutes longer.

To serve, use tongs to gently arrange the chicken in a rimmed serving dish or shallow bowl. Discard the bay leaves and coriander stalks. Taste and adjust the seasoning of the braising juices with salt as needed, then spoon the apricots and braising juices over the chicken. Garnish with coriander and serve with steamed couscous, garlic and herb labne, and green sauce.

Refrigerate leftover meat, apricots, and braising juices together in a covered container for up to 1 week or freeze for up to 3 months. Bring to a boil before serving.

VARIATION

To make a **Lamb Tagine,** substitute 1.8kg boneless **lamb shoulder,** cut into 7.5cm pieces and **salted** in advance, for the chicken. Before cooking the aromatics, melt 3 tablespoons of **Ghee** (page 62) **or oil** in the casserole over medium-high heat. Brown the lamb on all sides, about 4 minutes per side, then set the meat aside. Discard the used fat and continue the recipe as written, cooking the aromatics in fresh ghee. Note that the lamb may take up to 30 minutes longer than chicken thighs to become tender.

BONELESS CHICKEN
simple chicken thighs

MAKES 4 TO 6 THIGHS

4 to 6 boneless, skinless chicken thighs

Kosher salt

2 garlic cloves, finely grated

1 packed teaspoon finely grated lemon zest

3 tablespoons extra-virgin olive oil, plus more for the grill

This is the simplest, quickest way to cook up some chicken to add to a rice or noodle bowl, salad, taco, quesadilla, or pile of vegetables for dinner.

• • •

Spread the chicken thighs in a single layer on a baking tray. Use one hand to generously season with salt, and the other hand to turn the chicken over. Then use your dry hand to season the second side with salt.

In a medium bowl, stir together the garlic, lemon zest, and oil. Add the chicken to the bowl and stir to coat. Cook right away or marinate for up to 12 hours in the refrigerator. Bring up to room temperature before cooking.

When ready to cook, prepare a barbecue. If using charcoal, light a fire, let the flames die down, and wait until the coals ash over. Push the coals over to one side of the grill to create a medium-high zone and an indirect-heat zone. If using a gas grill, set up a medium-high-heat zone and an indirect-heat zone.

Scrub the grill grates clean, then rub the grates with a well-oiled tea towel. Begin the chicken over the hot part of the grill, moving to a cooler zone as needed if browning too fast, until well browned and cooked through, about 5 minutes per side.

Transfer to a chopping board and let rest at least 5 minutes before slicing.

VARIATIONS

For **Teriyaki-ish Chicken Thighs,** lightly season the **chicken** with salt. In an extra-large zip-lock plastic bag, combine 120ml **soy sauce**, 120ml **mirin**, 2 tablespoons finely grated **fresh ginger**, 2 finely grated **garlic** cloves, and 2 teaspoons **toasted sesame oil**. Add the chicken and toss to coat. Squeeze out excess air and seal the bag. Refrigerate for at least 2 hours (the chicken can remain in the marinade for up to 12 hours).

To cook, remove the chicken from the marinade and bring it up to room temperature. Cook as directed on page 306, but be aware that the mirin and soy sauce will encourage browning, so remain attentive and avoid excessively high heat to prevent burning.

•

For **Tex-Mex Thighs,** season with 2 teaspoons of **Teo's Chivi Spice** (page 348) after seasoning with salt, then grill as directed.

•

For **Souvlaki-ish Chicken Thighs,** season with salt in advance and marinate in **Creamy Oregano Dressing** (page 125) for 30 minutes before grilling as directed. Drizzle with more creamy oregano dressing after cooking.

BONELESS CHICKEN
chicken thigh schnitzel

I could eat this schnitzel every night. I prefer to make it with thighs, rather than breasts, because they're so tender and juicy. And this breading method, which has become my go-to for everything I fry, reliably produces a textbook-perfect crust. The secret here is twofold: First, replacing flour with potato starch in the initial step yields a coating that stays crisper for longer. And second, breaking down the panko allows the crumbs to coat every bit of the chicken and deliver an irresistible crunch.

• • •

Place the panko in a zip-lock plastic bag and use a rolling pin to grind the crumbs to a slightly finer consistency. (Alternatively, pulse the panko in a food processor for about 20 seconds.)

Prepare a dredging station using three large shallow bowls: Set the potato starch in one bowl. Whisk 2 eggs very well in a second bowl. Pour the panko into the third bowl. (Then use a sharp knife or scissors to cut the plastic bag along one seam so that you can open it up like a magazine. Set the plastic aside to use when pounding the chicken.) Season each bowl with a generous pinch of salt.

If the thighs are not already butterflied or uniformly thin, flatten them out a bit. Unfold the plastic bag so that one side is flat on your work surface and drizzle a little oil in the center. Place a cutlet onto the oil and top with a little more oil. Cover with the other side of the plastic bag and use a mallet or rolling pin to pound to a thickness of about 1cm. Repeat with the remaining cutlets.

Season the cutlets generously with salt on both sides. One cutlet at a time, dredge in potato starch, dip in egg, and coat with panko, pressing gently to adhere. Each step of the way, make sure that the cutlet is completely coated and then shake off the excess before moving to the next layer of coating. Use the third egg if needed to complete the breading process.

recipe continues

MAKES 6 THIGHS

160g panko breadcrumbs

80g potato starch

2 or 3 medium eggs

Kosher salt

6 boneless, skinless chicken thighs

600 to 720ml neutral oil, plus more as needed for pounding

Line a baking tray with a double layer of kitchen paper and set a wire rack inside it. Pour oil 6mm deep into a 30cm cast-iron frying pan over medium-high heat and add a pinch of panko. When the breadcrumbs sizzle, add as many pieces of chicken as will comfortably fit in a single layer without touching. Cook, moving the pieces around the pan periodically to ensure even cooking, until deep golden brown, 4 to 5 minutes on the first side, 2 to 3 on the second. Transfer the cutlets to the wire rack and repeat with the remaining cutlets. Season with salt to taste. Serve immediately.

USES AND VARIATIONS

Use the same breading method for anything you'd like to shallow- or deep-fry, from flaky white fish to all manner of vegetables. If working with something very wet, such as aubergines or tofu, allow time for the salt to penetrate, then pat it dry before proceeding with potato starch.

•

To use **chicken breasts** instead of thighs: If the breasts have the tenders still attached, use your hands to pull them off the breasts, then remove the bit of connective tissue at the top of the underside of each breast with a sharp knife. Lightly pound the underside of each breast with a kitchen mallet or rolling pin until it's evenly about 1.25cm thick. Bread and fry the breasts as directed on page 309, reducing the cooking time by a minute or two per side.

•

Make **Fried Chicken Sandwiches** with **Mark's Giardiniera** (page 69), **mayonnaise,** and thick slices of **iceberg lettuce** on soft **sandwich bread or buns**.

•

Serve alongside **Chicories Caesar with Focaccia Croutons** (page 131).

•

Slice and serve atop rice or **Simple Soba Salad** (page 174) with **Crunchy Cabbage Slaw** (page 121).

BONELESS CHICKEN
chilli crisp chicken salad

I spent the first year of the pandemic obsessed with bàng bàng chicken. It's a Sichuan-style chicken salad with perfectly balanced flavours and textures that leave your mouth tingling and just the slightest bit ravaged with heat. At some point, I realised that my Calabrian chilli crisp contains many of the same ingredients as bàng bàng chicken, from chilli oil to sesame seeds to Sichuan peppercorns. To streamline things, I started making the salad with chilli crisp. I tweaked a few other things along the way, so it's not exactly bàng bàng chicken anymore. But it's still so enjoyable that every time I make it for someone, they invariably exclaim, "What on earth *is* that?" and proceed to ask for the recipe.

• • •

In a large bowl, stir together the chilli crisp, mayonnaise, tahini, rice vinegar, oil, lemon zest, lemon juice, coriander, spring onions, and sugar until well combined. Add the chicken and mix until well coated. Taste and adjust the seasoning with salt and lemon juice as needed. Cover and refrigerate for 30 minutes to 1 hour to allow the flavours to meld.

Cover and refrigerate leftover salad for up to 3 days.

USE

For **Chilli Crisp Chicken Salad Sandwiches,** stir 75g **salted roasted peanuts** (coarsely chopped) into the chicken salad. Spread **mayonnaise** on soft **sandwich bread,** then top with the salad and thinly sliced **Persian cucumbers**.

SERVES 4

125g **Calabrian Chilli Crisp** (page 56)

6 tablespoons mayonnaise

3 tablespoons well-stirred tahini

2 tablespoons seasoned rice vinegar

1 tablespoon toasted sesame oil

1 packed teaspoon finely grated lemon zest

4 tablespoons freshly squeezed lemon juice

20g coarsely chopped coriander

4 spring onions, thinly sliced on a bias

1 teaspoon sugar

525g shredded cooked chicken

Kosher salt

BONES
chicken stock

MAKES 6 TO 7 LITRES

Requires 6 to 8 hours simmering

2.7kg chicken bones (at least half should be raw)

5.7 litres water

2 brown onions, unpeeled and quartered

2 carrots, peeled and cut into 4cm pieces

2 celery stalks, cut into 5cm pieces

1 head garlic, halved horizontally

5 sprigs parsley (or 10 stems)

4 sprigs thyme

2 bay leaves

1 teaspoon (3g) kosher salt

1 teaspoon black peppercorns

1 tablespoon apple cider vinegar

When I first read Nigella Lawson's thoughts on saving chicken bones for stock in her first book, *How to Eat,* I knew she was my kind of cook. "Do not throw away the chicken carcass after eating the chicken," she wrote. "Go so far, I'd say, as to scavenge from everyone's plate, picking up the bones they've left." I agree wholeheartedly. And if you can't bear the thought of repurposing bones that have been gnawed on by others, I implore you to save the carcass! Just wrap and store the bones in your freezer as you collect them until you've got about 1.4kg.

It's important to note, however, that some raw bones are essential for a rich stock. Long, gentle simmering transforms the collagen in the bones to gelatin, which lends body to stock. Since previously roasted bones will have already relinquished some of their collagen, make sure that at least half of the bones in the pot are raw. If you can get them, chicken feet, wings, and heads are particularly collagen-rich and make great stock fodder. And once your stock is cool, freeze it in a variety of 500ml and 1 litre containers so you have options when thawing.

• • •

In an 11-litre or larger pot, combine the bones, water, onions, carrots, celery, garlic, parsley, thyme, bay leaves, salt, and peppercorns. Bring the stock to a boil, then reduce the heat to bring the pot to a simmer. Use a fine-mesh skimmer to remove any foam that rises to the surface. Add the vinegar. (It helps draw out nutrients and minerals from the bones into the stock.)

Adjust the heat to keep the stock at a gentle simmer, cover, and cook the stock for at least 6 and up to 8 hours, keeping an eye on it to make sure it stays at a simmer. (If you have trouble keeping the stock at a simmer with the lid on, you can leave the lid ajar to help control the temperature.)

Strain the stock through a fine-mesh sieve. Refrigerate overnight, uncovered.

Once the stock has cooled completely, scrape away the fat, also known as schmaltz, that rises to the top. (I like to freeze it in ice cube trays, then store cubes in freezer bags to use in dishes like **Shaken Roast Potatoes,** page 264.) Refrigerate for up to 5 days or freeze for up to 6 months.

VARIATION

To make stock in a 6-litre pressure cooker, scale down the recipe. Use 1.4kg chicken bones, 2.8 litres water, 1 onion, 1 carrot, 1 celery stalk, ½ head garlic, 2 parsley stalks, 2 thyme sprigs, 1 bay leaf, ½ teaspoon (2g) kosher salt, ¼ teaspoon peppercorns, and 1 teaspoon apple cider vinegar. Cook at high pressure for 2 hours, with natural pressure release.

recipes to cook and eat in community

Several years ago, my friend Greta Caruso began having friends over to her apartment in New York City every Sunday night for dinner. Even though she's a wonderful cook, the dinners were never extravagant. Instead, each was an occasion for Greta to reconnect with close friends and a way for her to anchor her week. At the time, I visited New York often for work. The dinners were so special that I started planning my trips around them.

At Greta's table, I witnessed whims evolve into traditions. I watched my friend take pleasure in creating beauty as she set the table with her favourite vintage linens, candlesticks, and flower arrangements. Each week, when the bowl of Nocellara olives appeared, we'd all instinctively put our phones down—not because Greta had decreed it, but because it felt so nice to be together for a few hours no matter what was happening in the outside world.

I've spent my entire adult life gathering at rowdy tables for delicious meals, but something about those Sunday dinners was different. Greta's focus was less about what was on the table and more on who was around it. Though I sat there dozens of times, I could probably tell you only a couple things we ate. Yet I can recall scores of jokes and stories, and all the times I was kicked under the table for being dense. I remember the buzzy thrill of being introduced to new romantic partners and the heaviness of consoling grieving friends.

The deep sense of friendship and community I felt at Greta's dinners made me want to create a similar ritual for myself. At the time, my career was shifting—I was travelling constantly and felt unmoored in my own life. Though I'd been cooking for decades by then, it was rarely in such a casual, communal way for the people closest—and most important—to me. And something about that felt wrong. I made many excuses for it over the years, but the one I relied on most was this: My apartment was too small for a proper dining table—where would people sit? How could I host a weekly dinner without a table? On one level, I knew this was irrational—I've always encouraged others to think more expansively about space and let go of convention. Sit on the floor, I'd declare! Sit on the couch! Eat at the coffee table! And yet, I couldn't do it myself. My own hypocrisy weighed on me.

At any rate, I wasn't home. I was out in the world, filming and then promoting a documentary series, on book and speaking tours, out reporting my column in *The New York Times Magazine*. I didn't have time to institute any sort of ritual. And if I did, would my friends even come?

I turned these thoughts over in my mind until, exhausted, I stopped travelling so much. I moved out of the tiny apartment into a hand-built house in Oakland with its own little dining area. The first thing I did after unpacking was commission a woodworker friend to build me a table. Finally, I thought, I'd make my own Sunday dinners happen. But the pandemic shut down the world the week after the table arrived.

It didn't help that I'd also begun to descend into an abyss of depression. Sitting by myself at my gorgeous table in my beautiful home, I examined my life. What good was everything I'd achieved if I felt so unbearably sad and alone?

One morning a year and a half later, I was testing a recipe at home. I'd been working on a pork braise inspired by tacos al pastor. But—whether because I was depressed, unqualified, or the task itself was impossible—I kept failing miserably. And with each failure, I grew sadder and more unsure of myself.

My friend Sarah texted to see if I was up for a visit. Though we'd known each other for more than ten years, we were the kind of friends usually brought together by an outside force rather than of our own volition. She was at the farmers' market nearby with her kids, who wanted to come see my pup, Fava. "Of course," I responded. "I'm just here ruining some pork." While the kids played with Fava in the garden, Sarah asked what was wrong. "I don't know," I said. "I just can't get this braise right. It's haunting me. And to make matters worse, I'll be stuck with six pounds [13 kilos] of braised pork to eat by myself!"

"Well, we'll help you eat it," she offered with a coy smile.

Maybe it's because I was feeling so low at the time, or so deprived of casual gatherings that didn't require complicated arrangements and Covid tests, but I was so lonely and starved for connection that I received Sarah's casual offer like a vial of life-saving elixir. "When?" I quickly asked, worried that she might recant.

"How about Tuesday, at our house?" Sarah proposed. Two days later, I arrived at her door, pork in hand. We shredded it into a dinner of tacos, for which everyone was grateful—no one as much as me. The braise may not have been a major culinary achievement, but it did just fine for dinner on a Tuesday night in Oakland. It was so natural and nice to be together that as the evening ended, we all wondered, "Should we do it again next Tuesday?"

We've continued gathering weekly ever since, though Monday nights eventually became our standing date. It took nearly eight months of Monday dinners for me to realise I'd inadvertently built the ritual I'd so craved. It just looks different than I'd initially imagined. At our Monday dinners, I've learned how to share both responsibility and credit. I've learned that if I let other people care for me, they will. I've learned how it feels to build something sacred with people I love. We'll often say—only half-joking—that Monday dinner is our religion.

And while everyone in our group loves to cook and eat, no one person (not even me) directs the menus or does all of the cooking. Sure, sometimes I have a recipe or two I want to test and share, but other people's desires, interests, and constraints also influence what we eat. When we can, we take advantage of our many hands and make dumplings, tamales, ravioli, or another labour-intensive, assembly-line dish. And when I encounter a special-occasion ingredient while shopping—a perfect side of wild salmon, say, or first-of-the-season crab—I snag it for us, because while Monday dinner isn't a dinner party, it is a special occasion.

Four years in, this ritual and the community that sustains it are at the heart of my life. These friends have taught me what it means to belong. And I've finally found the sense of meaning—in cooking and in life—that I've sought for so long. It brings me indescribable joy to share food with my Monday dinner family; whenever I nail a new recipe or stumble upon a cache of ripe fruit, I immediately begin planning how to incorporate it into our next meal. But this isn't to say that we always make fancy or complicated food. When it's hot, we pull out the kiddie pool and eat hot dogs and popsicles. When we're too tired to cook, we'll order empanadas or pizza and throw together a salad. What we eat together matters far less than the fact that we eat together.

So, in the spirit of Monday dinner, this chapter is a compilation of dishes best shared with others, whether for the amounts they yield, the time and effort they require, or the communal pleasure they offer.

how to build an oasis in time

A GUIDE TO CREATING AND SUSTAINING A DINNER RITUAL OF YOUR OWN

In the years since we started our weekly dinner tradition, my friends and I have spent a lot of time thinking and talking about what makes it work so well. These, we believe, are the guiding principles of this oasis in time in our lives.

Choose a day and time and stick to it. The nature of modern life is a natural impediment to the formation of any ritual—that is, until you join or create a community that makes taking a collective break joyful. By committing as a group, you're pouring the foundation for "a cathedral in time," in the words of rabbi-philosopher Abraham Joshua Heschel. Over time, the day will begin to feel sacred. "I'm sorry, but no," you'll say, "I can't attend your birthday party, Beyoncé, because I have to attend Monday dinner." Furthermore, carving out a dedicated time and day together means there will be fewer logistics and far less correspondence to handle, making it that much more seamless.

Choose one location and stick to it. Though your instinct may be to share the burden of hosting, we've found that keeping the location consistent further streamlines everything. We always know when and where dinner is—Fava and I simply show up at the same time each week. We're all familiar with the kitchen and can navigate it comfortably, and we avoid the usual frantic last-minute scramble for serving utensils and olive oil typically involved with potlucks.

Perfect is the enemy of good. Abandon the idea that everything must be perfect, because it won't be. This is real life. You're not always going to have the very best ingredients, the right platter, or a lime instead of a lemon. It doesn't matter. No one will remember. What you will remember is the fact that you sat down to dinner together, week after week. As Heschel wrote in *The Sabbath*, "it is not a thing that lends significance to a moment; it is the moment that lends significance to things."

Make it feel holy. There are countless ways to create a sense of holiness. And while they don't need to involve religion, religious practices can be a helpful source of inspiration. Perhaps, for example, one of you is a committed baker, and your contribution each week is baking two loaves of bread—one for the meal and one to divide and send home with everyone. Maybe holiness for you looks like bringing nature inside with a bouquet of wildflowers each week before friends arrive. Maybe your version involves an old record player you've been meaning to hook up, trying a new dessert each week, or opening the bottles of wine you've been saving for . . . you're not sure why. Whatever it is, it should sanctify the occasion and be something that exists outside the chaos of everyday life.

Consistency is key. Sometimes, the dinner's a dud. Or everyone's in a bad mood. Or the three-year-old has a meal-ending meltdown. Or all the kids decide they're not going to eat the chicken even though they loved it last month. Other times, you won't get to check in with the friend you really wanted to talk to that night. But the stakes are much, much lower when you know there's always another dinner next week.

Make room for everyone. The only time I've ever made an excuse not to sit down at a weekly dinner was when we didn't have enough chairs. "I'll eat when the kids are done," I figured as I kept cooking. But by the time I made it outside, many of the parents were standing around, finishing half-eaten tacos off their kids' plates. It just wasn't the same. We'd relinquished the chance to experience that undefinable, sacred feeling that washes over us when we come to the table in unison, take in the array of colours and aromas, and have a moment of unspoken gratitude as our bodies begin to relax and we watch the kids begin to eat gleefully. The next day, I realised that I'd used the excuse of limited seating to slip into workhorse mode and unintentionally exclude myself from my favourite part of the evening. It was clear that we needed to institute a new rule: There must always be enough seats for everyone to eat at the same time.

Say the quiet parts out loud. If the group doesn't already have a framework in place for honest, judgement-free communication about fairly dividing costs and labour, you must create one. For example, the more socioeconomically secure members in our group take on a greater share of the financial burden so everyone can participate worry-free. As a nonparent, I'm happy to travel so that the parents don't have to schlep their kids to dinner. Alexis puts away the leftovers and does the dishes since the rest of us typically take time off to shop and cook. And since circumstances inevitably change, we take care to occasionally check in with one another about our contributions to make sure that resentments don't have a chance to build.

pane criminale

Back when I cooked monthly dinners at Tartine bakery, I tried to incorporate their extraordinary bread into every menu. At some point, I began scoring loaves destined to become garlic bread vertically rather than halving them horizontally. The brilliance of this small tweak is that it allows for a maximal ratio of garlic butter to bread. The resulting loaf was so laden with garlic, herb, and Parmesan butter that it was, well, criminally good. Friends soon started calling it *pane criminale*.

This recipe shines when made with a rustic loaf of farmhouse-style bread, but baguettes work well, too. Either way, use the most flavourful, crustiest bread you can find—it'll make all the difference.

• • •

Adjust an oven rack to the centre position and preheat to 200°C.

Mince 8 of the garlic cloves. Gently heat a small saucepan over medium-low and add the oil and minced garlic. Cook, stirring and swirling constantly, until the garlic is tender and fragrant, about 7 minutes. Do not allow it to take on any colour. (If you sense the garlic is starting to brown, remove the pan from the heat, and add a few drops of water.) Pour the garlic and oil into a medium heatproof bowl and set aside to cool.

Finely grate the remaining 2 garlic cloves. When the minced garlic and oil have cooled to room temperature, stir in the grated garlic, butter, chopped herbs, Parmesan, garlic powder, and salt and pepper to taste.

Deeply score the bread in 1-inch slices, but don't cut all the way through. Use an offset spatula to generously spread garlic butter on one side of each slice, as far down as you can reach. Wrap the bread in aluminium foil and place it on a baking tray.

Bake for 20 minutes (10 minutes for baguettes). Unwrap the top of the loaf and bake until the crust is browned and crisp, 5 to 8 minutes longer. Remove from the oven and let cool slightly before serving.

MAKES 1 X 450G LOAF OR 2 X 225G BAGUETTES

- 10 large garlic cloves, peeled
- 2 tablespoons extra-virgin olive oil
- 114g unsalted butter, at room temperature
- 20g finely chopped parsley leaves, basil leaves, and/or chives
- 30g finely grated Parmesan
- 1 teaspoon garlic powder
- Kosher salt
- Freshly ground black pepper
- 1 x 450g loaf rustic farmhouse-style bread or 2 x 225g baguettes

NOTE

You can prepare, wrap, and refrigerate the loaf up to 1 day ahead. Bring to room temperature before baking.

kuku-kopita

MAKES A 23 × 46CM PIE

Extra-virgin olive oil

1 leek, light-green and white parts, thinly sliced and washed

2 brown onions, cut into 8mm cubes

Kosher salt

3 large bunches of dill

1 large bunch of flat-leaf parsley

1 large bunch of coriander

3 bunches of spinach

340g feta or feta-style cheese, drained

115g cream cheese, cut into 1.25cm cubes

Freshly ground black pepper

3 medium eggs

450g package frozen filo pastry, thawed if frozen

I can always spot another Iranian's grocery trolley from across the store—it's the one packed to the brim with Persian cucumbers (naturally) and an obscene quantity of fresh herbs. Like all Iranians, I love herbs in all their forms—fresh, dried, sautéed, stewed, fried, you name it. When I cook from a recipe written by anyone else, I usually end up doubling—or tripling—the amount of herbs. This is especially true for American-style spanakopita, which typically contains only a modest amount of dill. One day, while preparing spanakopita filling, I realised I could intensify its herbiness by sautéing the herbs. The distinctly grassy aroma of herbs sizzling in oil was familiar—my mom often used the technique, common to Persian cooking, in stews and the herb frittata called kuku sabzi. Cooking the herbs down not only enhances their flavour, it also dramatically reduces their volume, meaning I could pack in even more of them.

The resulting dish, which I like to think of as the love child of a flaky, golden spanakopita and a herb-rich kuku, was so satisfyingly herby that I knew I'd never make the dish any other way.

• • •

Adjust an oven rack to the centre position and preheat to 220°C. Line a baking tray with parchment paper and set aside.

Heat a large frying pan over medium-high heat. When it's hot, add 3 tablespoons oil. When the oil shimmers, add the leek and onions. Reduce the heat to medium, season with a generous pinch of salt, and cook, stirring occasionally, until completely tender and just beginning to take on colour, about 15 minutes.

Meanwhile, use a sharp knife to quickly shave the tender leaves and stalks from the dill, parsley, and coriander. Discard the woody stalks and very coarsely chop the herbs. Pulse the herbs in a food processor until finely chopped. (Alternatively, finely chop the herbs by hand.)

recipe continues

When the onions and leeks are tender, add 2 tablespoons oil and the herbs. Season with salt and cook, stirring, until the herbs are completely wilted and turning dark green, about 3 minutes. Use a silicone spatula to scrape the onion mixture out into a large bowl and spread it out in the bottom of the bowl to allow it to cool. Set aside.

Wipe out the frying pan and set it over high heat. When it's hot, add 2 tablespoons oil and two or three big handfuls of the spinach. Season with a generous pinch of salt and sauté or toss with tongs to wilt. Cook until the stalks are tender, 2 to 3 minutes. Use tongs to transfer the spinach to the parchment-lined baking tray, spreading it out in a thin layer to cool. Wipe out the frying pan and repeat with the remaining spinach, then allow to cool.

Taking handfuls of the cooled spinach, squeeze out as much water as possible, then chop it coarsely. Add the chopped spinach to the onion and herb mixture. Crumble the feta cheese into the bowl in almond-sized pieces. Separate the pieces of the cream cheese as you add them into the bowl, add a few grinds of pepper, and then use your hands to combine everything until uniform. Taste and adjust the seasoning with salt as needed. The mixture should be very highly seasoned to account for the eggs that have yet to be added, and to stand up to the very flaky pastry. (The cheese and herb mixture can be made up to 1 day ahead if desired, then brought up to room temperature and combined with the eggs.)

Crack the eggs into the bowl and use your hands one last time to combine everything.

Brush the bottom and sides of a rimmed 33 × 46cm baking tin generously with oil. For the tidiest pie, you'll have to lay the bottom pastry sheets a little counterintuitively. Even though the pastry is likely the exact size of your pan, think of the bottom crust as a filo sling hanging over the long sides of the pan (you'll use the ends to wrap over the top of the pie and contain the filling when finishing assembly). Trimming with scissors as needed, use two sheets of pastry to entirely cover the bottom of the pan with minimal overlap, while leaving plenty of overhang along both long edges (work quickly here and keep the remaining filo pastry covered with a kitchen towel to prevent it from drying out). Brush the pastry generously with oil and repeat with 7 more layers of pastry, for a total of 8 layers.

Use a flexible spatula to spread the filling evenly over the pastry. Brushing each layer generously with oil as you go, top with 6 sheets of filo. Fold both sides of the overhang back over the pie, then top with 2 more sheets of filo, brushing generously with oil in between and on top. Use a sharp, serrated knife to score the pastry into serving-sized pieces.

Bake on the centre rack for 35 to 38 minutes, until the pastry is crisp and golden brown. Cool on a wire rack for 10 minutes before cutting and serving with a thin metal spatula.

Cover and store at room temperature for one night or refrigerate for up to 3 days. Eat at room temperature or warm gently in a toaster oven or oven to reheat and recrisp.

fluffy pork meatballs

While I've always been a fan of the old camp song "On Top of Spaghetti," I firmly believe that's the very last place a meatball belongs. No matter how many meatballs I'm served, the pasta-to-meatball ratio is never right, and I always end up with half a bowl of lonely spaghetti! No, I prefer to serve these tender meatballs atop a slice of olive oil–fried bread rubbed with garlic, with ample sauce spooned over both. And covered with lots and lots of cheese (grated Parmesan, naturally)—because that part of the song was spot on.

• • •

In a medium bowl, combine the panko and milk. Use your hands to massage the liquid into the crumbs, but do not overwork. Set aside to soak until completely absorbed.

Set a frying pan over low heat and add the olive oil. When the oil shimmers, add the onion and gently cook, stirring regularly, until soft but without colour, 10 to 12 minutes.

Add the garlic and cook until aromatic, but don't let it take on any colour, about 30 seconds. Scrape everything into a large bowl and allow it to cool.

Once the onion has cooled, add the pork, egg, Parmesan, parsley, fennel seeds, chilli flakes, black pepper, and salt. Use your hands to combine the mixture well. Add the panko and milk to the pork mixture and gently mix to combine. Avoid overworking or overcompressing the mixture, which can result in gummy or dense meatballs.

Make a small test patty to test the seasoning. Set a small frying pan over medium heat and add 1 tablespoon oil. Add the patty and cook until nicely browned on both sides and cooked through, 2 to 3 minutes per side. Taste and adjust the seasoning with salt, fennel, and chilli flakes as needed. Repeat with another test patty until the mixture is just right. Cover and refrigerate the mixture for 30 minutes to 1 hour.

recipe continues

MAKES 16 TO 18 MEATBALLS

120g panko breadcrumbs

180ml full-fat milk

3 tablespoons extra-virgin olive oil, plus more for cooking

1 onion, finely chopped

3 garlic cloves, minced

450g pork shoulder mince

1 medium egg

45g finely grated Parmesan, plus more for serving

20g minced parsley

1½ teaspoons fennel seeds, lightly crushed

1½ teaspoons chilli flakes

¼ teaspoon freshly ground black pepper

2 teaspoons (6g) kosher salt

1kg **Simple Tomato Sauce** (page 359)

240 to 360ml water

Olive Oil–Fried Bread (page 94), rubbed with garlic, for serving

Coat a baking tray with oil. Use wet hands to gently form the mixture into 16 to 18 meatballs, about 60g each, avoiding the urge to overcompress! Place the meatballs on the baking tray, making sure to leave space between them for browning to occur. Chill the formed meatballs for 30 minutes to 1 hour to help them keep their shape.

Preheat the grill.

In a large casserole, combine the tomato sauce and 240ml water and bring to a simmer, then reduce the heat to low.

Meanwhile, set the baking tray in the oven so that the meatballs are 5 to 10cm from the heat source and grill until browned on top, about 8 minutes. (Browning times will vary considerably depending on grill strength, so keep a close eye on your meatballs the first time you brown them.)

Remove the meatballs from the oven and transfer them to the simmering sauce. If needed, add another 120ml water to ensure all the meatballs are partially submerged. Simmer, stirring gently as needed, until the meatballs are cooked through, 6 to 10 minutes. Remove from the heat, cover, and leave the meatballs in the warm sauce until ready to serve.

Serve with olive oil-fried bread lightly swiped with a garlic clove, and abundant grated Parmesan.

Cool, cover, and store leftovers in remaining sauce. Refrigerate for up to 1 week or freeze for up to 3 months. Bring to a boil before using.

slow-cooked salmon

In 2003, I was working as a cook in Italy, dearly missing my friends back home. I often spent my lonely evenings reading food and art blogs. Eventually I decided to start my own. I called it *Ciao, Samin*—a phrase I heard dozens of times a day from co-workers and friends as I came and went. Mostly, I wrote about my days and, once in a while, my hopes and dreams. I had an audience of three or four people, tops.

Back in California, I continued blogging. Over time, I developed a modest but avid readership. And though I often wrote about working in a restaurant, it wasn't a traditional food blog. Me being me, there were no recipes.

Out of curiosity, I'd occasionally browse the list of search terms that regularly brought readers to my little-known corner of the internet. At some point, I noticed a strange pattern. Some of the most common phrases were "How to Cook Samin," "Samin Recipe," and my favourite, "Wild Samin." I couldn't make any sense of it. Why were there worldwide queries for my recipes and thoughts on how to cook, when I was just another twentysomething line cook? How did people hear about me? And why on earth did all those people think I was so wild?

Eventually, it hit me—no one was seeking my culinary wisdom. These folks were simply misspelling *salmon*. There was nothing to do but laugh and tell my friends about it. One urged me to post a "courtesy salmon recipe" on the sidebar for all those presumably confused readers, but I'd never written a recipe and didn't know where to begin. Plus, there were already a hundred other recipes for slow-roasted salmon, my favourite way to cook the fish, written by chefs with far more credibility than me.

I finally wrote that recipe a decade later, in *Salt Fat Acid Heat*. I now regularly hear from readers that slow-cooking has become their go-to method for cooking salmon, too. But my imposter syndrome has been flaring up, because when it comes to salmon, slow-cooking the fish—usually wrapped in a fig or banana leaf—is basically it for me. Whether it's a single portion in my toaster oven, or

SERVES 6 TO 8

8 to 10 large fig leaves or 225g banana leaves (fresh or thawed frozen)

900g skinless salmon fillet, preferably centre-cut, pin bones removed (see page 340)

Kosher salt

Extra-virgin olive oil

Optional for serving: **Green Sauce** (page 51), **Garlic and Herb Labne** (page 48), **Spicy Meyer Lemon Relish** (page 81), **House Dressing** (page 117), or a shower of fresh herbs

a fillet on the barbecue grill or in the oven, I only ever want to eat salmon that's cooked gently until its flesh is tender but still translucent. I want to feel the distinct pleasure of letting flakes of the rich, buttery fish melt on my tongue while I breathe in the faintly tropical aroma of the leaves in which it was wrapped. But since I'm not getting paid to write the same recipe over and over again, I've felt intense pressure to come up with something new. For years, I've been racking my brain to invent a dazzling new technique or more satisfying combination of seasonings.

Then, as I was doing research for a side project, I stumbled upon a recipe by the ancient Greek poet, humourist, and gastronomist Archestratus that made me reconsider. In a characteristically bossy passage on cooking tuna, he declared, "But here is the very best way for you to deal with this fish. You need fig leaves and oregano (not very much), no cheese, no nonsense. Just wrap it up nicely in fig leaves fastened with string, then hide it under hot ashes and keep a watch on the time: Don't overcook it."

Archie may have been talking about tuna (salmon aren't endemic to the Mediterranean, after all), but his advice still rings true: fig leaves, no cheese, no nonsense, gentle heat, keep an eye on the clock, and don't overcook it. I figured, if this recipe hasn't really changed in 2,300 years, who am I to suggest I've improved it since 2017? Sometimes, classic really is best.

And so, here's everything you need to know about slow-cooking salmon. Since the fish is spectacular served hot, at room temperature, or chilled, I usually slow-cook an entire side of salmon to feed a crowd. But keep in mind that the method works just as well for smaller pieces of salmon, as long as you keep the oven temperature low and heed the sensory cues to know when the fish is done.

recipe continues

A COUPLE OF THINGS BEFORE YOU BEGIN

Shopping: No matter how you plan to cook salmon, start with high-quality fish. Refer to the fish buying guide published by the Monterey Bay Aquarium's Seafood Watch for best practices. With very few exceptions, wild Alaskan salmon is an excellent choice. My favourite variety, Chinook, also known as king salmon, is the fattiest of all. When I can't get king, I look for the vibrant red flesh of sockeye.

Remove the pin bones: Each side of salmon has a line of thin pin bones that stretches about two-thirds of the way down the fillet from the head. Pin bones aren't connected to the fish's main skeleton and take a little extra work to remove, so your fishmonger may leave them behind. It's worth taking a few minutes to remove them so you and your guests don't spend the meal picking bones out of your teeth.

Lay the fillet skin-side down on a chopping board. Run your fingers lightly over the fish from head to tail to locate the pin bones and coax their ends out of the flesh. Starting at the head end, use a pair of tweezers or needle-nose pliers to tug at the bones, pulling at the same angle at which they are lodged in the fish. Once you get the bone out, dip your tweezers in a glass of cold water to release the bone. When you've finished, lightly run your fingers back and forth over the bone line to ensure you've gotten all the bones.

• • •

Adjust an oven rack to the centre position and preheat to 110°C.

If using fig leaves, trim the stalks and wipe the leaves with a damp cloth. If using banana leaves, unfold them and wipe with a damp cloth. Use a sharp paring knife to cut away the centre ribs. If using fresh banana leaves, pass them over a flame for a moment until they soften.

On a large baking tin, assemble a large bed of fig or banana leaves, shiny-side up. Season both sides of the fish with salt and tuck it, skin-side down, into the leaves. Drizzle with a little oil and use your hands to rub it in. Rustically wrap the leaves back over the fish, using more as needed to create a "package"—though I use that term very loosely, and you don't need to worry about creating a perfect seal or covering up every bit of fish.

Transfer to the oven and cook until the fish begins to flake in the thickest part of the fillet when poked with a knife or your finger, about 45 minutes. Because this method is so gentle on the salmon's proteins, the fish may appear translucent even though it's cooked.

To serve, unwrap the fish and discard the leaves. Gently tear the fish into large, rustic pieces and transfer to a platter. If you like, garnish with green sauce, garlic and herb labne, Meyer lemon relish, house dressing, or a shower of fresh herbs.

VARIATIONS

Substitute **cod or halibut** for the salmon.

•

To barbecue the fish, secure the leaf-wrapped "package" with a few lengths of kitchen string. Over a charcoal or gas grill, prepare a large indirect-heat cooking zone. Set the fish on the grill, lower the lid of the grill if there is one, and cook as directed above. If possible, monitor the temperature of the grill as you cook to keep it as close to 110°C as you can.

•

If you don't have fig or banana leaves, use **chard leaves** with the ribs removed to wrap the fish.

•

Omit the leaves entirely and cook the fish, uncovered, on a bed of **fennel fronds or parsley stalks**. If you like, lay a few paper-thin slices of **lemon, orange, or blood orange** over the fillet before baking.

dungeness crab with calabrian chilli butter

MAKES 6 CRABS (12 HALVES)

FOR THE CRABS
- 8 litres water
- 252g kosher salt
- 4 bay leaves
- 1 or 2 dried Calabrian chillies
- 2 lemons, halved
- 6 live Dungeness crabs (about 675g each)

FOR THE CHILLI BUTTER
- 175g unsalted butter
- 4 garlic cloves, minced
- 2 teaspoons cumin seeds, coarsely ground in a mortar and pestle
- 1 bay leaf
- 3 tablespoons Calabrian chilli paste
- 1 tablespoon aged sherry vinegar
- Kosher salt

Something about the way you have to work for the payoff makes each bite of Dungeness crab sweeter and more special. (If you can't find Dungeness crab, brown crab or spider crab are good substitutes.) Once or twice a winter, I'll line the dining table with newspaper, make **Pane Criminale** (page 329) and a huge chicory salad, and cook up a pile of crab for dinner. It's one of my favourite traditions, and I love watching everyone's personality come out at the table. Some people methodically clean the whole crab before taking a single bite. Others eat as they go, licking their fingers and dripping butter all over the place. I fall somewhere in the middle, accumulating a little pile of crab—I use the end of one of the littlest legs as a hook for picking meat—before heaping it onto a slice of garlic bread and drizzling it all with obscene amounts of chilli butter. For this messy eater, a tableful of crab shells and friends is a dream come true.

• • •

Preheat the oven to 220°C.

To make the crabs, in a 12-litre (or larger) soup pot, combine the water, salt, bay leaves, and dried chillies. Juice the lemons into the pot and add the rinds. Bring to a boil. One at a time, use tongs to pick up 3 of the crabs carefully by a back leg, then lower into the pot. Cook for 13 minutes (set a timer!), then remove the crabs to a baking tray and set aside. Repeat with the remaining crabs.

When the first batch of crabs is cool enough to handle, begin cleaning them in the sink. One at a time, remove the carapace, or top shell. Then flip the crab over and pull down the triangular apron and remove it. Working under cold running water, use your fingers to scrape away the yellow "butter." Remove the gills, intestines, and mouth. Finally, crack the body to split the crab in half. Repeat with the remaining crabs and discard all the detritus. Spread out the cleaned crab on two baking trays. (If not serving right away, refrigerate the crab.)

To make the chilli butter, melt 60g of the butter in a medium saucepan over medium-low heat. Add the garlic and cumin and cook, stirring occasionally, until fragrant and soft, but not taking on any colour, about 6 minutes. Reduce the heat to low and add the remaining 120g butter, the bay leaf, and the chilli paste. Simmer for 10 minutes to allow the flavours to meld, then add the vinegar and season with salt to taste. Transfer to a bain-marie to keep the butter hot at the table.

When ready to serve, slide the baking trays into the oven and heat the crab halves until steaming hot, about 6 minutes.

Make sure each guest has a set of crab crackers, a wooden or metal skewer, and a ramekin for the chilli butter. Place large bowls around the table for guests to discard shells as they eat.

VARIATION

For **Prawns with Calabrian Chilli Butter,** in a 7- to 9-litre pot, bring 6 litres water to a boil and season generously with **salt**, 480ml dry **white wine, 2 bay leaves,** and 1 dried **chilli de árbol**. Squeeze in the juice of 1 **lemon** and add the rinds. Add 1.4kg shell-on, deveined **prawns** ("king" size, aka 16–20 count) and cook until just cooked through and no longer translucent, 3 to 4 minutes. Serve immediately with the chilli butter.

NOTES

Chilli butter can be made without vinegar and refrigerated up to 1 day ahead. To finish, reheat in a bain-marie, then add vinegar and adjust the seasoning with salt.

Crabs can be boiled, cleaned, and refrigerated up to 1 day ahead. Bring to room temperature before heating in the oven to serve.

teo's brisket chivis

MAKES ENOUGH FILLING FOR ABOUT 24 SMALL BURRITOS

- 1.8kg beef brisket, cut into roughly 10 × 7.5cm pieces
- 1 brown onion, outermost layer peeled
- 8 garlic cloves, unpeeled
- 48g kosher salt
- 5 tablespoons **Teo's Chivi Spice** (see Note)
- 1.4 litres water
- 8 Roma tomatoes
- 8 fresh Anaheim chillies (see Note)
- 175g finely grated medium Cheddar cheese
- 350g finely grated Monterey Jack cheese
- 20 or 25cm flour tortillas
- Sliced radishes and lime wedges, for serving

After just one bite of Teo Diaz's brisket machaca at his Los Angeles taqueria, Sonoratown, I begged him for the recipe. The spicy beef filling, which Diaz mixes with cheese to fill small burritos called chivichangas, transported me straight back to my San Diego childhood. Teo grew up eating chivichangas (also known as chimichangas) almost every day in San Luis, Arizona, right on the border with Mexico. His single mother would prepare a big batch of them early each morning before heading out to pick produce in the fields of nearby Yuma, wrapping them individually in aluminium foil and leaving them on the counter for her six children to eat throughout the day.

Now the Brisket Chivi, as he calls it, is one of the most beloved items on the menu at Sonoratown. The kitchen is too small for a hob, so he simmers the beef in an industrial rice cooker before shredding and cooking it a second time with fire-roasted chillies, tomatoes, and heaps of grated cheese. The result, wrapped in a chewy flour tortilla, is perfectly spiced and mouthwateringly unctuous.

• • •

In a large casserole, combine the brisket, onion, garlic, salt, chivi spice, and water. Cover the pot and bring to a boil. Reduce the heat and simmer until the meat is tender when pierced with a fork, about 3 hours. (Alternatively, cook this mixture in a pressure cooker on high pressure for 90 minutes, with a 10-minute natural release, then finish the machaca on the hob.)

Meanwhile, preheat the grill. Position an oven rack 7.5 to 10cm from the grill.

Arrange the tomatoes and chillies on a baking tray and set in the oven so that the produce is 5 to 10cm from the heat source. Grill, rotating the tomatoes and chillies from time to time, until the skins are evenly blistered and charred. Depending on your grill, this could take anywhere from

NOTES

If you can't find Anaheim chillies, you can substitute 4 large green peppers.

To make **Teo's Chivi Spice,** in a small jar, combine equal parts **ground coriander, cumin, black pepper, cayenne pepper, garlic powder,** and **onion powder** and shake to combine. Store in an airtight container in a cool, dry place for up to 6 months. If you have a silica packet, add it to help keep the garlic and onion powder from clumping.

10 to 20 minutes—just keep a close eye on the pan and check on it every few minutes or so.

Place the blistered vegetables into a metal bowl and cover with a lid or plate. When they have cooled, peel the tomatoes and chillies and discard the skins and stalks. Use your hands to crush them into a rough salsa in the bowl. Set aside.

When the meat is tender, remove it from the pot and set aside. Discard the onion, the garlic, and all but 480ml of the cooking liquid. When the meat is cool enough to handle, shred it thoroughly with your hands or with two forks, scraping off any fat and setting it aside as you go. Finely chop the fat and add it back into the meat.

Return the pot to the hob and set it over medium heat. Add the meat, crushed salsa, and grated cheeses. Stir well to combine, then taste and adjust the seasoning with salt as needed. Bring to a gentle boil, then reduce the heat and simmer, uncovered, until thick and unctuous, 30 to 35 minutes—this is your machaca mixture.

To form chivichangas, spoon a heaping 4 tablespoons of machaca mixture into the centre of each tortilla and spread it into a 7.5cm rectangle. Fold the bottom half of the tortilla over the filling, then lift the top edge of the tortilla back towards the top of the filling to create a tight cylinder of filling. Fold both sides of the tortilla in, then tightly roll the chivichanga towards the top of the filling to yield a small, rectangular burrito.

Preheat a grill pan or frying pan to medium-hot. Cook the chivichangas until evenly crisp and golden brown all over, about 2 minutes per side. Serve hot with sliced radishes and wedges of lime.

Cover and refrigerate leftover machaca mixture for up to 1 week or freeze for up to 3 months. Reheat the machaca mixture gently with a splash of water, making sure to bring it to a boil, before serving.

fresh pasta sheets

Turning a mound of flour and eggs into silky, translucent sheets of pasta feels like the best kind of magic trick. And though every single person who makes their own pasta seems to swear by a slightly different recipe or bit of technical flair, the truth is, it's just not that complicated. If there is a secret, it's the value of familiarity—and that only comes with practice.

This has been my go-to recipe for more than twenty years, and I'm confident it'll work for you. But don't abandon your senses, because every batch of pasta is different, depending on everything from the weather to the type of flour and the size of your eggs. If your dough is sticky, lightly dust both the pasta and the work surface with flour. If the dough is still dry and crumbly after resting, knead in another yolk or a tablespoon of water. Your good judgement is the most important ingredient.

Making fresh pasta can be time-consuming and messy at first. To avoid unnecessary stress, clear off your counters to give yourself ample workspace and leave plenty of time to rest and roll the dough. And until you get the hang of using the pasta machine, enlist a friend or family member to help—one person can turn the crank while the other tends to the dough (kids are especially good at cranking!).

And before you begin, it's worth seeking out:

- A **pasta roller,** whether it's a hand-cranked model or a stand mixer attachment. It doesn't have to be fancy—even an inexpensive hand-cranked machine will save you time and frustration.
- **"00" flour** from Italy, which is milled far more finely than plain flour, will yield particularly smooth, satiny pasta.

• • •

Mound the flour in the centre of a large, wide bowl. Dig a well in the centre and add the whole eggs and egg yolks. Using a fork, beat the eggs together and begin to incorporate the flour, starting with the inner rim of the well. The dough will

**MAKES 375G DOUGH
(PLENTY FOR ONE
23 × 33CM LASAGNE)**

405g "00" or plain flour, plus more for dusting

3 medium eggs

4 medium egg yolks, plus more as needed

Semolina or rice flour, for dusting

start to form a shaggy mass when about half of the flour is incorporated.

Using your fingers, continue to mix the dough. Press any loose bits of flour into the mass of dough. If needed, add another egg yolk or a tablespoon of water to absorb all the flour. Once the dough coheres into a ball, remove it from the bowl.

Transfer the dough to a lightly floured surface and knead it by hand for 3 to 4 minutes, until it's smooth, elastic, and uniform in colour. Tightly wrap it in clingfilm and set aside for at least 30 minutes (and up to 4 hours) at room temperature.

Line three baking trays with parchment paper and lightly dust them with semolina flour. Set aside. Lightly dust a chopping board or countertop with "00" flour.

Cut off one-quarter of the dough. Rewrap the rest and set it aside. Use the heel of your hand to flatten the dough into an oval about the same width as the rollers on your pasta machine, about 15cm. Set the rollers to their thickest setting and pass the dough through.

Lay the dough out onto the floured chopping board and neatly fold it in half, keeping it about the same width as the pasta machine. Feed the dough through again at the thickest setting. Think of these first rolls as an extended kneading. Continue, now folding the dough into thirds and rolling it until it is smooth, silky, and even textured. Do your best to make the sheet the full width of the machine.

Once the dough is silky and smooth, you can begin to roll it out more thinly. Resist the temptation to watch the pasta as it comes out of the rollers, however hypnotic it may be. Instead, watch as it enters the machine, using one hand to ensure it goes in straight and doesn't ripple or fold over on itself. Roll it once through each of the next two or three settings, lightly sprinkling the dough with "00" flour as needed to keep it from sticking to itself, until the dough is about 6mm thick.

recipe continues

good things are better shared • 351

Once the pasta is about 6mm thick, begin rolling it twice through each setting. Continue to sprinkle both sides with flour to prevent sticking.

Roll out the pasta until you can just see the outline of your hand when you hold it under a sheet, about 2mm thick. (On most machines, you won't need to go to the thinnest setting.)

Cut the pasta into sheets 30 to 35cm long. Dust the sheets lightly with semolina flour, stack on one of the prepared baking trays, and cover with a clean, lightly dampened tea towel. Repeat with remaining dough.

Store fresh pasta in a single layer on a parchment-lined baking tray. Cover with clingfilm to keep it from drying out. Refrigerate for up to 1 night. Or freeze fresh pasta in a single layer on a parchment-lined baking tray. Freeze until rock hard, layer between pieces of parchment, and transfer to a zip-lock freezer bag. Freeze for up to 2 months. To cook, drop frozen sheets directly into boiling salted water—do not thaw. Cook for 4 to 7 minutes until tender.

VARIATIONS

For **Pasta Verde,** sauté 225g **baby spinach** until just wilted. Line a baking tray with parchment paper. Remove the spinach from the pan and spread it out in a single layer on the prepared pan. When cool, squeeze the leaves thoroughly, a palmful at a time, then chop coarsely. Purée in a blender with 3 medium **eggs** and 1 medium **egg yolk,** then add the spinach-egg mixture to the flour and proceed as described on pages 349 to 353.

For **Hand-Cut Noodles,** stack 4 sheets of pasta lightly dusted with semolina flour. Loosely roll the stack lengthways into thirds, as if you're folding a letter. Cut with a sharp knife (in 1.25cm increments for tagliatelle or fettuccine or 2cm increments for pappardelle), continuing until all the dough is sliced. Gently fluff and separate noodles and pile onto prepared baking trays into nests of single portions (about 85g). Cover until ready to use. Or freeze the nests on a baking tray in a single layer, then transfer to a zip-lock freezer bag and freeze for up to 2 months. To cook, drop frozen noodles directly into boiling salted water—do not thaw. Cook for 4 to 7 minutes until tender.

creamy spinach lasagne

In my early cooking days, I'd fantasise about opening a little lasagne joint. It'd have one or two daily options, a salad, a side of rapini, garlic bread, good wine, and communal tables at which to enjoy it all. And this—my take on a spinach and tomato lasagne—would be on the menu every day.

New York Times Cooking first published a version of this recipe in the spring of 2020, when so many of us found ourselves at home with ample time to take on cooking projects. Since then, I've tweaked it a bit—scaling it down to a more reasonable size and stirring the spinach into the béchamel sauce to yield an ooier, gooier dish. Making this lasagne—with its gossamer pasta sheets and many rich, creamy layers—involves a significant investment of time and labour. If you like, you can make the sauces and ricotta filling a day in advance and bring everything to room temperature before assembly. (And if you'd like to further simplify things, use shop-bought fresh pasta sheets and pasta sauce—I like Rao's.)

• • •

To make the creamy spinach, line a baking tray with parchment paper and set it near the hob. Set a large frying pan over high heat. When it's hot, add 2 tablespoons oil and two or three big handfuls of the spinach. Season with a generous pinch of salt and sauté until the stalks are tender and the leaves are wilted, 2 to 3 minutes. Use tongs to transfer to the parchment-lined tray. Wipe out the pan and repeat with more oil and the remaining spinach, then spread it out in a single layer and allow to cool.

Taking handfuls of the cooled spinach, squeeze out as much water as possible, then chop it coarsely. Place the chopped spinach in a large bowl. Add the béchamel and stir to combine. Taste the spinach mixture and season generously with salt. Press a piece of parchment paper or clingfilm against the surface of the mixture to prevent a skin from forming and set it aside until you're ready to assemble the lasagne.

recipe continues

MAKES A 23 × 33CM LASAGNE

FOR THE CREAMY SPINACH

Extra-virgin olive oil

900g spinach

Kosher salt

750g **Béchamel** (page 360), gently warmed

FOR THE RICOTTA FILLING

450g full-fat-milk ricotta

225g coarsely grated full-fat-milk mozzarella

100g finely grated Parmesan

20 large basil leaves, roughly chopped

Kosher salt

FOR ASSEMBLY

Neutral oil

Kosher salt

1 batch **Fresh Pasta Sheets** (page 349), rolled out and cut into 30cm pieces

750g to 1kg **Simple Tomato Sauce** (page 359)

185g **Béchamel** (page 360)

45g finely grated Parmesan

115g grated full-fat-milk mozzarella

To make the ricotta filling, in a large bowl, combine the ricotta, mozzarella, Parmesan, and basil. Use a large wooden spoon to combine everything with a whisking motion (this will ensure that the ricotta breaks up and the grated cheeses distribute evenly). Taste and adjust the seasoning with salt. Cover and set aside until you're ready to assemble the lasagne.

When ready to assemble, adjust an oven rack to the highest position and preheat to 220°C. Bring a large covered pot of water to a boil over high heat. Set a large colander in a baking dish and place it near the hob.

Season the boiling water generously with salt. Carefully ease 1 sheet of pasta into the water, using a slotted spoon to gently encourage the pasta to immerse. Then add the next sheet. Add 2 more pasta sheets in this way and cook until light in colour, floppy in texture, and completely cooked through, about 2 minutes. If the pasta bubbles above the surface of the water while cooking, encourage it back into the water with the slotted spoon. Use a sieve to gently remove the pasta from the water and place it in the prepared colander. Rinse under cold water until cool enough to handle, then begin assembly with the first batch of cooked pasta. Meanwhile, continue cooking, draining, and rinsing pasta in this way as you assemble the lasagne.

Coat the bottom and sides of a 23 × 33 × 5cm baking dish with oil. Gently press any remaining water from the pasta, then drape 2 or 3 sheets crossways to entirely cover the bottom of the pan with minimal overlap, and leave the ends hanging over the long sides (they'll be helpful for sealing the top). All four sides need not have overhang; two are plenty.

Evenly crumble a generous one-third of the ricotta filling over the pasta to create a foundation, then layer pasta sheets in from edge to edge of the pan. Trim the pasta with kitchen scissors to avoid overlap. Spread over about 310g tomato sauce and cover with another pasta sheet. Spread about half of the creamy spinach evenly over the pasta, sprinkle with 4 tablespoons grated Parmesan, and cover with another pasta sheet.

recipe continues

NOTE

To prepare the lasagne ahead and freeze, bake it for 30 minutes but do not brown, then cool and freeze for up to 4 weeks. Thaw completely overnight, then sprinkle with mozzarella and bake uncovered at 200°C until golden brown and bubbling on the surface, 25 to 30 minutes.

Repeat the layers using the same order, with pasta following each: one-third of the ricotta, about 310g of tomato sauce, and half the creamy spinach sprinkled with another 4 tablespoons Parmesan, then finish with a third layer each of ricotta and of tomato sauce. For the top, fold the overhanging pasta into the baking dish, to cover the top sheet and create a sealed pasta layer, and then spread with the béchamel. Gently cover with a piece of parchment and wrap tightly with foil. Place the lasagne on a baking tray to catch any overflow and bake for 40 minutes.

Pull the lasagne from the oven and carefully remove the foil and parchment. Sprinkle with the grated mozzarella and return to the oven until golden brown and bubbling on the surface, about 20 minutes.

Allow to cool for 15 minutes before slicing and serving. Wrap and refrigerate leftover lasagne for up to 4 days.

VARIATIONS

To make a **Courgette and Pesto Lasagne,** use the same ricotta filling and creamy spinach mixture. Instead of tomato sauce, toss sauteéd slices of **courgette** with **Basil Pesto** (page 67) and as you build the lasagne, drizzle each layer of courgette with a bit more pesto.

For **Winter Squash Lasagne,** make the creamy spinach as directed on page 355. Make the ricotta filling, but omit the basil. Instead, place 60g **unsalted butter** in a medium saucepan and set over medium heat. Cook, swirling, until the foam subsides and the butter begins to take on colour, then add 10 large **sage leaves**. Keep swirling the pan until the butter is golden brown and smells nutty and the sage is crisp, another 2 to 3 minutes. Allow to cool, then stir the butter and sage into the filling.

Assemble the lasagne with layers of creamy spinach, sage and ricotta filling, and roasted **winter squash**.

simple tomato sauce

As with much else in the kitchen and in life, I've streamlined the way I make tomato sauce. I no longer bother with sautéing a heap of onions, and I've dramatically reduced the cooking time, too. The resulting sauce has a much brighter tomato flavour. Quality ingredients are of the utmost importance in such a simple recipe. Make sure to use San Marzano or San Marzano–style tomatoes—I love the Bianco DiNapoli brand, as well as Pastene and Cento—and a flavourful extra-virgin olive oil.

• • •

Pour the tomatoes into a large bowl and use your hands to thoroughly crush them (have some fun!). Pour the water into the tins and swirl to rinse any remaining juice off the sides. Add the water to the crushed tomatoes and set aside.

Set a nonreactive medium casserole over medium heat and add 3 tablespoons of the oil and the garlic. Cook gently, stirring with a wooden spoon, until aromatic but not at all beginning to colour, 30 seconds to 1 minute.

Add the tomato purée and cook, stirring, until the oil turns orange, about 1 minute. Add the crushed tomatoes and season with salt. If using, add the basil and the chilli flakes to taste. Stirring regularly, bring the sauce to a boil, then reduce the heat and simmer until the flavours come together and any raw, tinny taste has cooked off, 22 to 25 minutes. If at any point the sauce starts to get too thick, add a little splash of water to thin it out.

Taste and adjust the seasoning with salt and sugar, if needed, then add the remaining olive oil (3 scant tablespoons). Use the sauce as is or use a food mill or immersion blender to purée.

Cool, cover, and refrigerate sauce for up to 1 week or freeze for up to 3 months. Bring to a boil before using.

MAKES ABOUT 1KG

2 x 400g tins whole tomatoes, preferably San Marzano

120ml water

70g extra-virgin olive oil

5 garlic cloves, minced

2 tablespoons tomato purée

Kosher salt

Handful of basil leaves or stalks (optional)

Chilli flakes (optional)

Sugar (optional)

béchamel

MAKES ABOUT 940G

114g unsalted butter
68g plain flour
960g full-fat milk
    Kosher salt
    Freshly ground black pepper
    Freshly grated nutmeg

This ratio of flour and butter to milk yields an ideal béchamel for lasagne—not so thin it's runny, and not so thick as to be gloopy. The most important thing is to keep a close eye on the pot—I recommend using both a whisk and a silicone spatula to stir and scrape the bottom once you add the milk to make sure the sauce doesn't scorch.

• • •

Set a large casserole over medium heat and add the butter. Once it melts, whisk in the flour, reduce the heat to very low, and cook for 10 minutes, stirring regularly to prevent browning. After the mixture foams a bit, it will visibly transform—the butter will separate, the bubbles will reduce in size, and the mixture will look like freshly wet fine sand.

Whisking vigorously, slowly pour in the milk. Increase the heat to medium and whisk until the mixture comes to a boil and thickens, about 2 minutes. Add salt, pepper, and a few zips of nutmeg to taste.

Return the heat to low. Continue cooking, whisking regularly, until the sauce is thick and smooth and no raw flour flavour remains, 10 to 15 minutes. Taste and adjust the seasoning with salt. If the béchamel is lumpy, strain through a fine-mesh sieve. Press a piece of parchment paper or clingfilm against the surface of the sauce to prevent a skin from forming and set aside until ready to use.

Béchamel can be made up to 1 day in advance and refrigerated. To reheat, place in a saucepan, add a splash of water or milk, and gently bring to a simmer while stirring over low heat.

lazy sugo

You might skim this recipe and think it looks anything but lazy. But compared to the way I've always made Bolognese, this sugo is a piece of cake. There's no soffritto to chop and fry, no endless browning of the meat, and no deglazing. You just get everything into the pot with minimum hassle and simmer it until it's tender, occasionally giving it a stir. The only real effort involves taking the cooked meat off the bone and shredding it, but even that's a small price to pay for three glorious kilos of rich, meaty sauce. Give some away, put some in the freezer to use in **Lasagne al Sugo** (page 364), and treat your loved ones to a comforting pasta with meat sauce you'll have made without breaking a sweat.

...

Pour the tomatoes into a large bowl and use your hands to thoroughly crush them (have some fun!). Pour the water into the tins and swirl to rinse any remaining juice off the sides. Add the water to the crushed tomatoes and set aside.

Set a large nonreactive casserole over medium heat. Add the oil and tomato purée. Cook, gently breaking up the paste with a wooden spoon, until the oil turns uniformly orange, about 3 minutes. Stir in the chilli flakes and wine and simmer for 2 minutes. Add the crushed tomatoes, pork, beef shin, onions, garlic, Parmesan rinds, and bay leaves. Season generously with salt and black pepper, increase the heat to medium-high and, stirring regularly, bring the sauce to a simmer.

Partially cover the pot and reduce the heat to keep the sauce at a gentle simmer. Stir and scrape occasionally to prevent scorching, especially in the centre of the pot, where the meat is most likely to stick. Cook until both the beef and the pork are falling off the bone, about 3½ hours for the beef, and 4½ hours for the pork, depending on the size of the pieces of meat. As the meat is cooked, use tongs or a slotted spoon to remove it from the sauce and set aside.

recipe continues

MAKES ABOUT 3KG

Requires 4½ to 5 hours cooking

4 x 400g tins whole tomatoes, preferably San Marzano

300ml water

75g extra-virgin olive oil

130g tomato purée

1 large pinch of chilli flakes

240ml dry red or white wine

900g bone-in pork shoulder, cut into 450g pieces, salted in advance (see page 281)

900g beef shin or osso buco (about 2 large pieces), salted in advance

2 brown onions, peeled and halved lengthways through the root

4 garlic cloves, thinly sliced

1 or 2 Parmesan rinds

2 bay leaves

Kosher salt

Freshly ground black pepper

1 to 2 tablespoons sugar (optional)

Once all the meat is cooked, turn off the heat and remove and discard the onions, Parmesan rinds, and bay leaves from the sauce. Once the meat is cool enough to handle, pick through it and discard the bones, gristle, and soft fat clumps, reserving the cartilaginous bits and hard fat strips. Use forks or your hands to shred the meat and return it to the sauce. Very finely chop the cartilaginous bits (they will add body!) from the shank and any hard fat (it will add so much texture and flavour!) from the pork and return it to the sauce.

Return the sauce to a simmer and adjust the seasoning with salt, black pepper, and sugar if needed. Cook until the flavours have melded and the sauce has reduced to your desired thickness, another 20 to 30 minutes.

Cover and refrigerate leftovers for up to 1 week or freeze in an airtight container for up to 6 months. Return to a boil before serving.

USE

To make **Pasta al Sugo,** for each serving, cook 100g of **Hand-Cut Noodles** (page 353) **or dried pasta** in a pot of boiling **salted water**. Meanwhile, in a nonreactive saucepan, bring 185g of **sauce** per serving to a simmer. Add the cooked pasta to the pan of sauce, along with 15g **unsalted butter** and a generous palmful of freshly grated **Parmesan** per serving. If the sauce clings too tightly to the pasta, loosen it with a few tablespoons of pasta cooking water (use tap water if you are worried things will get too salty) and simmer, swirling and tossing, until the sauce glossily and evenly coats the pasta. If the sauce is too watery, turn the heat up and reduce it a bit, stirring and swirling constantly, until the sauce clings to the pasta. Serve immediately with more Parmesan.

lasagne al sugo

MAKES A 23 × 33CM LASAGNE

Kosher salt

1 batch **Fresh Pasta Sheets** (page 349), rolled out and cut into 30cm sheets

Extra-virgin olive oil

1.2kg **Lazy Sugo** (page 361), gently warmed

1 batch **Béchamel** (page 360), gently warmed

100g finely grated Parmesan

115g coarsely grated full-fat-milk mozzarella

In Florence, I lived in a tiny studio around the corner from Rosticceria La Spada, where I'd pick something up for dinner a few nights a week—usually spit-roasted chicken and potatoes. But on the nights when I happened to walk in when the still-bubbling lasagne al forno emerged from the oven, I could never resist a slice. Baking transformed the distinct layers of hand-rolled pasta, rich béchamel, and meat sugo into a unified whole that I still fantasise about twenty years later.

Like all from-scratch lasagne, this is a big project. To work ahead, make the meat sauce well in advance and freeze it, and prepare the béchamel a day before you plan to assemble and bake the lasagne.

• • •

Adjust an oven rack to the highest position and preheat to 220°C. Bring a large covered pot of water to a boil over high heat. Set a large colander in a baking dish and place it near the hob.

Season the boiling water generously with salt. Carefully ease 1 sheet of pasta into the water, using a slotted spoon to gently encourage the pasta to immerse. Then add the next sheet. Add 2 more pasta sheets in this way and cook until light in colour, floppy in texture, and completely cooked through, about 2 minutes. If the pasta bubbles above the surface of the water while cooking, encourage it back into the water with the slotted spoon. Use a sieve to gently remove the pasta from the water and place it in the prepared colander. Rinse under cold water until cool enough to handle, then begin assembly with the first batch of cooked pasta. Meanwhile, continue cooking, draining, and rinsing pasta in this way as you assemble the lasagne.

Coat the bottom and sides of a 23 × 33 × 5cm baking dish with oil. Gently press any remaining water from the pasta, then use 2 or 3 sheets crossways to entirely cover the bottom of the dish with minimal overlap. Leave the ends hanging over the long sides (they'll be helpful for sealing the top). All four sides need not have overhang; two are plenty.

Evenly spread about 310g of the sugo over the pasta to create a foundation, then layer pasta sheets in from edge to edge of the pan. Trim the pasta with kitchen scissors to avoid overlap. Set aside 185g of the béchamel for the final layer, then evenly spread one-third of the remaining béchamel over the pasta, sprinkle with 30g Parmesan, and cover with another pasta sheet.

Repeat layering, alternating sugo with béchamel and Parmesan, following each with a layer of pasta. Your final layer will be sugo, topped with a last sheet of pasta. For the top, fold the overhanging pasta into the baking pan, to cover the final sheet and create a sealed pasta layer, and then spread with the reserved 185g béchamel. Gently cover with a piece of parchment and wrap tightly with foil. Place the lasagne on a baking tray to catch any overflow and bake for 40 minutes.

Pull the lasagne from the oven and carefully remove the foil and parchment. Sprinkle evenly with the mozzarella and return to the oven until golden brown and bubbling on the surface, about 20 minutes.

Allow to cool for 15 minutes before slicing and serving. Wrap and refrigerate leftover lasagne for up to 4 days.

NOTE

To prepare the lasagne ahead and freeze, bake it for 30 minutes but do not brown, then cool and freeze for up to 4 weeks. Thaw completely overnight, then sprinkle with mozzarella and bake uncovered at 200°C until golden brown and bubbling on the surface, 25 to 30 minutes.

yeasted breads and waffles

You can't swing a baguette in the California Bay Area without hitting an artisan baker. I'm grateful to them all for producing such extraordinary farmhouse-style bread, baguettes, and brioche. And since they're here, I've never felt much of a need to attempt making my own.

But occasionally, I bake bread at home just to experience the sorts of sensory pleasures that money can't buy. I love the instant sense of cosiness as the clean, sweet aroma of baking bread permeates my home. Or tearing into a just-baked pitta, allowing hot steam to pour out, and taking that first, chewy bite. It's the pleasure of breathing in the intermingling scents of honey and yeast as everyone reaches for the pan of hot, pillowy bread rolls and slathers them with butter. It's topping airy, olive oil–steeped focaccia with ripe slices of tomato, pyramids of flaky salt, and cream-steeped burrata.

This chapter, while brief, contains recipes for the breads, flatbreads, and yeasted waffles that I return to over and over again in search of those sensory delights. With the help of some of the aforementioned talented bakers—including Josey Baker, Jennifer Latham, and Laurie Ellen Pellicano—I've been tweaking and improving them for the last decade or so. Not only are these recipes foolproof and marvellous, but each time you try one you'll also get to luxuriate in the sublime human experience of eating and sharing still-warm bread.

the unbearable lightness of flour, or how much flour to use

Given that we tend to measure flour by volume rather than weight in the US, I've spent more time thinking about and discussing the weight of a cup of plain flour than anyone ever should, and I still don't have a definitive answer.

According to the King Arthur Baking Company, which has a terrific conversion guide for the weights of common baking ingredients on its website, a cup of flour weighs 120g. When I write recipes for *New York Times Cooking*, I adhere to their standard of 127g. Various cookbooks I've studied rely on standards ranging from 120 to 140g. Multiply that 20-g variation by 6 and, suddenly, you're adding an extra 120g of flour to your focaccia dough—an entire cup, by Artie's calculations!

How flour gets measured into a cup also accounts for part of the discrepancy. King Arthur and most other professionals agree that the best way to get an accurate measurement is by fluffing the flour in the container, gently spooning it into the measuring cup, and scraping away the excess with the back of a knife. But in my experience, even the most frantic fluffing, spooning, and scraping has never yielded a cup weighing less than 124g.

Furthermore, I spend a lot of time in other people's kitchens. I've watched countless people of all skill levels measure flour for baking, and nearly everyone measures flour by scooping it out of the bag with a measuring cup. Since unwieldy paper flour bags don't allow for proper fluffing and packaged flour is heavily compacted, the average scooped cup weighs 135g. Only the most avid home bakers know to fluff, spoon, and scrape. And almost anyone with that level of baking know-how generally chooses to use a scale for precision and ease.

This is why I believe the only way to entirely avoid all of this confusion is to use kitchen scales. So, based on my own extensive, if anecdotal, research, I'm adhering to using weights in my recipes. For the best results, using digital kitchen scales. If you need to upgrade from an old-fashioned balanced scales, choose one that can measure in increments of 1g or less—one with a precision of 0.1g is better. For ease of use, choose one with a tare function, that lets you reset to "0" with the press of a button. I'm aware that the flour used outside of the US may react differently in my recipes, and that individual ovens also vary, so bear this in mind as you try these recipes—you may need to do a little trial and error to get the final results right.

If you don't yet have a digital scale, I've got a few recommendations. I've used a $25 Escali Primo scale at home for more than ten years. Or, for about twice that price, the KD-8000 model from My Weigh comes with a plug-in adaptor, has a heavier capacity, and is the most consistently precise scale I've ever used.

sky-high focaccia

MAKES A 46 × 33CM FOCACCIA

Requires 4 hours, plus 12 to 24 hours for proofing and another 4 hours for final proof and bake

720g warm water

2¼ teaspoons (7g) fast-action dried yeast

½ teaspoon (4g) honey

800g strong white flour

2 tablespoons plus ½ teaspoon (20g) kosher salt

46g extra-virgin olive oil, plus more for dough handling and tin

Flaky salt, for sprinkling

NOTE

In warm weather, turns can be done every 20 minutes, and in colder weather, turns can take up to 40 minutes.

I've spent years tweaking and perfecting this golden, chewy focaccia recipe, which I originally developed for the *Salt Fat Acid Heat* documentary series. Since then, I've replaced plain flour with strong white flour, whose higher protein content allows for more height and chew. I also added a few strategic turns, or folds, of the dough as it proofs, to aid in gluten development. All of that focus on structure and gluten in the method has yielded a focaccia that's taller, airier, and chewier than ever before.

If you've never made focaccia, don't let any of that technical jargon scare you off. The beauty of this one-bowl recipe is that it requires only patience to achieve perfection. There's no stand mixer required, no endless kneading. One bite, and you won't believe you're not in Italy.

• • •

In a very large bowl, stir together 600g of the water, the yeast, and the honey. Let sit for 5 minutes, until frothy.

Use your hands or a large spoon to mix the flour into the yeast mixture until all the flour is incorporated. Cover with a clean, damp tea towel and let sit for 30 minutes.

Add the remaining 120g water, the kosher salt, and the oil. Use your hands to incorporate. As the dough absorbs the salt, it will behave sort of strangely, seeming to fall apart—this is fine. Just keep kneading and squeezing it with your hands—it'll come back together eventually, especially once it has a chance to rest.

Cover the bowl with a damp tea towel and set it in a warm spot to continue proofing. Every 30 minutes or so for the next 2½ hours, turn the dough. (Note that each turn consists of four quarter-turns, or folds.) With wet hands, gently loosen the dough from the north side of the bowl. Stretch the dough up until it resists, then fold it towards the south side of the bowl. Give the bowl a quarter-turn and repeat. Repeat twice more to end up where you started. Cover with the damp towel. During this first turn, the dough may not yet be relaxed

enough to tolerate all four folds, but do your best. As the dough relaxes, it'll become more elastic, and each turn will be more gratifying!

After about 3 hours total, the dough should be billowy and have doubled in volume. If not, continue to let rise and turn for up to 1 hour longer, moving the bowl to a warmer spot if necessary. After the final set of folds, gather up the edges of the dough into the centre as if you're making a massive dumpling, and then carefully flip it to tuck the join underneath. Gently coat the top of the dough with a little oil, seal the bowl with clingfilm or a lid, and refrigerate for 12 to 24 hours.

Generously coat the bottom and sides of a 33 x 46cm baking tin with nonstick cooking spray, then drizzle with 2 to 3 tablespoons oil. Gently transfer the dough to the tin, cover with clingfilm or a lid, and set in a warm spot to come to room temperature for 30 minutes.

With lightly oiled hands, gently stretch the dough to fill the tin, then drizzle with another 2 to 3 tablespoons oil. (Skip this oil on top if using the dough to make **Barbari Focaccia,** page 377.) Return the pan to a warm spot and allow to proof for 30 minutes.

Gently stretch the dough again to fill the entire tin. Repeat the stretching twice more over the next hour, then continue proofing the dough untouched until it's jiggly, bubbly, and flush with the top of the pan, 1 to 2 hours longer, depending on the ambient temperature. (Don't rush this step—it will make all the difference in getting the tallest, chewiest focaccia possible!)

Meanwhile, adjust an oven rack to the lowest position, place an overturned baking tray on the rack, and preheat to 230°C.

Once the dough is flush with the top of the tin, dip the pads of your fingers in any oil that's pooled in the corners of the tin. Spread your fingers wide like a piano impresario and make dimples across the entire tin of dough, pressing firmly to the bottom of the tin (this is the fun part!). Sprinkle evenly with flaky salt.

Place the baking tin with the focaccia on the overturned baking tray in the oven and bake for 25 to 28 minutes, until the corners are pulling away from the tin and the top is golden brown and glistening. If the top needs a little more browning, transfer to the top rack and bake for 3 to 5 minutes longer.

Cool the focaccia in the tin for 5 minutes, then use a thin flexible metal spatula to gently loosen it from the tin. Cool completely on a wire rack before slicing.

Store for up to 3 days wrapped in a paper bag inside of a plastic bag (this prevents the salt from dissolving). Bring back to life with a quick toast. Freeze for up to 3 months.

In Persian households, breakfast revolves around bread. When I travelled to Iran for the first time at age fourteen, I was baffled by the distinct lack of a toaster in every home I visited. Then I realised—who needs a toaster when you can get a fresh, steaming-hot flatbread from the corner bakery every morning?

Over the course of that summer, we travelled back and forth several times between Tehran and my grandparents' citrus orchard in the north. Perched on the lush Caspian coast, their village reminded me a lot of San Diego, where I'd spent my whole life. Unlike my grandmother, my grandfather didn't speak English, so we learned to make do with body language and my primary school–level Farsi. Even so, the bond between us was palpable. And it was strengthened by our shared love of noon barbari, a thick, chewy flatbread topped with sesame or nigella seeds. Any time I was there, he'd get up early to drive to the next village to get us barbari from his favourite baker. When he returned, we'd tear off pieces of warm bread to eat with sweet butter and caviar (him) or feta-style cheese and honey (me).

Come to think of it, my lifelong love of chewy, golden barbari explains my enthusiasm for focaccia. To try this barbari variation for yourself, simply brush the dough with a flour and water glaze and a sprinkling of nigella seeds and flaky salt before baking.

• • •

Prepare the focaccia dough as directed up to the point of putting it on the baking tin, but omit the 2 to 3 tablespoons of oil added before proofing. Then proof and stretch the dough as directed.

Adjust an oven rack to the lowest position, place an overturned baking tray on it, and preheat to 230°C.

Meanwhile, in a small saucepan, combine the flour, water, and bicarbonate of soda. Bring the mixture to a boil over medium

barbari focaccia

MAKES A 46 × 33CM FOCACCIA

Requires 4 hours, plus 12 to 24 hours for proofing and another 4 hours for final proof and bake

- 1 batch dough for **Sky-High Focaccia** (page 372)
- 1 tablespoon plain flour
- 120ml water
- ½ teaspoon bicarbonate of soda
- 1 tablespoon nigella seeds
- Flaky salt, for sprinkling

heat, then reduce to a simmer, stirring constantly. Cook until the mixture thickens enough to coat the spoon, about 1 minute. Remove from the heat and set the glaze aside.

When ready to bake, dimple the focaccia as directed, brush with the glaze, and sprinkle with the nigella seeds and flaky salt.

Place the baking tin with the focaccia on the overturned baking tray in the oven and bake for 25 to 28 minutes, until the corners are pulling away from the tin and the top is golden brown and glistening. If the top needs a little more browning, transfer to the top rack and bake for 3 to 5 minutes longer.

Cool the focaccia in the pan for 5 minutes, then use a thin flexible metal spatula to gently loosen it from the tin. Cool completely on a wire rack before slicing.

Store for up to 3 days wrapped in a paper bag inside of a plastic bag to prevent the salt from dissolving. Bring back to life with a quick toast. Freeze for up to 3 months.

USE

For a **Persian-Style Breakfast,** serve barbari focaccia with **Marinated Feta** (page 71), **cucumbers, fresh herbs, Apricot and Noyau Jam** (page 433), and piping-hot **black tea**.

oat and honey bread rolls

For several years, I collaborated with the bakers at San Francisco's Tartine on a series of monthly after-hours dinners. Over time, I grew to love their chewy oat bread above all the rest. Contained within its signature burnished crust is an interior crumb so soft and moist that it brings bread pudding to mind. As the name suggests, the bread owes its extraordinary texture to the two-thousand-year-old Scandinavian baking technique of folding a bit of oats into the dough.

If oats can turn a crusty loaf into a custardy delight, I figured it would perform magic on already-soft bread rolls. And it did just that. These rolls emerge from the oven as tender as can be, lightly sweet and nutty, and utterly ideal for slathering with salted butter.

• • •

In a spice grinder or high-powered blender, pulse the oats until they are about half their original size.

In a small saucepan, combine the oats, milk, and 90g of the water and bring to a boil while stirring over medium heat. Reduce the heat to medium-low and cook the oats to a very thick but still pliable consistency, 5 to 7 minutes. Use a silicone spatula to scrape the oats into the bowl of a stand mixer and refrigerate until cool.

Meanwhile, bloom the yeast in a small bowl with the remaining 2 tablespoons (30g) warm water. Let sit until the mixture is foamy, about 5 minutes.

Once the oats are cool, add the soured cream, honey, kosher salt, 1 egg, and the flour to the bowl. Scrape in the yeast mixture, snap on the dough hook, and mix until a shaggy dough forms. Cut 28g of the butter into 4 pieces and add them one at a time, allowing each piece to incorporate into the dough before adding the next. Increase the speed to medium and mix until the dough is evenly combined and begins to clump around the dough hook. Continue mixing for another 5 to 7 minutes, until the dough starts to strengthen—it will

MAKES 10 ROLLS

Requires 2½ hours proofing

50g rolled oats, plus more for sprinkling

20g full-fat milk

20g warm water

1¼ teaspoons (4g) fast-action dried yeast

120g soured cream, at room temperature

63g honey

1 tablespoon (9g) kosher salt

2 medium eggs, at room temperature

304g strong white flour, plus more for rolling

56g unsalted butter, at room temperature

Flaky salt, for sprinkling

look as smooth as a dough with some oats in it can look and appear "webby" as it pulls away from itself. In the end, the dough will remain very soft and sticky and won't completely pull away from the sides of the bowl. This is fine.

Lightly grease a large bowl with about 7g of the butter. Use a dough scraper or silicone spatula to scrape the dough into the bowl and cover tightly with a lid or plastic wrap. Set the bowl in a warm spot until the dough doubles in size, about 1½ hours.

Meanwhile, generously coat a 20- or 23cm round cake tin with the remaining 21g butter.

Uncover the dough and gently scrape it out onto a lightly floured work surface. Using flour as needed to keep the dough from sticking to the work surface and rolling pin, pat and then gently roll the dough into a round. (But avoid using too much flour—it'll prevent the friction needed to create a smooth ball.) Cut the dough into 10 equal pieces.

Take a piece of dough and tuck its corners together to form a rough ball or teardrop shape. Set the ball, seam-side down, on the work surface. Loosely cup your hand around the dough, then use a rapid circular motion to drag it across the surface. The friction between the dough and the countertop will create surface tension on the outside of the dough and result in a tight, even ball. Continue rolling the ball on the countertop until the skin is smooth and nearly no seam remains, then place it, seam-side down, into the prepared tin. Repeat with the remaining pieces of dough. Cover the pan with clingfilm and set in a warm spot until the rolls are soft, puffy, and nearly doubled in size, about 1 hour.

To bake, adjust an oven rack to the centre position and preheat to 200°C.

recipe continues

good things take time • 383

NOTES

Rolls can be formed and arranged in the pan 1 day ahead. Cover and refrigerate, then let them rise at room temperature before baking (this can take up to 3 hours).

This recipe doubles beautifully—simply bloom 7g of yeast in 2 tablespoons of lukewarm water and double all the remaining ingredients. Divide the dough into 24 equal pieces and bake in a 23 × 33cm baking tin.

In a small bowl, whisk the remaining egg. Gently and generously brush the tops of the rolls with the egg, then sprinkle with flaky salt and oats.

Bake the rolls until the tops are deep golden brown, 20 to 25 minutes.

Remove the tin from the oven and let the rolls cool for 5 minutes. Gently slide a thin flexible metal spatula around the sides of the tin to loosen the rolls, then underneath to loosen the bottom. Slide the entire grid of rolls out and onto a wire rack. Serve warm or let cool.

After cooling, store in an airtight container at room temperature for up to 3 days. Toast gently to refresh.

fluffy pitta pockets

It's thrilling to watch a pitta puff up with hot air as it bakes. And it's just as exciting to rip into one, steaming and fragrant, as soon as it emerges from the oven. A little wholemeal flour adds some nuttiness to this dough, while the strong white flour and generous kneading time lend it an unparalleled chewiness. If you've never baked bread before, start here. The dough is simple to make and—if you start in the morning—you'll be enjoying warm, fluffy pitta by afternoon.

• • •

In a measuring jug, stir together the warm water, yeast, and sugar. Let the mixture sit until it's foamy, about 5 minutes.

In a stand mixer, whisk together both flours and the salt. Add the yeast mixture and oil, snap on the dough hook, and mix on low speed to combine. Increase the speed to medium-high and knead until the dough forms a smooth, elastic ball that cleanly pulls away from the bowl, 8 to 10 minutes.

Remove the dough from the bowl. Lightly coat the bowl with oil, then return the dough to the bowl and cover tightly with clingfilm. Set in a warm place to double in size, 1½ to 2 hours.

Meanwhile, about 1 hour before baking, adjust the oven rack to the lowest position. Set a baking stone or overturned baking tray on the rack and preheat the oven to 260°C. Line a baking tray with parchment paper and set aside.

When the dough is ready, turn it out onto a clean work surface and divide it into 12 equal portions. Clear any flour, which will prevent the friction necessary for rolling a smooth ball, from the work surface. Take a portion of dough and tuck its corners together to form a rough ball or teardrop shape. Set the ball, seam-side down, on the work surface. Loosely cup your hand around the dough, then use a rapid circular motion to drag it across the surface. The friction between the dough and the countertop will create surface tension on the outside of the dough and result in a tight, even ball. Continue rolling the ball on the countertop until the skin is smooth and nearly no seam

MAKES 12 SMALL PITTAS

Requires 2 to 2½ hours proofing

360g warm water

2¼ teaspoons (7g) fast-action dried yeast

2 tablespoons (25g) sugar

360g strong white flour, plus more for dusting

90g wholemeal flour

1½ tablespoons (14g) kosher salt

55g extra-virgin olive oil, plus more for the bowl

remains. Repeat with the remaining balls. (Since this is a sticky dough, you may need to flour your hands as you divide and roll the balls, but avoid using too much flour.)

Arrange the dough balls on the parchment-lined baking tray, cover with a clean tea towel, and set the tray in the warm spot again to proof until the dough balls are light and pillowy to the touch, about 20 minutes. Line a large bowl with a clean tea towel and set aside.

Lightly flour the work surface and use a rolling pin to roll the balls into rounds 6mm to 1.25cm thick. Carefully lift a dough round and place it in the oven on the heated baking stone or overturned baking tray. (To transfer the dough to the stone or tray, it can help to first slide it onto a pizza peel or an upturned pie dish.) Once the dough puffs nicely, 3 to 4 minutes, flip and bake for another minute. The pitta should be a light golden brown. Transfer the pitta to the towel-lined bowl and cover to keep the bread soft. Repeat with the remaining dough. As you get more confident in your baking (and as the size of your baking stone allows), you can bake more than one pitta at a time.

Wrap and store leftovers in an airtight bag at room temperature, for up to 3 days. Toast gently to reheat.

NOTE

If you don't have a stand mixer, you can make this dough in a large bowl, then turn it out onto a lightly floured work surface and knead it until it's smooth, soft, and elastic, about 10 minutes.

chewy sesame flatbreads

MAKES 18 FLATBREADS

Requires 2 to 2½ hours proofing

360g warm water

2¼ teaspoons (7g) fast-action dried yeast

2 tablespoons (25g) sugar

450g strong white flour, plus more for dusting

3 tablespoons (27g) toasted sesame seeds

1½ tablespoons (14g) kosher salt

55g **Shallot Oil** (page 55), melted **Ghee** (page 62), or extra-virgin olive oil, plus more for the bowl and rolling the dough

This recipe comes from my friend Emily Su-Bowden, a talented chef who seamlessly weaves culinary techniques she grew up with into her Western-style professional cooking. I couldn't stop eating these flatbreads studded with sesame seeds when she served them at a celebratory lamb roast a few years ago. One side was brown and smoky from the grill, while the other was soft and chewy. Inspired by a technique for rolling mu shu pancakes she'd learned from her family, Emily pressed two dough balls together before rolling them out. Then she carefully grilled the double stack, charring its outer surfaces while allowing steam to gently cook the interior through. Finally, she peeled the stack apart, revealing a masterful combination of textures that couldn't be more enjoyable to eat. Serve them as you would pitta bread, with your favourite dips or alongside grilled meats and vegetables.

• • •

In a measuring jug, stir together the warm water, yeast, and sugar. Let the mixture sit until it's foamy on top, about 5 minutes.

In a stand mixer, whisk together the flour, sesame seeds, and salt. Add the yeast mixture and oil, snap on the dough hook, and mix on low speed to combine. Increase the speed to medium-high and knead until the dough forms a smooth, elastic ball that cleanly pulls away from the bowl, 8 to 10 minutes.

Remove the dough from the bowl. Lightly coat the bowl with oil, then return the dough to the bowl and cover tightly with clingfilm. Set in a warm place to double in size, 1½ to 2 hours.

Meanwhile, line a baking tray with parchment paper and set aside.

When the dough is ready, turn it out onto a clean work surface and divide it into 18 equal portions. Clear any flour, which will prevent the friction necessary for rolling a smooth ball,

from the work surface. Take a portion of dough and tuck its corners together to form a rough ball or teardrop shape. Set the ball, seam-side down, on the work surface. Loosely cup your hand around the dough, then use a rapid circular motion to drag it across the surface. The friction between the dough and the countertop will create surface tension on the outside of the dough and result in a tight, even ball. Continue rolling the ball on the countertop until the skin is smooth and nearly no seam remains. Repeat with the remaining balls. (Since this is a sticky dough, you may need to flour your hands as you divide and roll the balls, but avoid using too much flour.)

Arrange the dough balls on the parchment-lined baking tray, cover with a clean tea towel, and set the pan in the warm spot again to proof until the dough balls are light and pillowy to the touch, about 20 minutes.

Lightly flour the work surface. Brush a dough ball with enough oil to coat, then press a second ball of dough on top. Repeat with all of the dough balls until you have 9 stacks. Use a rolling pin to roll out each dough stack into a round 1.25cm thick.

Line a large bowl with a clean tea towel and set aside. Cook the dough rounds on a hot barbecue grill or in a hot cast-iron frying pan on the hob, rotating and turning to brown them evenly on both sides, 2 to 3 minutes per side. Brush with oil as you take them off the heat, then pile into the towel-lined bowl and allow to steam for a few minutes.

Peel the warm flatbreads apart and serve hot—one side will be steamy, chewy, and tender, the other toasty and golden brown.

Wrap and store leftovers in an airtight bag at room temperature for up to 3 days. Toast gently to reheat.

marion's yeasted waffles

MAKES 12 TO 16 WAFFLES

Requires overnight proofing

2¼ teaspoons (7g) fast-action dried yeast

1 tablespoon sugar

120g warm water

485g full-fat milk

114g unsalted butter, **Ghee** (page 62), or **Cardamom Ghee** (page 61), melted, plus more for cooking

1 teaspoon (3g) kosher salt

270g plain flour

2 medium eggs, lightly whisked

¼ teaspoon bicarbonate of soda

Salted butter and warm maple syrup or apricot jam, for serving

---

My brothers and I grew up eating toaster waffles. Our mom let us have them as a Saturday morning treat—or bribe, depending on how you look at it—before forcing us to spend the rest of the day at Persian school. They came eight to a pack, and since there were three of us, that meant that we each got two and two-thirds waffles. As the eldest, I became an expert at cutting circles into thirds—the start of a long career in preparing and portioning food.

It wasn't until years later that I tasted a truly perfect homemade waffle. One morning my kitchen sister Amy Dencler, then a cook and now the chef at Chez Panisse, invited me over for breakfast. I watched as she poured batter into her aged waffle iron, then carefully laid a rasher of crisp bacon into the centre before lowering the lid. A yeasty aroma permeated the kitchen, stoking my appetite. I couldn't wait to take a bite. When I did, my teeth shattered the lacy edges and sank into the centre, releasing more of that toasted yeast flavour. I begged Amy to share her secret.

Turns out, nothing much about the waffles was a secret. The recipe, by legendary cookbook author Marion Cunningham, was already widely beloved. Marion called them "the best waffle I know," and I couldn't agree more. Marion's recipe—and a couple variations on it—is the only one I'll allow in my kitchen.

• • •

In a large bowl, whisk together the yeast, sugar, and water. Set aside until foamy, about 5 minutes.

Add the milk, unsalted butter or ghee, and salt and whisk until combined. Finally, add the flour and whisk until smooth. Cover and refrigerate overnight (unless your kitchen is temperate, in which case you can leave the bowl on the counter).

To cook the waffles, set a baking tray with a wire rack in the oven and preheat to 100°C. Heat a waffle iron.

recipe continues

Whisk the eggs and bicarbonate of soda into the batter. Brush the waffle iron with melted butter, then pour a ladleful of batter onto each section of the iron. Let the batter set for 15 seconds or so, then close the lid. Cook at the highest setting, flipping as needed according to the manufacturer's instructions, until crisp, golden, airy, and emitting a yeasty aroma, 4 to 5 minutes. Repeat with the remaining batter. Keep prepared waffles warm in the oven.

Serve with salted butter and warm maple syrup or apricot jam. Store leftover waffles in an airtight bag in the freezer and toast to reheat.

VARIATIONS

To make **Amy's Bacon Waffles,** pour batter into the hot iron and let it set for about 30 seconds before adding 1 or 2 rashers of crisp-cooked **bacon**.

•

To make crisp, nutty **Buckwheat Waffles,** reduce the amount of plain flour in the batter to 180g and add 90g **buckwheat flour**.

a sweet note

I've spent most of my life denying myself pleasures great and small. For one thing, I've always struggled to believe I deserve to experience delight of any kind. And on the rare occasions when I've allowed myself a pleasure, it's only because I felt I'd earned the privilege. But pleasure is a right, an essential part of the human experience. And as I've grown older and more familiar with loss, I've become keenly aware of my own mortality, too. As a result, pleasure has become central to my life.

On a daily basis, this means using my most special mugs and plates, knowing that they could break or chip at any time. It means lighting a stick of my precious, fancy incense each morning so I can feel my body relax as I breathe in the sweet, grassy smoke. It means planting my garden full of heartbreakingly gorgeous flowers—knowing they'll quickly wither once they bloom—just so I can be engulfed by their splendour every time I approach my front door.

It also means always saying yes to dessert. We have to eat vegetables and proteins to survive, but dessert's entire raison d'être is pleasure. And to that end, each of the cakes, cookies, creamy desserts, sauces, and preserves in this chapter promises myriad forms of beauty and sensory delight. You'll feel a burst of pride (and maybe relief) as a decadent vanilla bean flan, bathed in caramel, slips effortlessly out of the pan and onto a platter. You'll hungrily breathe in the heady, almond-like perfume of *noyau* (apricot kernel extract) each time you open your jar of jam. You'll feel deep satisfaction as you whip up a perfectly moist, one-bowl chocolate cake in under an hour. You'll revel in the velvety texture of passion fruit curd as it melts on your tongue, releasing its floral perfume. And you'll feel your own sense of pleasure magnify when you share a jar of decadent burnt honey hot fudge with a friend.

    Our brains are hardwired to pursue not only pleasure but also sweetness. So to enjoy a dessert is to be utterly, beautifully human. It's worth making, eating, and sharing dessert—even the simplest one—because, as Zadie Smith put it, "we do not have so many reliable sources of pleasure in this life as to turn our nose up at one that is so readily available."

I was besotted with the Russian Honey Cake at San Francisco's now-closed 20th Century Cafe from the moment I tasted it. For years, I begged pastry chef and owner Michelle Polzine to share her recipe and let me write about it on my blog, but she refused. She said she was saving it for the day *The New York Times* came knocking, so when I began my monthly column for *The New York Times Magazine,* Michelle made good on her promise. The recipe for the twenty-layer cake was a beast. While I tested it, dozens of pancake-thin layers of the spiced cake cooled and rested on every flat surface in my home. The experience so overwhelmed me that I haven't attempted the cake again.

But I still crave it—I especially miss its ethereal whipped-cream icing, laced with burnt honey and dulce de leche. When a friend suggested using graham crackers to make a "lazy" version of the cake, I got straight to work. Holding fast to Michelle's icing recipe, I added only a little soured cream to offer the graham crackers a much-needed bit of tang. But, just as with the original cake, the graham crackers and icing transform overnight in the refrigerator—evolving from two distinct elements into a richly unified, perfectly balanced dessert that will stun everyone with the first bite.

• • •

To make the burnt honey filling, clip a sugar thermometer to a small saucepan and pour in the honey. Set over medium-high heat and bring to a simmer. After about 3 minutes, the honey will begin to foam intensely. Stirring occasionally with a silicone spatula, keep a close eye on the honey. When the honey begins to smoke, at about 150°C, turn off the heat and carefully add the water. When the honey stops bubbling, whisk to combine, pour it into a heatproof jug, and allow to cool to room temperature. You should have about 255g of burnt honey.

In a stand mixer fitted with the paddle, combine the burnt honey, dulce de leche, salt, and cinnamon and mix on low speed until smooth. Add the soured cream and continue

recipe continues

CAKES AND COOKIES

russian honey icebox cake

MAKES A 23 × 12.5CM LOAF CAKE

Requires 12 to 24 hours for chilling

FOR THE BURNT HONEY FILLING

255g honey

60g water

155g dulce de leche, shop-bought or homemade (page 432)

1½ teaspoons (5g) kosher salt

¾ teaspoon ground cinnamon

120g soured cream

480g double cream

FOR ASSEMBLY

400g graham crackers (or digestive biscuits)

mixing until homogeneous. Scrape this mixture into a small bowl and chill until completely cooled, about 2 hours. Rinse out the mixer bowl.

When ready to assemble, line a 23 × 12.5cm or larger loaf tin with clingfilm, leaving enough overhang on all sides to wrap the finished cake completely. Set aside.

Pour the double cream into the mixer bowl, return it to the stand mixer, and snap on the whisk attachment. Whip the cream on medium speed to soft peaks, about 3 minutes. Add the chilled honey mixture and continue whipping the filling to medium-stiff peaks, an additional 3 to 5 minutes.

Scoop about 240ml of the filling into the prepared tin and use an offset spatula to spread it out evenly. Line with whole and partial graham crackers or digestive biscuits to form a complete "cake" layer, going all the way to all four edges, then scoop in another 240ml of filling. Continue spreading filling and layering crackers for 4 to 5 layers of graham crackers or digestive biscuits, until just shy of the top of the tin, making sure to reserve 240ml of filling to top the cake. Top the cake with the remaining filling, spreading it out, and gently wrap the clingfilm overhang around the cake to cover it completely. Refrigerate for 12 to 24 hours.

To serve, unwrap the clingfilm, then place a serving platter or chopping board over the top of the loaf pan. Invert the platter and the pan to release the cake from the pan, then carefully peel the clingfilm off the cake. If you like, you can break up any remaining graham crackers or digestive biscuits into pieces and use to garnish, or grind them into crumbs and sprinkle on top of the cake. Slice and serve immediately.

Rewrap and refrigerate leftovers for up to 2 days.

CAKES AND COOKIES
yellow buttermilk cake

MAKES 2 X 23CM LAYERS

240g buttermilk, at room temperature (see Note)

1 teaspoon vanilla extract

190g plain flour whisked with 60g cornflour (see Note)

250g granulated sugar (see Note)

1½ teaspoons (5g) kosher salt

1½ teaspoons baking powder

½ teaspoon bicarbonate of soda

170g unsalted butter, at warm room temperature (18 to 24°C), cut into tablespoon-sizd pieces

2 tablespoons neutral oil

3 medium eggs, at room temperature, lightly whisked

1 batch **Soured Cream Fudge Icing** (page 407), at room temperature

Rainbow hundreds and thousands or sprinkles, for decorating (optional)

I was born in San Diego, but I never felt like I belonged there. My mom, desperate to instil some sense of cultural heritage in me and my brothers, constantly reminded us that we were Iranian first and American second. Outside our home, the messages that I didn't fit in were both implicit and explicit. My name tumbled awkwardly out of people's mouths. My skin tone, big nose, and massive head of curls—not to mention the unruly hair everywhere else on my body—all drew attention I didn't want. All I wanted as a kid was to blend in, to be "normal," to be like everyone else, to be known instead of judged. And somehow, very early on, "yellow box cake," baked from a readymade dried mix where you just add the wet ingredients, with chocolate icing came to represent the sense of belonging that was just out of reach.

My mom wasn't much of a baker, and when she did bake it wasn't from a box. For our birthdays, she ordered dense chocolate cakes covered in chocolate shavings from the most exquisite European bakery in town. The cakes were beautiful. They just weren't what I wanted.

Years later, when I started cooking and baking, I was drawn, of course, to yellow cake recipes. But while homemade versions often tasted better than boxed due to their higher-quality ingredients, their texture was always a disappointment. Too dense. Too dry. Too greasy. Nothing ever had that fork-tender, light-as-air texture that reminded me of the bake-sale cupcakes and slices of birthday cake at pool parties that always left me wanting more.

Eventually, I learned how cake mixes are made—by coating flour with tiny, solid fat particles (usually in the form of shortening) in industrial-sized mixers, so that when you add an egg, oil, and water at home, minimal gluten forms. That leads to that moist, melt-in-your-mouth texture I so love. I set out to replicate the technique using quality ingredients and eventually learned about "reverse creaming." It's a method popularised by Rose Levy Beranbaum, author of *The Cake Bible*. Instead of the typical creaming process, in which butter and sugar are whipped together, butter—very soft but still

solid—is mixed into the dry ingredients to completely coat them with fat, mimicking commercial cake mix. The result was exactly what I'd been looking for. After three decades, victory was mine.

This recipe also owes a great debt to the late Flo Braker, whose tender buttermilk cake, long a favourite of mine, served as a starting point. And to the very much alive Alice Medrich, who, upon tasting the cake, was kind enough to let me know I'd finally nailed the assignment.

• • •

Adjust an oven rack to the centre position and preheat to 180°C. Coat 2 x 23cm round cake tins with nonstick cooking spray, line the tin bottoms with rounds of parchment, then spray the parchment and set the tins aside.

Pour the buttermilk into a jug. Add the vanilla and stir to combine. Set aside.

In a stand mixer fitted with the paddle, combine the flour, sugar, salt, baking powder, and bicarbonate of soda and mix on low speed for 30 seconds. Add the butter and continue mixing until the mixture resembles a coarse meal, about 2 minutes. Add the oil and continue mixing until the mixture comes together into a pasty dough.

Increase the speed to medium and gradually add the whisked eggs in 3 batches, beating for 20 seconds after each addition to allow the eggs to incorporate. Stop the mixer and scrape the sides and bottom of the bowl, as well as the whisks. Return the mixer to medium and add the buttermilk mixture. Mix just until evenly combined and no thick lumps remain. Use a silicone spatula to scrape down to the bottom of the bowl to make sure that all the dry ingredients are incorporated. At this point, the batter should be light, shiny, creamy, and beautifully emulsified. (If you are worried about the emulsion breaking, remove the bowl from the mixer, add a few chips of ice, and whisk rapidly by hand to stabilise the mixture.)

Evenly divide the batter between the prepared tins. For the utmost precision, use a scale to weigh the batter, about 540g per tin.

Transfer to the centre rack and bake for 15 minutes. Rotate the tins 180 degrees and switch their positions for more even browning. Bake for an additional 9 to 11 minutes (24 to 26 minutes total), until the surface of the cake springs back slightly when touched lightly in the centre and the sides begin to pull away from the pan.

Let the cakes cool in the tins for 10 minutes. Carefully unmould the cakes onto a parchment-lined baking tin and leave them upside down to create an evenly flat surface that will make the cake assembly easier. Set the tin on a wire rack and cool completely before icing.

To prepare the cake for icing, use a serrated knife to even the tops of the layers if needed (and by all means, eat the trimmings!). Place one cake layer on a serving plate, cut-side down, and use a pastry brush to gently wipe away any crumbs. Use an offset spatula to spread about 280g of the icing evenly across the cake. Carefully set the second cake layer on top, trimmed-side down, being careful to centre it. Brush away any more crumbs.

Place about 140g of the icing in a small bowl and thin it out with a little water so it's very easy to spread. Use an offset spatula to spread a thin layer of this thinned icing on the top and sides of the cake, then chill until set, about 15 minutes. Repeat as necessary until no crumbs show through the icing.

Use the offset spatula to generously ice the cake with the remaining (unthinned) icing. Begin with the top of the cake, then ice the sides. You may have a little icing left over, but you can eat that straight from the fridge with a spoon in the middle of the night. (Or do as Laurie Ellen suggests and load it up on your cake in peaks and valleys—because who doesn't love getting a slice with extra icing?) Decorate the cake with

NOTES

It's crucial that everything be at room temperature here. Don't skimp on this step! If you haven't had the chance to prepare ahead of time, you can gently heat the buttermilk while you preheat the oven.

This recipe won't work with organic sugar, which will break the delicate emulsion. Use white granulated or caster sugar.

My original recipe uses bleached cake flour, which isn't available in the UK, but mixing cornflour with plain flour will get you similar results.

The cake can be baked 1 day in advance, cooled completely, and wrapped tightly in plastic before icing the day of serving.

hundreds and thousands or sprinkles if you like. Chill for 30 minutes to set before serving.

Wrap and store leftover iced cake at room temperature for up to 3 days.

VARIATIONS

To make **Confetti Cake,** stir 100g cylindrical **rainbow sprinkles** (artificially coloured, since naturally coloured will fade, and not hundreds and thousands, which will bleed) into the batter before dividing into two tins. (Listen, if you want a fun cake, you must let go of your hippie inclinations for one moment and let the joy, sugar, and red no.40 lake pump through your veins!)

•

For true boxed cake flavour, use **imitation vanilla extract**.

•

For **Yellow Cupcakes,** spoon the batter into greased muffin tins and bake for 16 to 18 minutes. Cool completely before icing with an entire batch of **Soured Cream Fudge Icing** (page 407).

•

For a 23 × 33cm cake, bake for 30 to 35 minutes. Let cool completely in the tin. Make a half-batch of the fudge icing to ice this cake.

CAKES AND COOKIES
soured cream fudge icing

Soured cream gives this smooth, shiny icing the tang of cultured dairy to balance its sweetness. Use chocolate that's 56 per cent to 60 per cent cacao and a quality, dark Dutch-process cocoa powder, such as Guittard or Valrhona, to guarantee the richest, most luscious icing.

• • •

Fill a medium pot to a depth of 5cm of water and bring to a simmer over medium heat. Place the butter and chocolate in a heatproof medium bowl and set it over the pot. Turn the heat to low and, stirring occasionally with a silicone spatula, melt the butter and chocolate until the mixture is completely smooth. (Alternatively, melt the butter and chocolate in the microwave in 30-second increments, stirring until completely smooth.)

Whisk the sugar, cocoa, and salt into the melted chocolate and butter mixture. Allow to cool to room temperature for 10 minutes. Stir in the soured cream and vanilla and whisk vigorously until completely smooth and shiny. (If whisking by hand doesn't yield a completely smooth, shiny icing, or if you sense that the emulsion is breaking, add a couple small chips of ice and use an immersion blender or food processor to blend the icing until smooth and shiny, about 30 seconds.)

Cover and refrigerate icing for up to 3 days. Bring to room temperature before using.

MAKES ABOUT 985G (ENOUGH TO GENEROUSLY FROST 2 X 23CM LAYERS; FOR A 23 × 33CM SHEET CAKE, HALVE THE RECIPE)

228g unsalted butter, cut into pieces

114g plain dark chocolate, finely chopped

240g icing sugar, sifted

68g Dutch-process cocoa powder, sifted

1 teaspoon (3g) kosher salt

320g soured cream, straight from the fridge

2 teaspoons vanilla extract

CAKES AND COOKIES
one-bowl chocolate cake

This is my go-to when I need to make a cake in under an hour. It's a variation on the same boiling-water-and-cocoa cake I've been making for more than twenty years (the hot water or coffee encourages the cocoa to "bloom," intensifying its flavour). I tweaked a few things to streamline the method while also making it richer, moister, and more chocolaty. While it's wonderful served on its own, it's also a fantastic palette for all sorts of icings, including lightly sweetened vanilla cream and cream cheese icing. And if you *really* want to impress folks, slather it with a generous layer of burnt honey icing. For all the options, see page 410.

• • •

Adjust an oven rack to the upper-middle position and preheat to 180°C. Coat a 23 × 33cm baking tin with nonstick cooking spray, line with a parchment sling, then spray the parchment to coat. Set aside.

Sift the flour, cocoa, baking powder, and bicarbonate of soda into a large bowl. Add the salt, brown sugar, and granulated sugar and whisk to combine.

In a jug, whisk together the eggs, soured cream, oil, and vanilla until smooth.

Make a well in the centre of the dry ingredients and gradually whisk in the oil mixture until it's mostly incorporated. Keep whisking as you add the boiling water or hot coffee in a thin stream. Stir until smooth. Pour the batter into the prepared tin.

Bake for 30 minutes, or until the top of the cake springs back when touched, its sides are pulling away from the tin, and an inserted cocktail stick comes out clean.

Let the cake cool completely in the tin. Cover with icing if desired before serving.

Tightly wrapped, this cake will keep for 4 days at room temperature.

recipe continues

MAKES A 23 × 33CM CAKE

236g plain flour

75g Dutch-process cocoa powder

1 teaspoon baking powder

1 teaspoon bicarbonate of soda

2 teaspoons (6g) kosher salt

150g soft dark brown sugar

150g granulated sugar

2 medium eggs, at room temperature

180g soured cream

110g neutral oil

2 teaspoons vanilla extract

240g boiling water or freshly brewed strong coffee

1 batch **Cream Cheese Icing, Burnt Honey Icing,** or **Whipped Vanilla Cream** (see page 410)

ICINGS

To make **Cream Cheese Icing,** beat 227g **cream cheese**, 85g **unsalted butter,** both at room temperature, and 1 teaspoon (3g) kosher **salt** with an electric mixer on low speed. When it's smooth, gradually add 240g **icing sugar** and beat until incorporated. Add 1 tablespoon **vanilla extract,** increase the speed to medium, and beat for 2 minutes until fluffy, stopping to scrape the bowl as needed. Spread onto the cooled cake with an offset spatula.

•

To make **Whipped Vanilla Cream,** chill a large deep metal bowl (or the bowl of a stand mixer) and a whisk (or whisk attachment) in the freezer for at least 20 minutes. Place 240g **double cream,** 1½ teaspoons **granulated sugar**, 2 teaspoons **vanilla extract,** and a pinch of **salt** in the bowl and whip the cream by hand or at low speed until soft peaks appear. If using a mixer, finish whisking the cream by hand until all the liquid is incorporated and the cream is soft and billowy. Keep chilled, then spread onto the cooled cake with an offset spatula.

•

Use the filling from **Russian Honey Icebox Cake** (page 399) as an icing. Use an offset spatula to spread it onto the cooled cake.

CAKES AND COOKIES
preserved lemon and labne cake

I spent three years testing lemon cakes before I thought to make one with two of my beloved kitchen staples. Labne offers tang and contributes to the cake's tender crumb. Replacing fresh lemon with preserved Meyer lemon paste not only streamlines the preparation, it also provides the salt, acid, and welcome hint of funk that make this cake an undeniable pleasure to eat. And the simple lemon-turmeric glaze brightens both the colour and flavour of the cake.

• • •

Adjust an oven rack to the centre position and preheat to 180°C. Coat a 23cm round cake tin with nonstick cooking spray, line the bottom with a round of parchment, then spray the parchment and set the tin aside.

To make the cake, in a medium bowl, whisk together the granulated sugar, labne, oil, Meyer lemon paste, water, and eggs.

In a large bowl, whisk together the flour, baking powder, and bicarbonate of soda. Whisk the wet mixture into the dry mixture until smooth. Scrape the batter into the prepared tin and smooth it out into an even layer.

Bake for 40 to 45 minutes, until an inserted cocktail stick emerges free of crumbs.

Let the cake cool in the tin for 10 minutes, then transfer to a wire rack to cool completely.

To make the glaze, in a medium bowl, whisk together 1 tablespoon lemon juice and the turmeric, then let the mixture sit for a few minutes to bloom. Whisk in the icing sugar and salt until smooth, adding more lemon juice as needed to get a drizzly consistency.

Spread the glaze over the cooled cake, letting it drip down the sides. Allow to set for 30 minutes before slicing the cake.

Store leftover cake in an airtight container at room temperature for up to 2 days.

MAKES A 23CM ROUND CAKE

FOR THE CAKE

250g granulated sugar

180g labne, soured cream, or Greek yogurt

110g neutral oil

80g **Preserved Meyer Lemon Paste** (page 79)

2 tablespoons (30g) water

2 medium eggs, at room temperature

180g plain flour

1 teaspoon baking powder

¼ teaspoon bicarbonate of soda

FOR THE GLAZE

1 to 2 tablespoons freshly squeezed lemon juice

⅛ teaspoon ground turmeric

125g icing sugar

Pinch of kosher salt

CAKES AND COOKIES
sparkling banana bread

MAKES A 20 X 20CM SQUARE

FOR THE BANANA BREAD

203g plain flour

2 teaspoons (6g) kosher salt

1 teaspoon bicarbonate of soda

1 teaspoon baking powder

1 teaspoon ground cinnamon

288g well-mashed ripe bananas (about 3 bananas; see Note)

150g soft dark brown sugar

140g neutral oil

80g buttermilk or soured cream, at room temperature

1½ teaspoons vanilla extract

2 medium eggs, at room temperature

FOR THE TOPPING

6 tablespoons granulated sugar

1½ teaspoons ground cinnamon

½ teaspoon flaky sea salt

2 very ripe bananas, halved lengthways

Packed with both mashed and whole bananas, this is my ideal banana bread. To maximise the ratio of the cinnamon-sugar topping to the moist, flavourful interior, I bake it in a cake tin. In the oven, the topping transforms into a sparkling crust that releases wave after wave of cinnamon aroma with each bite.

•••

Adjust an oven rack to the upper-middle position and preheat to 180°C. Coat a 20cm square baking tin with nonstick cooking spray. Line with a parchment sling and spray the parchment.

To make the banana bread, in a large bowl, whisk together the flour, kosher salt, bicarbonate of soda, baking powder, and cinnamon.

In a medium bowl, whisk together the mashed bananas, brown sugar, oil, buttermilk, vanilla, and eggs until evenly combined.

Stir the banana mixture into the dry ingredients and mix to combine, making sure to incorporate all the dry flour at the bottom of the bowl.

To make the topping, in a small bowl, combine the granulated sugar, cinnamon, and flaky salt.

Pour the batter into the prepared pan and then let the pan drop from a height of 7.5cm onto the countertop a couple times to release any air bubbles that might have gotten trapped inside the batter. Sprinkle the topping in a thick, even layer over the batter, then gently place the banana halves, cut-side up, atop the batter, cutting into pieces as needed to make them fit.

Bake for 50 to 55 minutes, until a cocktail stick inserted around the halved bananas emerges clean.

Let the cake cool in the tin for 10 minutes, then transfer to a wire rack to cool completely before slicing. (Alternatively, leave the cake to cool in the tin and serve it directly from there.)

Wrap and store at room temperature for up to 3 days.

I first met Laurie Ellen Pellicano when I was a young cook and she was working the bread counter at Berkeley's legendary Acme Bread Company. A few years later, we reconnected at Tartine in San Francisco, where she worked her way up to head pastry chef and I cooked monthly dinners. Along the way, her help has been indispensable to every one of my projects, including this book. Now, she's got her own eponymous business, giving new life to classic shortbread biscuits by creating exciting flavour combinations, including matcha and caramelised white chocolate, lemon poppy seed, and panettone.

To be honest, I was never much of a shortbread person until I tasted Laurie Ellen's version, but I get it now. Her biscuits are both crisp and melt-in-your-mouth tender, rich with butter and salt. Aware of my tendency to add cardamom to everything I cook, Laurie Ellen offered to develop a version of her recipe studded with the spice. To bump up the flavour, she suggested dipping the biscuits in cardamom sugar before baking. "I love the sparkle it gives," she said, "and functionally, it's the first thing to hit your tongue and activate the aromatic notes in the cardamom on your palate." These biscuits are perfect for dunking into a cup of tea, and they make wonderful gifts, too. I like to keep a log or two of dough in the freezer (see Note), so I can bake some off whenever anyone drops by.

• • •

CAKES AND COOKIES
laurie ellen's cardamom shortbread

MAKES 40 LITTLE BISCUITS, (4CM ROUNDS), PLUS ENOUGH DOUGH FOR 80 MORE

370g plain flour

½ teaspoon baking powder

228g unsalted butter, at room temperature

180g icing sugar

1 tablespoon plus ½ teaspoon freshly ground cardamom

1½ teaspoons (5g) kosher salt

1 medium egg, lightly whisked

1½ teaspoons **Noyau Extract** (page 438) or vanilla extract

50g granulated sugar

In a medium bowl, whisk together the flour and baking powder. Set aside.

In a stand mixer fitted with the paddle, combine the butter, icing sugar, 1 tablespoon of the cardamom, and the salt. Beat on medium-high speed until the mixture is light and fluffy, 3 to 5 minutes. Stop the mixer and scrape down to the bottom of the bowl with a silicone spatula. With the mixer on low speed, stream in the egg to combine, then increase the speed to medium for 30 seconds. Stop and scrape the bowl again, then add the extract and mix to combine.

recipe continues

NOTES

For perfectly round cookies, tightly cinch the dough logs when you wrap them with parchment to avoid forming a flat bottom. First, fold the parchment over the log and roll it back and forth to smooth it out. Keeping the parchment against the dough, press a ruler into the crevice where the dough meets the cutting board at a 45-degree angle. Holding the ruler in place, gently tug on the top of the parchment to roll and round out the log.

To freeze the dough, tightly wrap the parchment-covered logs with plastic. To use the frozen dough, slice and sugar the cookies as directed and add 1 to 2 minutes to the baking time.

With the mixer off, add the flour mixture. Pulse the mixer a bit to avoid coating yourself in flour, then mix on low until just a few streaks of flour remain. Stop and scrape down the bowl, paying extra attention to the paddle and bottom of the bowl where undermixed bits tend to hide. Return to low speed and mix until the dough comes together, 10 to 15 seconds. The dough should cling to the paddle and start to pull away from the sides of the bowl. Remove the bowl from the mixer and use a spatula to fold the dough over a few times to ensure it is homogenous. Wrap the dough in clingfilm, patting into a rectangle roughly 11.4 × 25cm and 4cm thick.

Chill the dough for 15 minutes, then cut it lengthways into three pieces. Let the dough warm up a bit, then roll each piece into a log about 3cm in diameter. Wrap each log with a piece of parchment (see Note) and transfer to a baking tray. Refrigerate the dough until firm, at least 1 hour.

When ready to bake, adjust oven racks to the upper-middle and lower-middle positions and preheat to 160°C. Line two baking sheets with parchment paper.

In a small bowl, combine the granulated sugar and the remaining ½ teaspoon cardamom. Use a sharp knife to trim the ends of one log and slice it into coins 6mm thick.

Dip the top of each biscuit in cardamom sugar and set on the prepared baking sheets, leaving 1.25cm space between each (they won't spread much). About 20 will fit on each sheet.

Bake for 16 to 19 minutes, switching racks and rotating the sheets front to back after 10 minutes. The edges should just begin to take on colour, and the bottoms should be a light golden brown.

Transfer the biscuits to wire racks to cool completely.

Store in covered containers for up to 1 month. (Laurie Ellen prefers a biscuit tin for its remarkable ability to keep biscuits crisp.)

CUSTARDS AND CREAMY DESSERTS
vanilla bean flan

MAKES A 23CM FLAN

Requires 2 hours or overnight chilling

- 200g granulated sugar
- 80g water
- 400g tin sweetened condensed milk
- 240g full-fat milk, at room temperature
- 240g single cream, at room temperature
- 6 medium eggs, at room temperature
- 1 teaspoon (3g) kosher salt
- 1 vanilla pod, halved lengthways

When learning how to cook, I was taught to make custards with fresh dairy. But once I learned that practically every Latin recipe for flan begins with a tin of sweetened condensed milk, I grew curious. As it turns out, the store cupboard staple not only obviates the need for sugar in the custard, its rich texture also contributes to the flan's seductive creaminess. And a generous amount of cream not only ensures a decadent custard, it also tempers the distinct "cooked" taste of condensed milk. The gentle heat of a bain-marie and a low baking temperature further ensure that the vanilla bean–speckled flan will be as smooth as silk.

• • •

Adjust an oven rack to the centre position and preheat to 160°C. Bring 3 litres water to a boil for the bain-marie. Set a wire rack inside a 23 × 33cm baking tin and have it and a 23 × 13cm loaf tin ready to go.

In a medium saucepan, combine the sugar and water and bring to a simmer. Use a wet pastry brush to dissolve any sugar crystals clinging to the sides of the pan. Swirling the pan, cook the caramel to a dark amber, then pour it into the loaf tin. Immediately pick up the tin to swirl the caramel and evenly coat the bottom and sides. Set aside.

In a large bowl, combine the sweetened condensed milk, milk, cream, eggs, and salt. Use a sharp paring knife to scrape the vanilla seeds from both halves of the pod and add them to the bowl (reserve the pod for another use). Use an immersion blender to blend the mixture just until no streaks of egg remain.

Set a fine-mesh sieve over the prepared loaf tin and pour the custard mixture through it to catch any errant eggshells or egg bits. Cover the tin with foil. Set the loaf tin on the rack in the 23 × 33cm tin. Pull out the oven rack and set the tin on it, then add enough boiling water to come halfway up the sides of the loaf tin.

recipe continues

all good things come to an end

Bake until an instant thermometer reads 76.6°C when inserted into the centre, about 1 hour 30 minutes. The surface of the flan should be just set to the touch, and the centre should jiggle just enough to make you a little bit uncomfortable. The custard will continue cooking as it cools due to the loaf tin's depth, so be brave and pull it from the oven a little earlier than you might feel it's ready.

Refrigerate the custard until it cools completely (at least 2 hours, and preferably overnight). To serve, run a thin paring knife or offset spatula along the edge of the pan to loosen the flan from the tin and flip it onto a rimmed plate to catch the caramel.

Cover and refrigerate leftovers for up to 5 days.

a small, good thing: strawberries with soured cream and brown sugar

I loved how Robin Wall Kimmerer, in her lyrical memoir, *Braiding Sweetgrass,* reminisced about harvesting wild strawberries as a child. "You could smell ripe strawberries before you saw them," she wrote, "the fragrance mingling with the smell of sun on damp ground."

Sadly, these days we tend to see our strawberries long before we smell them— if we get to smell them at all. Many of the volatile aromatic compounds responsible for the striking scents Kimmerer described have been bred out of most modern strawberries because they also hasten spoilage. And as we've shifted away from small-scale farming over the last century, commercial growers have prioritised qualities like shelf life and size over flavour and aroma.

Happily, it's not impossible to experience the heady aroma—and flavour—of Kimmerer's childhood for yourself. Wild strawberries— sometimes called alpine strawberries, fraises des bois, and mignonettes—are easy enough to grow in a home garden or even on a sunny patio; try the Mara des Bois variety. I've also had great success with larger Sparkle, Albion, and Tristar varieties, all bred for fragrance. And if you don't have the patience to grow your own, seek out wild strawberries at farmers' markets and specialist produce markets. Failing that, simply sniff all the strawberries at the supermarket and let your nose—rather than your eyes—be your guide.

To prepare, rinse, drain, and halve or quarter **strawberries,** then toss them with a bit of **granulated sugar** and a tiny pinch of **salt**. Let them sit for 15 minutes or so to get their juices flowing, then spoon them into individual bowls. Top with a dollop of **soured cream** and, at the very last second, a sprinkling of **brown sugar**. It's a perfect dessert.

I don't remember much about the circumstances of my first cherry clafoutis. But I must have loved the classic French farmhouse dessert, because I've been trying to reproduce that first custardy, almond-scented pancake ever since. As with many simple recipes, doing it well turned out to be a challenge. Over the last twenty years, I've made so many rubbery fruit omelettes that if I didn't have the vague memory of that warm, tender, cherry-filled custard as a touchstone, I'd have given up completely.

A few years ago, when I had a glut of cherries, I decided to try clafoutis again. This time, though, I invested in a little forethought. After noticing the similarities in their batters, I wondered if I might not apply the main lesson I've learned from making crepes to clafoutis. If what makes a crepe tender is rest—and lots of it—then perhaps a long, post-mix rest would yield a more tender clafoutis, as well. To my utter surprise, it worked!

• • •

In a large bowl, whisk together the eggs, granulated sugar, 1 teaspoon (3g) of the salt, the soured cream, milk, and noyau extract until smooth. Sprinkle 68g of the flour over the custard mixture and whisk until smooth. Transfer the custard to a 1-litre container, cover, and refrigerate for 4 hours or overnight.

About 1 hour before you plan to bake, pull the custard mixture out of the refrigerator and let it come to room temperature. Adjust oven racks to the upper-middle and lower-middle positions, place a clean, well-seasoned 30cm cast-iron frying pan on the lower rack, and preheat to 220°C.

Line a baking tray with parchment and lay out the cherries, cut-side up (it's fine if they crowd each other a bit). Roast on the upper rack for 15 minutes, until tender and beginning to dry out. Let the cherries cool a bit, then transfer to a medium bowl and sprinkle with the remaining 1 tablespoon flour, the

CUSTARDS AND CREAMY DESSERTS
cherry clafoutis

MAKES ONE 30CM CLAFOUTIS

Requires 4 hours or overnight resting

- 4 medium eggs
- 134g granulated sugar
- 1¼ teaspoons (4g) kosher salt
- 240g soured cream
- 160g full-fat milk
- 2 tablespoons **Noyau Extract** (page 438) or 1 teaspoon almond extract
- 68g plus 1 tablespoon plain flour
- 675g sweet cherries, pitted and halved
- ⅛ teaspoon ground cinnamon
- 14g unsalted butter
- Icing sugar, for serving

NOTE

If you don't have a 30cm cast-iron frying pan, you can use a 25cm and increase the cooking time by 2 to 3 minutes. Or use a 30cm stainless-steel frying pan, but keep a closer eye on the clafoutis, as it may cook more quickly.

cinnamon, and ¼ teaspoon (1g) kosher salt. Toss to coat the cherries evenly.

Carefully remove the hot frying pan from the oven and add the butter. Swirl it around the pan to coat the bottom and sides as it melts. Pour in the batter and arrange the cherries evenly on top of the batter (it's fine if some of them sink).

Return the pan to the lower rack and bake for 18 to 20 minutes, until the clafoutis puffs and browns. If the top of the clafoutis isn't browning after 15 minutes, rotate and transfer the pan to the upper rack and continue baking until the centre of the custard barely jiggles and the temperature registers 90°C.

Allow to rest for 5 minutes, then serve warm, either straight from the pan or flipped out onto a serving platter. Shower with icing sugar.

VARIATION

For an **Apricot Clafoutis,** substitute 675g of quartered **fresh apricots** for the cherries.

CUSTARDS AND CREAMY DESSERTS
passion fruit curd

Fruit curd is a case study in balance. The sweet must even out the tart. The butter and eggs must not overpower the fresh fruit flavour. And the curd must cook just enough to set, but not so far that the eggs within it scramble and ruin its velvety texture. This recipe heroically manages that tightrope walk, yielding a curd that's sweet, rich, and creamy without being cloying. And passion fruit lends the curd both a floral dimension and a pleasant tang with its musky flavour.

While my favourite way to eat this curd is straight from the jar, I also like layering it into small glasses or jars with softly whipped cream and shortbread biscuits to make tiny, individual parfaits.

Look for fresh passion fruit at Latin grocers or use frozen pulp or frozen, unsweetened juice to make the curd. Avoid tinned or bottled juice if you can—it's usually heat-treated and sweetened and won't taste the same.

• • •

MAKES ABOUT 660G

- 300g fresh passion fruit juice (see Note)
- 150g granulated sugar
- 1½ teaspoons (5g) kosher salt
- 3 medium eggs
- 5 medium egg yolks
- 114g cold unsalted butter, cut into tablespoon-sized pieces

Pour 5cm depth of water into a wide medium pot and bring to a gentle simmer over medium heat. Set a fine-mesh sieve over a medium stainless-steel bowl (avoid glass, plastic, or ceramic, which are insulators and will slow down the cooling process) and set aside.

In a large heatproof bowl, whisk together the juice, sugar, salt, whole eggs, and egg yolks. Set the bowl over the pot of simmering water. Stirring and scraping constantly with both a whisk and a silicone spatula, cook the curd until it just barely begins to thicken. Beware—this will take a while (about 12 minutes) and then happens all at once. The moment you notice the curd thickening (the temperature will be in the 68 to 71°C range), remove the bowl from the heat and pass the curd through the prepared sieve. Avoid vehemently pressing the curd through the sieve to prevent any eggy bits from passing through.

Add the cold butter and use an immersion blender to emulsify the curd, but do not overblend—20 to 30 seconds is plenty.

recipe continues

Cover immediately with clingfilm pressed against the curd to prevent a skin from forming. Chill completely—overnight if possible—before using.

Keep refrigerated for up to 5 days, but it's doubtful the curd will last that long.

USE

For **Passion Fruit Parfaits,** layer curd and **Whipped Vanilla Cream** (page 410) into small jars, glasses, or bowls. Garnish with **passion fruit pulp with seeds** and **Laurie Ellen's Cardamom Shortbread** (page 417).

NOTES

To make passion fruit juice, use a spoon to scoop out the pulp and the seeds (it's fine if a little of the membrane comes along). Pulse the seedy pulp with an immersion blender or in a food processor for about a minute to break it up. Strain through a fine-mesh sieve into a medium bowl and press on the pulp with a large spoon or the back of a ladle to squeeze as much juice out as possible. Save 4 tablespoons of the seeds if you like, for spooning over the curd or parfait, and discard the rest. You'll need about 900g of passion fruit to get about 500g pulp, which will yield about 320ml juice.

CUSTARDS AND CREAMY DESSERTS

vanilla bean rice pudding

MAKES ABOUT 1.1KG

720g full-fat milk

240g double cream

75g sugar

    Kosher salt

 1 vanilla pod, halved lengthways

110g medium- or long-grain rice (I like jasmine and Arborio)

 2 medium egg yolks

When I find myself awash in cherries, plums, nectarines, berries, or mangoes, I make a pot of this subtly sweet rice pudding. While the pudding cooks, the seeds and pod of an entire vanilla pod infuse it with a host of rich, floral aromas. The result is an ideal complement to ripe fruits of all kinds. It's also pretty darned good with a spoonful of **Apricot and Noyau Jam** (page 433), or simply on its own.

• • •

In a medium casserole, combine 480g of the milk, the cream, the sugar, and 1 teaspoon (3g) kosher salt. Use a sharp paring knife to scrape the vanilla seeds from both halves of the pod, and add both the seeds and the pod to the pot. Stirring regularly, bring the milk to a boil over medium heat, then turn off and let steep until the rice is ready.

Meanwhile, in a medium pot, bring 2 litres of water to a boil. Season the water lightly with salt, then add the rice and cook for 2 minutes.

Drain the rice and add it to the pot of milk. Stirring regularly, bring to a simmer over medium heat, then reduce the heat to low—the milk should be barely simmering—and cover. Cook, stirring occasionally, until most of the liquid is absorbed, about 1 hour.

In a medium bowl, whisk together the egg yolks and remaining 240g milk. Whisking constantly, ladle about 480ml of the hot rice mixture into the bowl with the eggs to temper them. Whisk the warmed egg mixture into the pot and continue cooking the pudding over low heat, stirring constantly until thickened, 8 to 10 minutes longer. Taste and adjust the seasoning and remove the vanilla pod.

Serve warm, at room temperature, or cold. To prevent a skin from forming, press a piece of parchment or clingfilm onto the surface of the pudding as it cools.

Cover and refrigerate leftovers for up to 5 days.

SAUCES AND PRESERVES

pressure cooker dulce de leche

MAKES ABOUT 420G

400g tin sweetened condensed milk, label removed

A pressure cooker simplifies the formerly laborious (picture hours of sweaty stirring) or terrifying (picture tins of hot caramel exploding all over the kitchen ceiling and walls) process of making dulce de leche. All it takes is a tin of sweetened condensed milk, some water, and a bit of time. No stirring or fear involved!

• • •

Closely inspect the tin to make sure it doesn't have any dents or other inconsistencies. Place it inside a pressure cooker (or Instant Pot) and add enough water to reach the pot's maximum capacity.

Set over high heat. Once the cooker has reached full pressure, set a timer for 24 to 30 minutes depending on your desired colour and texture. (On Instant Pots and other electric pressure cookers, this feature is automatic once you turn the pot on and set the time.) I like my dulce de leche very dark and thick, so I cook mine for 30 minutes, but if you prefer a lighter colour and slightly softer texture, reduce the cooking time a bit.

When the time is up, turn the cooker off and allow the pressure to release naturally. Once the tin has cooled completely to room temperature, remove it from the water. Use a tin opener to open the tin and scoop out the dulce de leche with a small silicone spatula.

Refrigerate leftovers in an airtight container for up to 6 months.

A ripening fruit heeds no one's schedule but its own, so my most sacred culinary ritual begins in early May each year with a call to my favourite orchard. I check on the timing of their apricots—depending on the year, they're ready to harvest sometime between late May and mid-July—and clear my calendar accordingly.

Apricots are a temperamental wonder. Unique among stone fruits for the way they ripen—from the inside out—they make us wait until it's nearly too late before revealing their secrets. My two favourite varieties are Blenheim (sometimes called Royal Blenheim) and Bonny Royal. Floral and delicate, these apricots don't travel very well and are quick to spoil. So when I get word that the fruit is ready to harvest, I drop everything and make my annual pilgrimage.

Waves of pleasure wash over me as I pick—and snack on—kilos of honey-sweet apricots warmed by the morning sun. And then a desperate need to extend the moment indefinitely overtakes me.

So as I leave the orchard, panic sets in and a countdown begins—few things underscore the relentless passage of time like a car full of ripe stone fruit. A single warm day can mean the difference between ripe and rotten. But a person can eat only so many apricots in a day, so I try to stop the clock by turning the fruit to jam, most of which I'll offer as gifts. In the words of writer Rebecca Solnit, "Making preserves is an art of stalling time, of making the fruit that is so evanescent last indefinitely … Each container is a capsule in which time stands still."

This method for making jam may be labour- and time-intensive, but its results are also unparallelled. The various steps of this sticky, finicky process—macerating the fruit overnight, cooking the liquid and fruit separately, cracking the apricot stones to extract their fragrant kernels—are all in service of faithfully preserving the flavour, texture, and, yes, glory of the fruit. Though this ritual is often one I undertake privately—picking, processing, and canning the fruit on my own—I never feel alone. Every jar I give away is not only a time

SAUCES AND PRESERVES

apricot and noyau jam

MAKES SEVEN TO EIGHT 250ML JARS

Requires overnight steeping

2kg ripe apricots, preferably Blenheim or Bonny Royal variety (about 25 apricots)

700g granulated sugar, plus more if needed

1 teaspoon (3g) kosher salt

½ teaspoon (3g) ascorbic acid powder (optional; see Note)

3 tablespoons freshly squeezed lemon juice

4 tablespoons **Noyau Extract** (optional; page 438)

capsule but also a time machine. It's a way for me to share the sublime beauty of that dry, hot morning in the apricot orchard with whoever opens it.

• • •

The night before you plan to make the jam, stone and quarter the apricots, reserving the stones. Trim away any soft or mouldy bits. Place the fruit in a large bowl or pot, and toss with the sugar, salt, and ascorbic acid (if using). Cover with a piece of parchment or lid and refrigerate. Place the stones on a plate in a single layer and freeze.

The following day, bring the fruit to room temperature before beginning the jam-making process.

Lay a tea towel across a chopping board. Place the frozen apricot stones on the towel in a single layer. Cover with a second towel and use a hammer to gently crack each stone open, then remove the kernel—the *noyau*—from each stone (it's fine if the kernels break into pieces). Discard the shells, place the kernels in a jelly bag or muslin pouch, and secure with kitchen string.

Place the fruit, the liquid it released overnight, and the pouch of noyaux in a 6-litre or larger nonreactive pot, as heavy as possible, and set over high heat. Set a colander inside a large heatproof bowl and set aside. Stirring occasionally with a wooden spoon or silicone spatula, bring the fruit to a boil, then carefully pour everything into the colander to drain the fruit. Return the drained syrup and kernel pouch to the pot and set the fruit aside.

Stirring constantly over high heat, bring the syrup to 110°C, or until the rapid boil slows, the bubbles grow large, and the syrup thickens, about 15 minutes.

Return the fruit to the pot and allow the jam to return to 110°C, stirring constantly to prevent scorching. If the temperature gets stuck below 105°C, the syrup seems to stop thickening, or the jam tastes too tart, add up to 200g of sugar

to balance. Add a pinch of salt if needed to adjust the seasoning. The hot jam should taste uncomfortably sweet—once it cools, its flavour will mellow. Keep stirring and cooking until all the fruit softens completely and the jam reaches a slow, thick boil, about 20 minutes. Add the lemon juice. Taste and adjust the sugar, salt, and lemon juice as needed—the jam should be mouth-smackingly sweet and tart. Add the noyau extract (if using). Remove the pot from the heat.

Remove the pouch with the kernels and set aside. When it's cool enough to handle, squeeze as much liquid (and noyau essence) from the bag as you can and stir it into the jam. Rinse off the noyaux from the pouch and save the kernels to make extract. Divide the jam into seven or eight 250ml jars. Cover and refrigerate for up to 6 months. (Or heat-process the jars for 10 minutes to seal and store at room temperature for up to 1 year.)

NOTES

Your best bet for finding ripe apricots is at a local farmers' market.

Ascorbic acid powder, also called vitamin C powder, is readily available at natural foods stores and online. Adding it to the fruit while it macerates will delay oxidation and yield a more brightly coloured jam that'll retain its vibrancy for months.

SAUCES AND PRESERVES

noyau extract

MAKES 360ML

25 to 30 noyaux (apricot kernels)

420ml vodka, bourbon, or light rum

Hidden within the stone of an apricot is a kernel, or *noyau*, rife with the perfume of almonds, vanilla, apricots, and lilies. The fragrance is intoxicating, simultaneously familiar and indescribable, and entirely worth extracting and capturing in a jar to add to whipped cream, rice pudding, custard, cake batter, and even cocktails all year long. But the highest use of noyau extract—and the reason I'll never stop making it—is in apricot jam, whose flavour it elevates from delicious to downright heavenly. Another bonus: You get to use a hammer to crack the pits! And while this recipe uses only a few dozen noyaux, there's no such thing as too many kernels in a jar of extract. You can't go wrong as long as you use enough vodka to completely submerge the kernels.

Apricot kernels contain a compound called amygdalin, which human bodies can convert to cyanide. To disable the amygdalin, give the kernels a quick toast before steeping them in the alcohol.

• • •

Preheat the oven to 150°C.

If the kernels are wet, allow them to dry, then spread them on a baking tray and toast them for 10 minutes. The noyaux shouldn't take on any colour. Remove them from the oven and allow to cool.

Place the noyaux and liquor in a 500ml jar. Cover and place in a dark, cool, dry place for 3 months or longer. Give the jar a shake occasionally when you think of it.

Strain the extract to remove debris as you use it—the longer the kernels remain in the liquor, the more aromatic and flavourful the extract will become. You can also add more toasted kernels as they accumulate, topping off with more liquor, resulting in an infinite supply of extract.

This recipe traces its roots to an excellent 2004 *Gourmet* magazine recipe for brown sugar hot fudge sauce. From there, Deb Perelman, of the blog *Smitten Kitchen,* went on to tweak and simplify it in her signature way, adding the option of using honey. Then my best friend Laurel's mother, Lynn, changed the recipe yet again by increasing the honey and decreasing the sugar.

When Laurel shared her mom's recipe with me, I was in my "burnt honey" era (see: **Russian Honey Icebox Cake,** page 399). I suspected burning the honey for this sauce would deepen and complicate its flavour, and I was right. The result is a sauce that's dark and bitter, yet shiny and sweet. It's salty and chewy, and it clings to ice cream in just the right way. A jar—if you can bear to part with it—makes an excellent gift.

• • •

Place the honey and golden syrup in a small saucepan, clip a sugar thermometer to the pan, set over medium-high heat, and bring to a simmer. After about 3 minutes, the mixture will begin to foam intensely. Stirring occasionally with a silicone spatula, keep a close eye on the honey. When the honey begins to smoke, at about 150°C, turn off the heat and carefully add the cream.

Stand back and allow the honey to sputter away until it stops bubbling, then whisk to combine. Add the butter, brown sugar, cocoa powder, and salt and return the heat to low. Simmer, stirring, for a few more minutes, until everything melts and comes together. Remove the pan from the heat, stir in the chocolate, and continue whisking until the residual heat yields a smooth, shiny sauce. Stir in the vanilla and taste and adjust the salt if needed.

Serve immediately on ice cream, or if you prefer a thicker texture, wait 5 to 10 minutes for the sauce to set.

Cover and refrigerate leftovers in a glass jar for up to 2 months.

Reheat in a microwave or gently over low heat to serve.

SAUCES AND PRESERVES

burnt honey hot fudge

MAKES ABOUT 480G

170g honey

   1 tablespoon golden syrup

160g double cream

28g unsalted butter, cut into pieces

50g soft dark brown sugar

25g cocoa powder

1½ teaspoons (5g) kosher salt

170g chopped dark chocolate or chips

   1 teaspoon vanilla extract

references and influences

I'm deeply grateful to the following writers and thinkers for keeping me company and paving the way for my work. Their words and ideas have generously guided mine.

COOKING

Rose Levy Beranbaum, *The Cake Bible*
Abra Berens, *Ruffage*
Marion Cunningham, *The Fannie Farmer Cookbook (1994)*
Rose Gray and Ruth Rogers, *The River Cafe Cookbook*
Christopher Hirsheimer and Melissa Hamilton, *Cook Something*
Sarah Kieffer, *100 Cookies*
Alana Kysar, *Aloha Kitchen*
Nigella Lawson, *Cook, Eat, Repeat; How to Eat*
Lara Lee, *Coconut & Sambal*
Deborah Madison, *Vegetarian Cooking for Everyone*
Joshua McFadden, *Six Seasons*
Yotam Ottolenghi (complete works)
Michelle Polzine, *Baking at the 20th Century Cafe*
Chad Robertson, *Tartine Bread*
Judy Rodgers, *The Zuni Café Cookbook*
Claire Saffitz, *Dessert Person*
Nigel Slater (complete works)
David Tanis, *David Tanis Market Cooking*
Alice Waters, *The Art of Simple Food; Chez Panisse Fruit; Chez Panisse Vegetables*

ON LIFE, NATURE, TIME, COMMUNITY, AND HAPPINESS

Priya Basil, *Be My Guest*
Annie Dillard, *Pilgrim at Tinker Creek*
Ross Gay, *The Book of Delights; The Book of (More) Delights; Inciting Joy*
Abraham Joshua Heschel, *The Sabbath*
bell hooks, *All About Love*
Carrie Jenkins, *Sad Love*
Chloé Cooper Jones, *Easy Beauty*
Dacher Keltner, *Awe*
Robin Wall Kimmerer, *Braiding Sweetgrass*
Ezra Klein, *The Ezra Klein Show* (podcast)
Audre Lorde, *The Cancer Journals*; "Poetry Is Not a Luxury"
John McPhee, *Giving Good Weight*
Jenny Odell, *How to Do Nothing*
Mary Oliver (complete works)
Judith Shulevitz, *The Sabbath World*
Zadie Smith, "Joy"
Rebecca Solnit, *The Faraway Nearby; Orwell's Roses*

FOOD WRITING

Archestratus, *Fragments from the Life of Luxury*
Laurie Colwin, *Home Cooking*
M. F. K. Fisher, *The Art of Eating*
Patience Gray, *Honey from a Weed*
Jane Grigson, *Good Things; Jane Grigson's Fruit Book; Jane Grigson's Vegetable Book*
Edna Lewis, *In Pursuit of Flavor*
Tejal Rao, essays in *The New York Times* and *The New York Times Magazine*
Helen Rosner, essays in *The New Yorker*
Vertamae Smart-Grosvenor, *Vibration Cooking*
Ruby Tandoh, *Cook as You Are; Eat Up*; essays in *The New Yorker*

resources

INGREDIENTS

Blenheim apricots: Andy's Orchard; Frog Hollow Farm
French specialist ingredients: Sous Chef; Market Hall Foods
Italian specialist ingredients: Sous Chef; Gustiamo; Mad Rose Specialty Foods; Market Hall Foods
Japanese specialist ingredients: Sous Chef; The Japanese Pantry
Olive oil: Honey & Co., Leila's Shop, Ottolenghi, Sous Chef, EXAU; Fat Gold; Mad Rose Specialty Foods; Séka Hills
Seville oranges: Rising C Ranches
Spices: Honey & Co., Ottolenghi; Burlap & Barrel; Diaspora Spice Co.; Kalustyan's; Oaktown Spice Shop
Vinegar: Tart Vinegar

HOUSEWARES

Ceramics: 1690 Store; ANK Ceramics; Eric Bonnin Ceramics; Grandmont Street; Heath Ceramics; Helen Levi Ceramics; MARCH San Francisco; MHCeramics; Mt. Washington Pottery; Poterie Barbotine; Sarah Kersten Studio; Zoe Dering
Enamelware: Falcon Enamelware
Linens: Block Shop Textiles; Gregory Parkinson; MADRE Linen; SUAY; TABLE
Pewter: Salter House
Puglian splatterware: MARCH San Francisco; Francesco Fasano; Tancredi & Morgen
Venetian glassware: Carlo Scarpa for Venini; R+D.Lab; Striulli Vetri d'Arte
Woodwork: The Boardsmith; Courtney Petley; Elise McLauchlan

TOOLS

Carbon-steel pans: Blanc Creatives
Knives: Everett Noel Knives; Hida Tool & Hardware
Pasta-making tools: q.b. Cucina
Wine bottles and corkers: Oak Barrel Winecraft

acknowledgements

This book would not exist without the friendship, hard work, care, support, and inspiration the following people have offered me:

- Ilana Alperstein
- Karim Arem
- Mansour Arem
- Paige Arnett
- Anandamayi Arnold
- Josey Baker
- Steven Barclay
- Rebecca Berlant
- Felicity Blunt
- Kate Bolen
- Richard Booth
- Aya Brackett
- Laurel Braitman
- Flo Braker
- Milena Brown
- Greta Caruso
- Sam and Sam Clark
- Ama Codjoe
- Ken Concepcion
- Steve Costa
- Matthew Craven
- Chris Crawford
- Corey Creasey
- Miya and Niko Creasey
- Jenny Davis
- Mark Davis
- Terry Deal
- Cara DeFabio
- Vega Michelle DeFabio
- Teodoro Diaz-Rodriguez, Jr.
- Brooke Ehrlich
- Richard Elman
- Alice Erb
- Susan Eslick
- Jennifer Feltham
- Eliza Fischer
- Jonathan Safran Foer
- Rose Fox
- Sally Franklin
- Mara Greenaway
- Erica Gonzalez
- Twilight Greenaway
- Gina Guilinger
- Claire Gutierrez
- Ebony Haight
- Sam Hamilton
- Julia Harrison
- Hrishikesh Hirway
- Emily Isayeff
- Robbie Jeanne
- Alex Johnson
- Lillian Kang
- Jayne Yaffe Kemp
- Azraf Khan
- Jessica Koslow
- Kevin Kwan
- Cynthia Lasky
- Jennifer Latham
- Gary Lee
- Kate Levinson
- Justin Limoges
- Marlow CG Limoges
- Jaylen Lopez
- Wendy MacNaughton
- Alexis Madrigal
- Orion and Flora Madrigal
- Josh Maricich
- Amalia Mariño
- Amanda Marsalis
- Alice Medrich
- Thao Nguyen
- Pasha Nosrat
- Loren Noveck
- Zora O'Neill
- Yotam Ottolenghi
- Sarit Packer
- Gregory Parkinson
- Adriano Pedreira
- Laurie Ellen Pellicano
- Lori Podraza
- Michelle Polzine
- Kimbo Prichard
- Tejal Rao
- Alison Rich
- Sarah Rich
- David Riland
- Tess Rossi
- Celia Sack
- David Sangalli
- Vanessa Santos
- Kate Slate
- Kari Stuart
- Lexi Sparrow
- Itamar Srulovich
- Emily Su-Bowden
- Mei Mei Su-Bowden
- Carrie Sullivan
- Bridget Sweet
- Adriana Taranta
- Dana Velden
- Alvaro Villanueva
- Andy Ward
- Emily Weinstein
- Amy Wilson
- Stacey Witcraft
- Malia Wollan
- Hannah Wright
- Rebecca Zaharia

index

a

Adas Polo, 158
agave syrup
   Cucumber-Chia Agua Fresca, 222
   Peanut-Ginger Dressing, 176
   Salty Lemon Soda, 81
   Sesame-Soy Dressing, 174–76
   Spicy Meyer Lemon Relish, 81
   Sweet and Spicy Courgette with Meyer Lemon, 241
   Tahini Sbagliato, 132–34
Aioli, 236
   in **Runner Beans with Tomatoes and Aioli**, 236
   in **Summer Salad Matrix**, 214–17
   in **Tomato Salad Matrix**, 247
almonds
   Roasted Almonds with Fried Sage, 98
   Roasted Vegetable Salad Matrix, 272–75
   Sarit's Ashura Cereal, 146–48
   toasting, 37
Amy's Bacon Waffles, 393
Anaheim chillies
   Calabrian Chilli Crisp, 56–59
   Teo's Brisket Chivis, 346–48
ancho chillies
   Tortilla Soup, 295–96
anchovy fillets
   Classic Caesar, 128
   Fava's Caesar, 128–31
   Sautéed Greens, 258
   Spicy Tuna Pantry Pasta, 177–79
apples
   Autumn Chicory Salad, 118
   Shaved Fennel and Apple Salad, 124
Apricot and Noyau Jam, 433–37
   with **Ricotta Custard Pancakes**, 145
apricot kernels
   Noyau Extract, 438
apricots, dried
   Chicken Braised with Apricots and Harissa, 302–5
   Lamb Tagine, 305

apricots, fresh
   Apricot and Noyau Jam, 433–37
   Apricot Clafoutis, 426
aquafaba
   about, 115
   Creamy Lemon-Miso Dressing, 122–24
   Creamy Oregano Dressing, 125–27
   Fava's Caesar, 128–31
   Summer Salad Matrix, 214–17
Arroz Rojo, 154
Arroz Verde, 154
Artichoke Hearts and Goat's Cheese, Butter Beans Braised with, 162
asparagus
   Blanched Asparagus, 201
   Boiled Spring Vegetable Matrix, 208–11
   preparing, 201
   sautéing, 199
   Spring Chopped Salad, 124
   Stewed Spring Vegetables, 207
   Vegetable Extravaganza, 176
   Warm Asparagus Vinaigrette, 201
aubergine
   Grilled Aubergines, 223
   Italian-Style Marinated Aubergines, 225
   preparing, 223
   Roasted Aubergines, 223
   Roasted Aubergine Parmesan, 225
   sautéing, 199
   Summer Salad Matrix, 214–17
   Whipped Baba Ghanoush, 100–102
Autumn Chicory Salad, 118
Autumn Chopped Salad, 137
avocados
   Autumn Chopped Salad, 137
   Avocado Toast, 94
   California Citrus Salad, 266
   Summer Salad Matrix, 214–17

b

bacon
   Amy's Bacon Waffles, 393
   Sautéed Greens, 258
Baghali Polo, 158
Baked Goat's Cheese Salad, 75

Banana Bread, Sparkling, 414
banana leaves
   Slow-Cooked Salmon, 337–41
Barbari Focaccia, 377–78
Basic Crispy Rice, 155–58
   in **Adas Polo**, 158
   in **Baghali Polo**, 158
   in **Persian-Style Herbed Rice**, 158
   in **Saffron-Flecked Crispy Rice**, 156
basil
   Basil Pesto, 67
   Broad Bean Crostini, 202
   Confit of Little Tomatoes, 242
   Courgette and Pesto Lasagne, 358
   Courgette Antipasto, 241
   Creamy Corn and Squash Sauté, 213
   Creamy One-Pot Pasta with Ricotta and Peas, 182
   Creamy Spinach Lasagne, 355–58
   Creamy Tomato and Goat's Cheese Pasta, 244
   Crunchy Shaved Pepper Salad, 230
   Herb Salad, 218
   Marinated Shell Bean Salad, 235
   Pane Criminale, 329
   Peperonata, 230
   Roasted Aubergine Parmesan, 225
   Roasted Tomato Sauce, 244
   Runner Beans with Tomatoes and Aioli, 236
   Sugar Snap Pea Chopped Salad, 205
   Sweet and Spicy Courgette with Meyer Lemon, 241
   Sweet Pepper Antipasto, 229
   Three-Bean Salad, 238
Basil Pesto, 67
   in **Roasted Vegetable Salad Matrix**, 272–75
   in **Courgette and Pesto Lasagne**, 358
basmati rice
   about, 150
   Adas Polo, 158
   Arroz Rojo, 154
   Arroz Verde, 154
   Baghali Polo, 158
   Basic Crispy Rice, 155–58
   Persian-Style Herbed Rice, 158
   Saffron-Flecked Crispy Rice, 156
   water ratios, 153

beans
  Adas Polo, 158
  Baghali Polo, 158
  Broad Bean and Preserved Meyer Lemon Dip, 202
  Butter Beans Braised with Artichoke Hearts and Goat's Cheese, 162
  Classic Chopped Salad, 127
  cooking, 159
  Cuban-Style Black Beans, 162
  Frijoles con Todo, 161
  Marinated Gigante Beans, 161
  Marinated Shell Bean Salad, 235
  Pasta with Broad Beans and Mint, 202
  Refried Beans, 161
  Roasted Vegetable Salad Matrix, 272–75
  soaking, 159
  Spring Salad with Broad Beans, 202
  Stewed Spring Vegetables, 207
  substitutions, 39
  Summer Salad Matrix, 214–17
  White Bean, Celery, and Tuna Salad, 127
  White Bean Stew with Tomatoes and Saffron, 186
  See also chickpeas; shell beans; string beans
Béchamel, 360
  in Courgette and Pesto Lasagne, 358
  in Creamy Spinach Lasagne, 355–58
  in Lasagne al Sugo, 364–65
  in Winter Squash Lasagne, 358
beef
  Lazy Sugo, 361–63
  Teo's Brisket Chivis, 346–48
beetroot
  Marinated Roast Beetroot, 248
  Roasted Vegetable Salad Matrix, 272–75
  Vibrant Beetroot Labne, 248
biscuits
  Laurie Ellen's Cardamom Shortbread, 417–18
black beans
  Cuban-Style Black Beans, 162
  Refried Beans, 161
Blanched Asparagus, 201
Blanched Greens, 256
Blanched String Beans, 236

Boiled Spring Vegetable Matrix, 208–11
Boiled Summer Squash, 239
Braised Kale with Feta-Style Cheese and Chillies, 258–59
breads
  Barbari Focaccia, 377–78
  Broad Bean Crostini, 202
  Chewy Sesame Flatbreads, 388–90
  croutons, 37–38
  Fluffy Pitta Pockets, 385–87
  Oat and Honey Bread Rolls, 381–84
  Olive Oil–Fried Bread, 94
  Pane Criminale, 329
  panzanella, 245
  panzanella with torn croutons, 247
  Sky-High Focaccia, 372–76
  Sparkling Banana Bread, 414
  in Summer Salad Matrix, 214–17
  tearing, 32
Bright Pickled Onions, 52
  in California Citrus Salad, 266
  in Chickpea Salad with Cucumbers and Dill, 163
  in Classic Egg Salad, 149
  in Crunchy Shaved Pepper Salad, 230
  in Greek Salad with Farro and Souvlaki-ish Chicken Skewers, 127
  in Grilled Summer Salad, 229–30
  in panzanella with torn croutons, 247
  in Roasted Vegetable Salad Matrix, 272–75
  in Sicilian Citrus Salad, 266
  substitutions, 39
  in Summer Salad Matrix, 214–17
  in Tomato Salad Matrix, 247
  in Torn Charred Courgette with Chillies and Mint, 239–41
  in White Bean, Celery, and Tuna Salad, 127
broad beans
  Baghali Polo, 158
  Boiled Spring Vegetable Matrix, 208–11
  Broad Beans and Preserved Meyer Lemon Dip, 202
  Broad Bean Crostini, 202
  Pasta with Broad Beans and Mint, 202
  preparing, 202
  Spring Salad with Broad Beans, 202

Stewed Spring Vegetables, 207
broccoli
  Dark-Roasted Broccoli, 251
  Long-Cooked Broccoli, 252
  Pasta with Long-Cooked Broccoli, 252
  Roasted Vegetable Salad Matrix, 272–75
  sautéing, 199
  shopping for, 251
  stalks, 251
  Vegetable Extravaganza, 176
brown rice
  about, 151
  Brown Rice Bowl, 121
  water ratios, 153
Brown Sugar, Strawberries with Soured Cream and, 422
Buckwheat Waffles, 393
Burnt Honey Hot Fudge, 441
Burnt Honey Icing, 410
burrata
  Boiled Spring Vegetable Matrix, 208–11
  Roasted Vegetable Salad Matrix, 272–75
  Summer Salad Matrix, 214–17
  in Tomato Salad Matrix, 247
butter
  Béchamel, 360
  Cacio e Pepe Butter, 181
  Cardamom Ghee, 61–62
  Dungeness Crab with Calabrian Chilli Butter, 342–43
  Ghee, 62
  Prawns with Calabrian Chilli Butter, 343
  Winter Squash and Green Curry Soup, 171
Butter Beans Braised with Artichoke Hearts and Goat's Cheese, 162
buttermilk
  Joojeh Kabob Roast Chicken, 284–86
  Sparkling Banana Bread, 414
  Yellow Buttermilk Cake, 402–6

C

cabbage
  Chicken Kabob Wraps, 134
  Crunchy Cabbage Slaw, 121
  Gingery Roasted Cabbage Wedges, 259
  sautéing, 199

index • 447

Spring Chopped Salad, 124
Cacio e Pepe Butter, 181
   on Corn on the Cob, 213
Cacio e Pepe Farro, 181
cakes
   Confetti Cake, 406
   One-Bowl Chocolate Cake, 409–10
   Preserved Lemon and Labne Cake, 413
   Russian Honey Icebox Cake, 399–401
   Sparkling Banana Bread, 414
   Yellow Buttermilk Cake, 402–6
Calabrian Chilli Crisp, 56–59
   in Boiled Spring Vegetable Matrix, 208–11
   in Braised Kale with Feta-Style Cheese and Chillies, 258–59
   in Charred Courgettes with Labne, 239
   in Chilli Crisp Chicken Salad, 313
   on Corn on the Cob, 213
   in Peanut-Ginger Dressing, 176
   in Sesame-Soy Dressing, 174–76
   in Smashed Cucumber Salad, 221–22
   in Summer Salad Matrix, 214–17
   in Sweet and Spicy Winter Squash, 271
Calabrian chilli purée
   about, 29
   Dungeness Crab with Calabrian Chilli Butter, 342–43
   Prawns with Calabrian Chilli Butter, 343
   Sautéed Greens, 256–58
   Spicy Gem Caesar with Golden Panko, 131
   Stewed Clams with Tomatoes and Saffron, 185–86
   Torn Charred Courgettes with Chillies and Mint, 239–41
Calabrian chillies
   about, 29
   Bright Pickled Onions, 52
   Calabrian Chilli Crisp, 56–59
   Dungeness Crab with Calabrian Chilli Butter, 342–43
   Marinated Feta, 71–72
   substitutions, 39
California Citrus Salad, 266
Calrose rice, about, 150
cardamom
   Cardamom Ghee, 61–62
   Golden Chicken Soup, 293–94

Laurie Ellen's Cardamom Shortbread, 417–18
Cardamom Ghee, 61–62
   in Chicken Braised with Apricots and Harissa, 302–5
   with Dark-Roasted Carrots, 255
   in Marion's Yeasted Waffles, 391–93
   in Ricotta Custard Pancakes, 145
   substitutions, 39
carrots
   Chicken Braised with Apricots and Harissa, 302–5
   Chicken Stock, 314–15
   Crunchy Cabbage Slaw, 121
   Curried Carrot and Coconut Soup, 169–71
   Dark-Roasted Carrots, 255
   Golden Chicken Soup, 293–94
   Kid Crudités, 91
   Lamb Tagine, 305
   Mark's Giardiniera, 69–70
   Roasted Vegetable Salad Matrix, 272–75
   Shaved Carrot Salad, 255
   Vegetable Extravaganza, 176
cauliflower
   Dark-Roasted Cauliflower, 251
   Mark's Giardiniera, 69–70
   Roasted Vegetable Salad Matrix, 272–75
   sautéing, 199
   shopping for, 251
celery
   Autumn Chopped Salad, 137
   Chicken Stock, 314–15
   Classic Egg Salad, 149
   Creamy Tomato Soup, 172–73
   Golden Chicken Soup, 293–94
   Mark's Giardiniera, 69–70
   Roasted Vegetable Salad Matrix, 272–75
   Shaved Fennel and Apple Salad, 124
   Warm Potato Salad, 263
   White Bean, Celery, and Tuna Salad, 127
Cereal, Sarit's Ashura, 146–48
Charred Courgettes with Labne, 239
Charred Sweet Potatoes, 268
cheese
   Autumn Chicory Salad, 118
   Braised Kale with Feta-Style Cheese and Chillies, 258–59

Butter Beans Braised with Artichoke Hearts and Goat's Cheese, 162
Chickpea Salad with Cucumbers and Dill, 163
Classic Chopped Salad, 127
Courgette and Pesto Lasagne, 358
Creamy Corn and Squash Sauté, 213
Creamy Spinach Lasagne, 355–58
Creamy Tomato and Goat's Cheese Pasta, 244
Crispy Open-Faced Quesadillas, 168
crumbling, 35
Elote-Style Salad, 213
Kuku-kopita, 330–33
Lasagne al Sugo, 364–65
Marinated Feta, 71–72
Marinated Goat's Cheese, 74–75
Roasted Aubergine Parmesan, 225
Roasted Vegetable Salad Matrix, 272–75
Roquefort Dressing, 135–37
Shaved Fennel and Apple Salad, 124
Sugar Snap Pea Chopped Salad, 205
Summer Salad Matrix, 214–17
tearing, 32
Teo's Brisket Chivis, 346–48
See also cream cheese; Parmesan; ricotta
Cherry Clafoutis, 425–26
Chewy Sesame Flatbreads, 388–90
chia seeds
   Cucumber-Chia Agua Fresca, 222
chicken
   Chicken Braised with Apricots and Harissa, 302–5
   Chicken Kabob Wraps, 134
   Chicken Stock, 314–15
   Chicken Thigh Schnitzel, 309–10
   Chilli Crisp Chicken Salad, 313
   Chilli Crisp Chicken Salad Sandwiches, 313
   Chivi Spice Chicken Thighs, 298–99
   Crunchy and Refreshing Green Salad, 118
   Fried Chicken Sandwiches, 310
   Golden Chicken Soup, 293–94

Greek Salad with Farro and
  Souvlaki-ish Chicken
  Skewers, 127
Joojeh Kabob Roast
  Chicken, 284–86
Joojeh Kabobs, 286
One-Pot Chicken with Giant
  Couscous and Preserved
  Lemon, 290–91
Piri Piri Chicken, 287–89
Roast Chicken and Potato
  Dinner, 265
Roast Chicken with Bread
  Salad, 94
salting, 281
shopping for, 281
Shoyu Chicken, 300–301
Shoyu Chicken Wings, 301
Simple Chicken Thighs, 306–7
Simple Spatchcocked
  Chicken, 282–83
Souvlaki-ish Chicken Thighs, 307
Teriyaki-ish Chicken Thighs, 306–7
Tex-Mex Thighs, 307
Tortilla Soup, 295–96
Chicken Stock, 314–15
  about, 30
  in Arroz Rojo, 154
  in Arroz Verde, 154
  Chicken Braised with Apricots
    and Harissa, 302–5
  in Chivi Spice Chicken
    Thighs, 298–99
  in Coconut-Lemongrass Soup with
    Chickpeas, 167
  in Creamy Tomato Soup, 172–73
  in Curried Carrot and Coconut
    Soup, 169–71
  in Lamb Tagine, 305
  in Winter Squash and Green Curry
    Soup, 171
Chicken Thigh Schnitzel, 309–10
  in Brown Rice Bowl, 121
  with Chicories Caesar with
    Focaccia Croutons, 310
  with Crunchy Cabbage Slaw, 310
  with Simple Soba Salad, 310
chickpeas
  aquafaba, 115
  Chickpea Salad with Cucumbers
    and Dill, 163
  Classic Chopped Salad, 127
  Coconut-Lemongrass Soup with
    Chickpeas, 167
  Crispy Snacking Chickpeas, 165

Roasted Vegetable Salad
  Matrix, 272–75
soaking, 159
Spring Chopped Salad, 124
Stewy Harissa Chickpeas with
  Winter Squash, 166
substitutions, 39
chicories
  Chicories Caesar with Focaccia
    Croutons, 131
  Roasted Vegetable Salad
    Matrix, 272–75
Chilli Crisp Chicken Salad, 313
Chilli Crisp Chicken Salad
  Sandwiches, 313
Chilli Vinegar, 76
  in Green Sauce, 51
  in Shaved Carrot Salad, 255
  in Spicy Whipped Tahini, 64
  substitutions, 39
  in Whipped Baba
    Ghanoush, 100–102
  in White Bean, Celery, and Tuna
    Salad, 127
chillies de árbol
  Curried Carrot and Coconut
    Soup, 169–71
  Marinated Feta, 71–72
  Prawns with Calabrian Chilli
    Butter, 343
Chilled Melon with Mint, 226
chipotle peppers in adobo sauce
  Chivi Spice Chicken
    Thighs, 298–99
  Tortilla Soup, 295–96
chives
  Broad Bean Crostini, 202
  Herb Salad, 218
  Miso and Labne Onion Dip, 93
  Pane Criminale, 329
  Spring Salad with Fava Beans, 202
Chivi Spice Chicken Thighs,
  298–99
chocolate
  about, 31
  Burnt Honey Hot Fudge, 441
  One-Bowl Chocolate Cake, 409–10
  Soured Cream Fudge Icing, 407
cider vinegar
  Bright Pickled Onions, 52
  Chilli Vinegar, 76
  Creamy Lemon-Miso
    Dressing, 122–24
  Pickled Thai Chillies, 76
  Tahini Sbagliato, 132–34

citrus fruits
  California Citrus Salad, 266
  preparing, 266
  Preserved Meyer Lemon Paste, 79
  Sicilian Citrus Salad, 266
  Vin d'Orange, 106–8
  Winter Citrus Salad, 266
  zesting, 28–29
Clams, Stewed, with Tomatoes and
  Saffron, 185–86
Classic Caesar, 128
Classic Egg Salad, 149
Classic Chopped Salad, 127
cocoa, about, 31. *See also* chocolate
coconut chips/flakes
  Curried Carrot and Coconut
    Soup, 169–71
  Thai Pomelo Salad, 266
coconut milk/cream
  Coconut Rice, 154
  Coconut-Lemongrass Soup with
    Chickpeas, 167
  Curried Carrot and Coconut
    Soup, 169–71
  Winter Squash and Green Curry
    Soup, 171
cod
  Saffron and Tomato Fish Stew, 186
  Slow-Cooked Salmon
    (variation), 341
  Tomato-Poached Fish, 244
coffee
  One-Bowl Chocolate Cake,
    409–10
condiments
  Calabrian Chilli Crisp, 56–59
  Cucumber and Herb Labne, 48
  Garlic and Herb Labne, 48
  Green Sauce, 51
  Mark's Giardiniera, 69–70
  Shallot and Spring Onion
    Labne, 48
  Spicy Meyer Lemon Relish, 81
  Spicy Whipped Tahini, 64
  Toasty Whipped Tahini, 64
  Whipped Green Tahini, 64
  Whipped Tahini, 63–64
Confetti Cake, 406
Confit of Little Tomatoes, 242
  in Tomato Salad Matrix, 247
coriander
  Arroz Verde, 154
  Brown Rice Bowl, 121
  Chicken Braised with Apricots
    and Harissa, 302–5

coriander (cont'd):
    Chilli Crisp Chicken Salad, 313
    Chivi Spice Chicken Thighs, 298–99
    Creamy Corn and Squash Sauté, 213
    Crunchy and Refreshing Green Salad, 118
    Crunchy Cabbage Slaw, 121
    Cucumber and Herb Labne, 48
    Elote-Style Salad, 213
    Garlic and Herb Labne, 48
    Green Sauce, 51
    Grilled Summer Salad, 229–30
    Herb Salad, 218
    Kuku-kopita, 330–33
    Lamb Tagine, 305
    Persian-Style Herbed Rice, 158
    Quick Cucumber Salad, 221
    Shakshuka, 244
    Shaved Carrot Salad, 255
    Simple Soba Salad, 174–76
    Smashed Cucumber Salad, 221–22
    Spicy Meyer Lemon Relish, 81
    Spring Chopped Salad, 124
    Sweet and Spicy Courgettes with Meyer Lemon, 241
    Tahini Sbagliato, 132–34
    Thai Pomelo Salad, 266
    Tortilla Soup, 295–96
corn
    Corn on the Cob, 213
    Corn Salad, 213
    Creamy Corn and Squash Sauté, 213
    Elote-Style Salad, 213
    Grilled Summer Salad, 229–30
    preparing, 213
    Sautéed Corn, 213
    sautéing, 199
    Summer Salad Matrix, 214–17
    Vegetable Extravaganza, 176
courgettes
    Boiled Summer Squash, 239
    Charred Courgettes with Labne, 239
    Courgette and Pesto Lasagne, 358
    Courgette Antipasto, 241 in Summer Salad Matrix, 214–17
    Grilled Summer Squash, 239
    Sweet and Spicy Courgettes with Meyer Lemon, 241
    Torn Charred Courgettes with Chillies and Mint, 239–41
    in Three-Bean Salad, 238

    in White Bean, Celery, and Tuna Salad, 127
Crab, Dungeness, with Calabrian Chilli Butter, 342–43
cream
    Burnt Honey Hot Fudge, 441
    Creamy Tomato Soup, 172–73
    Russian Honey Icebox Cake, 399–401
    Whipped Vanilla Cream, 410
cream cheese
    Cream Cheese Icing, 410
    Kuku-kopita, 330–33
Creamy Corn and Squash Sauté, 213
Creamy Lemon-Miso Dressing, 122–24
    in Boiled Spring Vegetable Matrix, 208–11
    with Dark-Roasted Carrots, 255
    in Grilled Summer Salad, 229–30
    in Roasted Vegetable Salad Matrix, 272–75
    in Shaved Fennel and Apple Salad, 124
    in Sugar Snap Pea Chopped Salad, 205
    in Spring Chopped Salad, 124
    in Spring Salad with Broad Beans, 202
    in Summer Salad Matrix, 214–17
Creamy One-Pot Pasta with Ricotta and Peas, 182
Creamy Oregano Dressing, 125–27
    in Boiled Spring Vegetable Matrix, 208–11
    in Chickpea Salad with Cucumbers and Dill, 163
    in Classic Chopped Salad, 127
    in Crunchy Shaved Pepper Salad, 230
    with Dark-Roasted Carrots, 255
    in Greek Salad with Farro and Souvlaki-ish Chicken Skewers, 127
    in Roasted Vegetable Salad Matrix, 272–75
    in Souvlaki-ish Chicken Thighs, 307
Creamy Sesame-Ginger Dressing, 119–21
    in Brown Rice Bowl, 121
    in Crunchy Cabbage Slaw, 121
    in Roasted Vegetable Salad Matrix, 272–75

    in Steamed Kabocha with Sesame-Ginger Dressing, 271
    in Summer Salad Matrix, 214–17
Creamy Spinach Lasagne, 355–58
Creamy Tomato and Goat's Cheese Pasta, 244
Creamy Tomato Soup, 172–73
crème fraîche
    Creamy Corn and Squash Sauté, 213
    Crème Fraîche Devilled Eggs, 97
    Summer Salad Matrix, 214–17
Crisp Hash Browns, 264
Crispy Fried Shallots, 55
    in Boiled Spring Vegetable Matrix, 208–11
    in Butter Beans Braised with Artichoke Hearts and Goat's Cheese, 162
    in Roasted Vegetable Salad Matrix, 272–75
    in Shallot and Spring Onion Labne, 48
    in String Beans with Ginger and Shallots, 238
    in Summer Salad Matrix, 214–17
Crispy Open-Faced Quesadillas, 168
Crispy Snacking Chickpeas, 165
    in Roasted Vegetable Salad Matrix, 272–75
croutons
    Chicories Caesar with Focaccia Croutons, 131
    making, 37–38
    panzanella with torn croutons, 247
    in Roasted Vegetable Salad Matrix, 272–75
    Spring Chopped Salad, 124
    Spring Salad with Broad Beans, 202
    Summer Salad Matrix, 214–17
Crudités, Kid, 91
Crunchy and Refreshing Green Salad, 118
Crunchy Cabbage Slaw, 121
Crunchy Shaved Pepper Salad, 230
Cuban-Style Black Beans, 162
cucumbers
    Chicken Kabob Wraps, 134
    Chickpea Salad with Cucumbers and Dill, 163
    Chilli Crisp Chicken Salad Sandwiches, 313
    Cucumber and Herb Labne, 48
    Cucumber-Chia Agua Fresca, 222

Greek Salad with Farro and
    Souvlaki-ish Chicken
    Skewers, 127
Grilled Summer Salad, 229–30
Kid Crudités, 91
preparing, 221
Quick Cucumber Salad, 221
Shirazi salad, 247
Smashed Cucumber Salad, 221–22
Spring Chopped Salad, 124
Summer Salad Matrix, 214–17
Vegetable Extravaganza, 176
Cupcakes, Yellow, 406
currants
    Autumn Chopped Salad, 137
    Roasted Vegetable Salad
        Matrix, 272–75
    Sautéed Greens, 256–58
curry paste
    Curried Carrot and Coconut
        Soup, 169–71
    Winter Squash and Green Curry
        Soup, 171

d

Dark-Roasted Broccoli, 251
Dark-Roasted Carrots, 255
Dark-Roasted Cauliflower, 251
Dark-Roasted Winter Squash, 271
    in Sweet and Spicy Winter
        Squash, 271
dates. See Medjool dates
delicata squash, about, 271
desserts
    Apricot Clafoutis, 426
    Burnt Honey Hot Fudge, 441
    Cherry Clafoutis, 425–26
    Confetti Cake, 406
    Cream Cheese Icing, 410
    Laurie Ellen's Cardamom
        Shortbread, 417–18
    One-Bowl Chocolate Cake, 409–10
    Passion Fruit Curd, 427–29
    Passion Fruit Parfaits, 429
    Preserved Lemon and Labne
        Cake, 413
    Pressure Cooker Dulce de
        Leche, 432
    Russian Honey Icebox
        Cake, 399–401
    Soured Cream Fudge Icing, 407
    Sparkling Banana Bread, 414
    Strawberries with Soured Cream
        and Brown Sugar, 422

Vanilla Bean Flan, 419–21
Vanilla Bean Rice Pudding, 430
Yellow Buttermilk Cake, 402–6
Yellow Cupcakes, 406
Dijon mustard
    Classic Caesar, 128
    Classic Egg Salad, 149
    Creamy Lemon-Miso
        Dressing, 122–24
    Creamy Oregano Dressing, 125–27
    Fava's Caesar, 128–31
    Green Sauce, 51
    House Dressing, 117–18
dill
    Baghali Polo, 158
    Broad Bean and Preserved Meyer
        Lemon Dip, 202
    Broad Bean Crostini, 202
    Chickpea Salad with Cucumbers
        and Dill, 163
    Classic Egg Salad, 149
    Crunchy and Refreshing Green
        Salad, 118
    Cucumber and Herb Labne, 48
    Garlic and Herb Labne, 48
    Greek Salad with Farro and
        Souvlaki-ish Chicken
        Skewers, 127
    Herb Salad, 218
    Kuku-kopita, 330–33
    Persian-Style Herbed Rice, 158
    Quick Cucumber Salad, 221
    Spring Salad with Broad
        Beans, 202
    Sweet and Spicy Courgettes with
        Meyer Lemon, 241
    Tahini Sbagliato, 132–34
    Warm Potato Salad, 263
dinner rituals, creating, 323–25
dips and spreads
    Apricot and Noyau Jam, 433–37
    Broad Bean and Preserved Meyer
        Lemon Dip, 202
    Cucumber and Herb Labne, 48
    Garlic and Herb Labne, 48
    Miso and Labne Onion Dip, 93
    Pressure Cooker Dulce de
        Leche, 432
    Shallot and Spring Onion
        Labne, 48
    Spicy Whipped Tahini, 64
    spooning and smearing, 35–36
    Toasty Whipped Tahini, 64
    Vibrant Beetroot Labne, 248
    Whipped Baba Ghanoush, 100–102

    Whipped Green Tahini, 64
    Whipped Tahini, 63–64
dressings
    Classic Caesar, 128
    Creamy Lemon-Miso
        Dressing, 122–24
    Creamy Oregano Dressing,
        125–27
    Creamy Sesame-Ginger
        Dressing, 119–21
    Fava's Caesar, 128–31
    House Dressing, 117–18
    Peanut-Ginger Dressing, 176
    Roquefort Dressing, 135–37
    Sesame-Soy Dressing, 174–76
    Tahini Sbagliato, 132–34
drinks
    Cucumber-Chia Agua Fresca, 222
    Salty Lemon Soda, 81
    Sekanjebin (Sweet and Sour Mint
        Shrub), 105
    Vin de Pamplemousse, 108
    Vin d'Orange, 106–8
Dungeness Crab with Calabrian
    Chilli Butter, 342–43

e

eggs
    bringing to room temperature, 38
    Crème Fraîche Devilled Eggs, 97
    Passion Fruit Curd, 427–29
    7½-Minute Eggs, 149
    Shakshuka, 244
    10-Minute Eggs, 149
Elote-Style Salad, 213
extra-virgin olive oil, about, 25–26

f

farro
    Cacio e Pepe Farro, 181
    Greek Salad with Farro and
        Souvlaki-ish Chicken
        Skewers, 127
    Kale and Farro Caesar Salad, 131
    Roasted Vegetable Salad
        Matrix, 272–75
fattoush, 211, 245, 247
Fava's Caesar, 128–31
    in Chicories Caesar with Focaccia
        Croutons, 131
    in Kale and Farro Caesar Salad, 131
    in Spicy Gem Caesar with Golden
        Panko, 131

fennel
  Crunchy and Refreshing Green Salad, 118
  Mark's Giardiniera, 69–70
  Roasted Vegetable Salad Matrix, 272–75
  sautéing, 199
  Shaved Fennel and Apple Salad, 124
  Snap Pea Chopped Salad, 205
feta-style cheese
  Braised Kale with Feta-Style Cheese and Chillies, 258–59
  Chickpea Salad with Cucumbers and Dill, 163
  Creamy Corn and Squash Sauté, 213
  Kuku-kopita, 330–33
  Marinated Feta, 71–72
  Marinated Shell Bean Salad, 235
  Summer Salad Matrix, 214–17
fig leaves
  Slow-Cooked Salmon, 337–41
filo pastry
  Kuku-kopita, 330–33
fish
  Saffron and Tomato Fish Stew, 186
  Slow-Cooked Salmon, 337–41
  Spicy Tuna Pantry Pasta, 177–79
  Tomato-Poached Fish, 244
  White Bean, Celery, and Tuna Salad, 127
fish sauce
  Creamy Tomato and Goat's Cheese Pasta, 244
  Curried Carrot and Coconut Soup, 169–71
  Thai Pomelo Salad, 266
  Tomato-Poached Fish, 244
flaky salt, about, 25
Flame-Roasted Peppers, 229
Flan, Vanilla Bean, 419–21
Flatbreads, Chewy Sesame, 388–90
Fluffiest Mashed Potatoes, 265
Fluffy Pitta Pockets, 385–87
  in **Chicken Kabob Wraps**, 134
  in croutons, 37–38
  with **Broad Bean and Preserved Meyer Lemon Dip**, 202
Fluffy Pork Meatballs, 335–36
Fluffy Steamed Sweet Potatoes, 268
Forever Popcorn, 88–90
Fresh Pasta Sheets, 349–54
  in **Creamy Spinach Lasagne**, 355–58
  in **Lasagne al Sugo**, 364–65
  in **Courgette and Pesto Lasagne**, 358

  in **Winter Squash Lasagne**, 358
Fresno chillies
  Piri Piri Chicken, 287–89
Fried Chicken Sandwiches, 310
Frijoles con Todo, 161

g

garlic
  about, 26, 28
  Braised Kale with Feta-Style Cheese and Chillies, 258–59
  Calabrian Chilli Crisp, 56–59
  Chicken Braised with Apricots and Harissa, 302–5
  Chicken Stock, 314–15
  Chivi Spice Chicken Thighs, 298–99
  Confit of Little Tomatoes, 242
  Creamy Sesame-Ginger Dressing, 119–21
  Garlic and Herb Labne, 48
  Golden Chicken Soup, 293–94
  Lamb Tagine, 305
  One-Pot Chicken with Giant Couscous and Preserved Lemon, 290–91
  Pane Criminale, 329
  Roasted Tomato Sauce, 244
  Shoyu Chicken, 300–301
  Simple Tomato Sauce, 359
  Summer Salad Matrix, 214–17
  Teo's Brisket Chivis, 346–48
  Tortilla Soup, 295–96
Garlic and Herb Labne, 48
  in **Boiled Spring Vegetable Matrix**, 208–11
  in **Broad Bean and Preserved Meyer Lemon Dip**, 202
  in **Charred Courgettes with Labne**, 239
  in **Roasted Vegetable Salad Matrix**, 272–75
  substitutions, 39
  in **Summer Salad Matrix**, 214–17
  in **Tomato Salad Matrix**, 247
  in **Vibrant Beetroot Labne**, 248
Ghee, 62
  in **Amy's Bacon Waffles**, 393
  in **Buckwheat Waffles**, 393
  Cardamom Ghee, 61–62
  in **Chewy Sesame Flatbreads**, 388–90
  in **Chicken Braised with Apricots and Harissa**, 302–5
  in **Lamb Tagine**, 305

  in **Marion's Yeasted Waffles**, 391–93
  in **Sautéed Greens**, 256–58
  in **Shaken Roast Potatoes**, 264
  substitutions, 39
  Giant Couscous and Preserved Lemon, One-Pot Chicken with, 290–91
  Giardiniera, Mark's, 69–70
ginger
  Coconut-Lemongrass Soup with Chickpeas, 167
  Creamy Sesame-Ginger Dressing, 119–21
  Curried Carrot and Coconut Soup, 169–71
  Gingery Roasted Cabbage Wedges, 259
  Golden Chicken Soup, 293–94
  Peanut-Ginger Dressing, 176
  Sesame-Soy Dressing, 174–76
  Shaved Carrot Salad, 255
  Shoyu Chicken, 300–301
  Smashed Cucumber Salad, 221–22
  Spicy Meyer Lemon Relish, 81
  String Beans with Ginger and Shallots, 238
  Summer Salad Matrix, 214–17
  Teriyaki-ish Chicken Thighs, 306–7
  Winter Squash and Green Curry Soup, 171
goat's cheese
  Butter Beans Braised with Artichoke Hearts and Goat's Cheese, 162
  Creamy Corn and Squash Sauté, 213
  Creamy Tomato and Goat's Cheese Pasta, 244
  Marinated Goat's Cheese, 74–75
  Marinated Shell Bean Salad, 235
  Summer Salad Matrix, 214–17
Golden Chicken Soup, 293–94
Gouda
  Roasted Vegetable Salad Matrix, 272–75
  Shaved Fennel and Apple Salad, 124
  Sugar Snap Pea Chopped Salad, 205
graham crackers
  Russian Honey Icebox Cake, 399–401
grapefruit
  California Citrus Salad, 266
  Sicilian Citrus Salad, 266
  Thai Pomelo Salad, 266
  Vin de Pamplemousse, 108

Winter Citrus Salad, 266
Greek Salad with Farro and Souvlaki-ish Chicken Skewers, 127
green coriander seeds
   about, 233
   Charred Courgettes with Labne, 239
   Green Coriander Vinegar, 233
   Green Coriander Vinegar, 233
     in **Whipped Green Tahini**, 64
Green Sauce, 51
   in **Boiled Spring Vegetable Matrix**, 208–11
   on **Corn on the Cob**, 213
   in **Creamy Corn and Squash Sauté**, 213
   in **Roasted Vegetable Salad Matrix**, 272–75
   in **Summer Salad Matrix**, 214–17
greens. *See* leafy greens; *specific greens*
Grilled Aubergines, 223
Grilled Summer Salad, 229–30
Grilled Summer Squash, 239
   in **Charred Courgettes with Labne**, 239
   in **Torn Charred Courgettes with Chillies and Mint**, 239–41
   in **Courgette Antipasto**, 241
guajillo chillies
   Calabrian Chilli Crisp, 56–59

h

haiga rice, about, 151, 153
halibut
   Saffron and Tomato Fish Stew, 186
   Slow-Roasted Salmon (variation), 341
   Tomato-Poached Fish, 244
Hand-Cut Noodles, 353–54
   in **Pasta al Sugo**, 363
harissa paste
   Chicken Braised with Apricots and Harissa, 302–5
   Lamb Tagine, 305
   Shakshuka, 244
   Stewy Harissa Chickpeas with Winter Squash, 166
Hash Browns, Crisp, 264
herbs, fresh
   about, 29
   Avocado Toast, 94
   in **Boiled Spring Vegetable Matrix**, 208–11
   Cucumber and Herb Labne, 48
   Garlic and Herb Labne, 48
   Herb Salad, 218

Pea Purée, 205
Roasted Vegetable Salad Matrix, 272–75
Shirazi salad, 113, 247
Summer Salad Matrix, 214–17
tearing, 32
Whipped Green Tahini, 64
Homemade Labne, 29
   in **Joojeh Kabob Roast Chicken**, 29
honey
   Burnt Honey Icing, 410
   Burnt Honey Hot Fudge, 441
   Creamy Sesame-Ginger Dressing, 119–21
   House Dressing, 117–18
   Oat and Honey Bread Rolls, 381–84
   Roasted Vegetable Salad Matrix, 272–75
   Russian Honey Icebox Cake, 399–401
   Shoyu Chicken, 300–301
   Sweet and Spicy Winter Squash, 271
Honeynut squash
   pie preparation, 271
   Stewy Harissa Chickpeas with Winter Squash, 166
   Winter Squash and Green Curry Soup, 171
House Dressing, 117–18
   in **Autumn Chicory Salad**, 118
   in **Baked Goat's Cheese Salad**, 75
   in **Boiled Spring Vegetable Matrix**, 208–11
   in **Crunchy and Refreshing Green Salad**, 118
   with **Dark-Roasted Carrots**, 255
   in **Herb Salad**, 218
   in **Roast Chicken with Bread Salad**, 94
   in **Roasted Vegetable Salad Matrix**, 272–75
   in **Runner Beans with Tomatoes and Aioli**, 236
   in **Summer Salad Matrix**, 214–17, 247
   in **Tomato Salad Matrix**, 247
   in **Warm Asparagus Vinaigrette**, 201
   in **Warm Potato Salad**, 263

i

Iceberg Slice, 137
icing
   Cream Cheese Icing, 410

Soured Cream Fudge Icing, 407
Italian-Style Marinated Aubergine, 225

j

jalapeños
   Arroz Verde, 154
   Chicken Kabob Wraps, 134
   Creamy Sesame-Ginger Dressing, 119–21
   Cuban-Style Black Beans, 162
   Summer Salad Matrix, 214–17
Jam, Apricot and Noyau, 433–37
jars, sterilising, 38
jasmine rice
   about, 150
   Coconut Rice, 154
   Vanilla Bean Rice Pudding, 430
   water ratios, 153
Joojeh Kabob Roast Chicken, 284–86
Joojeh Kabobs, 286
   in **Chicken Kabob Wraps**, 134

k

kabocha squash
   about, 271
   Steamed Kabocha with Sesame-Ginger Dressing, 271
Kalamata olives
   Greek Salad with Farro and Souvlaki-ish Chicken Skewers, 127
kale
   Braised Kale with Feta-Style Cheese and Chillies, 258–59
   Golden Chicken Soup, 293–94
   Kale and Farro Caesar Salad, 131
   sautéing, 199
Kamut
   Sarit's Ashura Cereal, 146–48
Kid Crudités, 91
kidney beans
   Classic Chopped Salad, 127
kitchen tools, 40–41
kosher salt, about, 25
Kuku-kopita, 330–33
kumquats
   Marinated Feta, 71–72

l

labne
   about, 29
   Basic Crispy Rice, 155–58

labne (cont'd):
   Charred Courgettes with Labne, 239
   Cucumber and Herb Labne, 48
   Garlic and Herb Labne, 48
   Homemade Labne, 29
   Miso and Labne Onion Dip, 93
   Preserved Lemon and Labne Cake, 413
   Shallot and Spring Onion Labne, 48
   Vibrant Beetroot Labne, 248
Lamb Tagine, 305
Lasagne al Sugo, 364–65
Laurie Ellen's Cardamom Shortbread, 417–18
   in Passion Fruit Parfaits, 429
Lazy Sugo, 361–63
   in Lasagne al Sugo, 364–65
   in Pasta al Sugo, 363
leafy greens
   Baked Goat's Cheese Salad, 75
   Blanched Greens, 256
   Sautéed Greens, 256–58
   sautéing, 199
   stripping, 256
   See also specific greens
leeks
   Kuku-kopita, 330–33
lemongrass
   Coconut-Lemongrass Soup with Chickpeas, 167
   Curried Carrot and Coconut Soup, 169–71
   Thai Pomelo Salad, 266
   Winter Squash and Green Curry Soup, 171
lemons, lemon juice, and lemon zest
   Aioli, 236
   Boiled Summer Squash, 239
   Braised Kale with Feta-Style Cheese and Chillies, 258–59
   Butter Beans Braised with Artichoke Hearts and Goat's Cheese, 162
   Chilli Crisp Chicken Salad, 313
   Classic Caesar, 128
   Creamy Lemon-Miso Dressing, 122–24
   Creamy Oregano Dressing, 125–27
   Creamy Sesame-Ginger Dressing, 119–21
   Dark-Roasted Broccoli, 251
   Dungeness Crab with Calabrian Chilli Butter, 342–43
   Fava's Caesar, 128–31
   Golden Chicken Soup, 293–94
   Green Sauce, 51
   Kale and Farro Caesar Salad, 131
   Long-Cooked Broccoli, 252
   Marinated Goat's Cheese, 74–75
   Marinated Shell Bean Salad, 235
   One-Pot Chicken with Giant Couscous and Preserved Lemon, 290–91
   Pea Purée, 205
   Prawns with Calabrian Chilli Butter, 343
   Preserved Lemon and Labne Cake, 413
   Preserved Meyer Lemon Paste, 79–81
   Spicy Meyer Lemon Relish, 81
   Spicy Tuna Pantry Pasta, 177–79
   Spicy Whipped Tahini, 64
   Stewed Spring Vegetables, 207
   Sweet and Spicy Courgettes with Meyer Lemon, 241
   Tahini Sbagliato, 132–34
   Toasty Whipped Tahini, 64
   Vin d'Orange, 106–8
   Warm Nocellara Olives, 87
   Whipped Baba Ghanoush, 100–102
   Whipped Green Tahini, 64
   Whipped Tahini, 63–64
   White Bean, Celery, and Tuna Salad, 127
   zesting, 28–29
lettuce
   Autumn Chopped Salad, 137
   Chicken Kabob Wraps, 134
   Classic Chopped Salad, 124
   Crunchy and Refreshing Green Salad, 118
   Iceberg Slice, 137
   Fried Chicken Sandwiches, 310
   Roasted Vegetable Salad Matrix, 272–75
   Spicy Gem Caesar with Golden Panko, 131
   Spring Chopped Salad, 124
   Spring Salad with Broad Beans, 202
   tearing, 32
limes and lime juice
   Chilled Melon with Mint, 226
   Cucumber-Chia Agua Fresca, 222
   Grilled Summer Salad, 229–30
   Joojeh Kabob Roast Chicken, 284–86
   Peanut-Ginger Dressing, 176
   Sesame-Soy Dressing, 174–76
   Shirazi salad, 113, 247
   Thai Pomelo Salad, 266
Long-Cooked Broccoli, 252
   in Pasta with Long-Cooked Broccoli, 252

m

mangetout
   Boiled Spring Vegetable Matrix, 208–11
   sautéing, 199
   Stewed Spring Vegetables, 207
   Vegetable Extravaganza, 176
maple syrup
   Peanut-Ginger Dressing, 176
   Roasted Vegetable Salad Matrix, 272–75
   Sesame-Soy Dressing, 174–76
   Spicy Meyer Lemon Relish, 81
   Sweet and Spicy Courgettes with Meyer Lemon, 241
   Sweet and Spicy Winter Squash, 271
   Tahini Sbagliato, 132–34
Mara's Tofu, 187
   in Brown Rice Bowl, 121
Marinated Feta, 71–72
   in Braised Kale with Feta-Style Cheese and Chillies, 258–59
   in Crunchy Shaved Pepper Salad, 230
   in Roasted Vegetable Salad Matrix, 272–75
   substitutions, 39
   in Summer Salad Matrix, 214–17
Marinated Gigante Beans, 161
Marinated Goat's Cheese, 74–75
   in Baked Goat's Cheese Salad, 75
   in Butter Beans Braised with Artichoke Hearts and Goat's Cheese, 162
   on Corn on the Cob, 213
   in Crunchy Shaved Pepper Salad, 230
   in Broad Bean Crostini, 202
   in Roasted Vegetable Salad Matrix, 272–75
   substitutions, 39
   in Summer Salad Matrix, 214–17
Marinated Roast Beetroot, 248

Marinated Shell Bean Salad, 235
Marion's Yeasted Waffles, 391–93
Mark's Giardiniera, 69–70
   in **Fried Chicken Sandwiches**, 310
   in **Roasted Vegetable Salad Matrix**, 272–75
mayonnaise
   Aioli, 236
   Chilli Crisp Chicken Salad, 313
   Classic Egg Salad, 149
   Crème Fraîche Devilled Eggs, 97
   Elote-Style Salad, 213
   Summer Salad Matrix, 214–17
Meatballs, Fluffy Pork, 335–36
Medjool dates
   One-Pot Chicken with Giant Couscous and Preserved Lemon, 290–91
   Roasted Vegetable Salad Matrix, 272–75
   Shaved Carrot Salad, 255
   Sugar Snap Pea Chopped Salad, 205
melons
   Chilled Melon with Mint, 226
   Summer Salad Matrix, 214–17
milk
   Apricot Clafoutis, 426
   Béchamel, 360
   Cherry Clafoutis, 425–26
   Creamy Tomato Soup, 172
millet, puffed
   Sarit's Ashura Cereal, 146–48
mint
   Broad Bean Crostini, 202
   Chilled Melon with Mint, 226
   Cucumber and Herb Labne, 48
   Garlic and Herb Labne, 48
   Herb Salad, 218
   Pasta with Broad Beans and Mint, 202
   Quick Cucumber Salad, 221
   Sekanjebin (Sweet and Sour Mint Shrub), 105
   Snap Pea Chopped Salad, 205
   Thai Pomelo Salad, 266
   Torn Charred Courgettes with Chillies and Mint, 239–41
mirin
   Shoyu Chicken, 300–301
   Teriyaki-ish Chicken Thighs, 306–7
miso
   about, 29
   Creamy Lemon-Miso Dressing, 122–24
   Creamy Sesame-Ginger Dressing, 119–21
   Miso and Labne Onion Dip, 93
   Tahini Sbagliato, 132–34
Miso and Labne Onion Dip, 93
   in **Roasted Vegetable Salad Matrix**, 272–75
mozzarella
   Classic Chopped Salad, 127
   Creamy Spinach Lasagne, 355–58
   Lasagne al Sugo, 364–65
   Roasted Aubergine Parmesan, 225
   Roasted Vegetable Salad Matrix, 272–75
   Summer Salad Matrix, 214–17
   Winter Squash Lasagne, 358
   Zucchini and Pesto Lasagne, 358

n

Nardello peppers
   Grilled Summer Salad, 229–30
   Summer Salad Matrix, 214–17
neutral oil, about, 26
nigella seeds
   Barbari Focaccia, 377–78
   Roasted Vegetable Salad Matrix, 272–74
Nocellara olives
   Mark's Giardiniera, 69–70
   Warm Nocellara Olives, 87
nonstick cooking spray, about, 30
Noyau Extract, 438
   in **Apricot and Noyau Jam**, 433–37
   in **Apricot Clafoutis**, 426
   in **Cherry Clafoutis**, 425–26
   in **Laurie Ellen's Cardamom Shortbread**, 417–18
nutritional yeast
   Forever Popcorn, 88–90
nuts
   crumbling, 36
   toasting, 37
   See also specific nuts

o

Oasis in Time, creating, 323–25
Oat and Honey Bread Rolls, 381–84
olive oil, about, 25–26
Olive Oil–Fried Bread, 94
   in **Avocado Toast**, 94
   in **Broad Bean Crostini**, 202
   with **Long-Cooked Broccoli**, 252
   with **Marinated Gigante Beans**, 161
   with **Pea Purée**, 205
   with **Rapini Pesto**, 258
   in **Roast Chicken with Bread Salad**, 94
   in **Roasted Vegetable Salad Matrix**, 272–75
   with **Sweet Pepper Antipasto**, 229
   in **Tomato Salad Matrix**, 247
olives
   Sicilian Citrus Salad, 266
   See also Nocellara olives; Kalamata olives
One-Bowl Chocolate Cake, 409–10
One-Pot Chicken with Giant Couscous and Preserved Lemon, 290–91
onions
   Adas Polo, 158
   Arroz Rojo, 154
   Arroz Verde, 154
   Braised Kale with Feta-Style Cheese and Chillies, 258–59
   Bright Pickled Onions, 52
   Chicken Braised with Apricots and Harissa, 302–5
   Chicken Stock, 314–15
   Chivi Spice Chicken Thighs, 298–99
   Creamy Tomato Soup, 172–73
   Cuban-Style Black Beans, 162
   Golden Chicken Soup, 293–94
   Kuku-kopita, 330–33
   Lamb Tagine, 305
   Lazy Sugo, 361–63
   Miso and Labne Onion Dip, 93
   Peperonata, 230
   Refried Beans, 161
   Roasted Vegetable Salad Matrix, 272–75
   sautéing, 199
   Shirazi salad, 113, 247
   Shoyu Chicken, 300–301
   Spicy Tuna Pantry Pasta, 177–79
   Teo's Brisket Chivis, 346–48
   Tortilla Soup, 295–96
oranges
   California Citrus Salad, 266
   Sicilian Citrus Salad, 266
   Vin d'Orange, 106–8
   Winter Citrus Salad, 266

oregano
- **Creamy Oregano Dressing,** 125–27
- **Sweet Pepper Antipasto,** 229

p

Pancakes, Ricotta Custard, 145
Pane Criminale, 329
Pan-Fried Potato Gratin, 263–64
panko breadcrumbs
- **Baked Goat's Cheese Salad,** 75
- **Chicken Thigh Schnitzel,** 309–10
- **Fluffy Pork Meatballs,** 335–36
- **Roasted Aubergine Parmesan,** 225
- in **Roasted Vegetable Salad Matrix,** 272–75
- **Spicy Gem Caesar with Golden Panko,** 131
- in **Spring Salad with Broad Beans,** 202
- in **Summer Squash au Gratin,** 241

panzanella, 245, 247
Parmesan
- about, 28
- **Autumn Chicory Salad,** 118
- **Basil Pesto,** 67
- **Boiled Summer Squash,** 239
- **Chicories Caesar with Focaccia Croutons,** 131
- **Classic Caesar,** 128
- **Courgette and Pesto Lasagne,** 358
- **Creamy One-Pot Pasta with Ricotta and Peas,** 182
- **Creamy Spinach Lasagne,** 355–58
- **Fava's Caesar,** 128–31
- **Fluffy Pork Meatballs,** 335–36
- **Kale and Farro Caesar Salad,** 131
- **Lasagne al Sugo,** 364–65
- **Lazy Sugo,** 361–63
- **Long-Cooked Broccoli,** 252
- **Pane Criminale,** 329
- **Pasta al Sugo,** 363
- **Pasta with Broad Beans and Mint,** 202
- **Pasta with Long-Cooked Broccoli,** 252
- **Rapini Pesto,** 258
- **Roasted Aubergine Parmesan,** 225
- **Roasted Vegetable Salad Matrix,** 272–75
- **Skillet Potato Gratin,** 263–64
- **Spicy Gem Caesar with Golden Panko,** 131
- **Spicy Tuna Pantry Pasta,** 177–79

- **Summer Squash au Gratin,** 241
- **White Bean Stew with Tomatoes and Saffron,** 186
- **Winter Squash Lasagne,** 358

parsley
- **Arroz Verde,** 154
- **Broad Bean Crostini,** 202
- **Butter Beans Braised with Artichoke Hearts and Goat's Cheese,** 162
- **Chicken Stock,** 314–15
- **Crunchy and Refreshing Green Salad,** 118
- **Cucumber and Herb Labne,** 48
- **Fluffy Pork Meatballs,** 335–36
- **Garlic and Herb Labne,** 48
- **Golden Chicken Soup,** 293–94
- **Herb Salad,** 218
- **Kuku-kopita,** 330–33
- **Pane Criminale,** 329
- **Persian-Style Herbed Rice,** 158
- **Sweet and Spicy Courgettes with Meyer Lemon,** 241
- **Sweet and Spicy Winter Squash,** 271
- **Tahini Sbagliato,** 132–34
- **White Bean, Celery, and Tuna Salad,** 127

parsnips
- **Boiled Spring Vegetable Matrix,** 208–11
- **Roasted Parsnips,** 260
- **Silky Parsnip Purée,** 260

passion fruit
- juice, 429
- **Passion Fruit Curd,** 427–29
- **Passion Fruit Parfaits,** 429

pasta
- **Courgette and Pesto Lasagne,** 358
- **Creamy One-Pot Pasta with Ricotta and Peas,** 182
- **Creamy Spinach Lasagne,** 355–58
- **Creamy Tomato and Goat's Cheese Pasta,** 244
- **Fresh Pasta Sheets,** 349–54
- **Hand-Cut Noodles,** 353–54
- **Lasagne al Sugo,** 364–65
- **Pasta al Sugo,** 363
- **Pasta Verde,** 353
- **Pasta with Broad Beans and Mint,** 202
- **Pasta with Long-Cooked Broccoli,** 252
- **Spaghetti Cacio e Pepe,** 180–81
- **Spicy Tuna Pantry Pasta,** 177–79

- **Winter Squash Lasagne,** 358
Pea Purée, 205
Peanut-Ginger Dressing, 176
- in **Simple Soba Salad,** 174–76

peanuts
- **Brown Rice Bowl,** 121
- **Calabrian Chilli Crisp,** 56–59
- **Chilli Crisp Chicken Salad Sandwiches,** 313
- **Crunchy Cabbage Slaw,** 121
- **Curried Carrot and Coconut Soup,** 169–71
- **Smashed Cucumber Salad,** 221–22
- **Thai Pomelo Salad,** 266

pears
- **Autumn Chicory Salad,** 118

peas
- **Boiled Spring Vegetable Matrix,** 208–11
- **Creamy One-Pot Pasta with Ricotta and Peas,** 182
- frozen, 205
- **Pea Purée,** 205
- preparing, 205
- sautéing, 205
- **Stewed Spring Vegetables,** 207
- **Vegetable Extravaganza,** 176
- See also mangetout; sugar snap peas

pecans
- **Autumn Chicory Salad,** 118
- **Rapini Pesto,** 258
- **Roasted Vegetable Salad Matrix,** 272–75
- **Sarit's Ashura Cereal,** 146–48
- **Shaved Fennel and Apple Salad,** 124
- toasting, 37

Pecorino Romano
- **Cacio e Pepe Butter,** 181
- **Cacio e Pepe Farro,** 181
- **Spaghetti Cacio e Pepe,** 180–81
Peperonata, 230
- in **Shakshuka,** 244

peperoncini
- **Chicken Kabob Wraps,** 134
- **Classic Chopped Salad,** 127

peppers
- **Crunchy Shaved Pepper Salad,** 230
- **Cuban-Style Black Beans,** 162
- **Flame-Roasted Peppers,** 229
- **Mark's Giardiniera,** 69–70
- **Grilled Summer Salad,** 229–30
- **Peperonata,** 230
- sautéing, 199

456 • good things

Summer Salad Matrix, 214–17
Sweet Pepper Antipasto, 229
Vegetable Extravaganza, 176
Persian-Style Herbed Rice, 158
persimmons
   Autumn Chicory Salad, 118
   Autumn Chopped Salad, 137
pesto
   Basil Pesto, 67
   Courgette and Pesto Lasagne, 358
   Rapini Pesto, 258
Pickled Thai Chillies, 76
   in Avocado Toast, 94
   in Braised Kale with Feta-Style Cheese and Chillies, 258–59
   Creamy Sesame-Ginger Dressing, 119–21
   in Green Sauce, 51
   in Roasted Vegetable Salad Matrix, 272–75
   in Shaved Carrot Salad, 255
   in Spicy Meyer Lemon Relish, 81
   in Spicy Whipped Tahini, 64
   substitutions, 39
   in Summer Salad Matrix, 214–17
   in Sweet and Spicy Courgettes with Meyer Lemon, 241
   in Thai Pomelo Salad, 266
   in Tomato-Poached Fish, 244
   in Whipped Baba Ghanoush, 100–102
   in White Bean, Celery, and Tuna Salad, 127
pickles
   Bright Pickled Onions, 52
   Pickled Thai Chillies, 76
pine nuts
   Autumn Chopped Salad, 137
   Basil Pesto, 67
   Roasted Vegetable Salad Matrix, 272–75
   Sautéed Greens, 256–58
   Sugar Snap Pea Chopped Salad, 205
   Summer Salad Matrix, 214–17
   toasting, 37
pinto beans
   Frijoles con Todo, 161
   Refried Beans, 161
Piri Piri Chicken, 287–89
Pitta Pockets, Fluffy, 385–87
poblano chillies
   Arroz Verde, 154

pomegranate seeds
   Autumn Chopped Salad, 137
Pomelo Salad, Thai, 266
Popcorn, Forever, 88–90
poppy seeds
   Creamy Lemon-Miso Dressing, 122–24
pork
   Fluffy Pork Meatballs, 335–36
   Lazy Sugo, 361–63
potatoes
   Coconut-Lemongrass Soup with Chickpeas, 167
   Crisp Hash Browns, 264
   Fluffiest Mashed Potatoes, 265
   Pan-Fried Potato Gratin, 263–64
   Roast Chicken and Potato Dinner, 265
   Shaken Roast Potatoes, 264
   Warm Potato Salad, 263
Prawns with Calabrian Chilli Butter, 343
Preserved Lemon and Labne Cake, 413
Preserved Meyer Lemon Paste, 79–81
   in Avocado Toast, 94
   in Boiled Spring Vegetable Matrix, 208–11
   in Broad Bean and Preserved Meyer Lemon Dip, 202
   in Chickpea Salad with Cucumbers and Dill, 163
   in Creamy Lemon-Miso Dressing, 124
   in Marinated Gigante Beans, 161
   in Marinated Roast Beetroot, 248
   in One-Pot Chicken with Giant Couscous and Preserved Lemon, 290–91
   in Preserved Lemon and Labne Cake, 413
   in Salty Lemon Soda, 81
   in Spicy Meyer Lemon Relish, 81
   substitutions, 39
   in Sweet and Spicy Courgettes with Meyer Lemon, 241
   in Warm Nocellara Olives, 87
   in White Bean, Celery, and Tuna Salad, 127
Pressure Cooker Dulce de Leche, 432
puffed wheat
   Sarit's Ashura Cereal, 146–48

pumpkin seeds
   Roasted Vegetable Salad Matrix, 272–75
   Sarit's Ashura Cereal, 146–48
   Summer Salad Matrix, 214–17

q

Quick Cucumber Salad, 221

r

radicchio
   Autumn Chicory Salad, 118
   Autumn Chopped Salad, 137
   Classic Chopped Salad, 127
   Roast Chicken with Bread Salad, 94
radishes
   Roasted Vegetable Salad Matrix, 272–75
   Spring Salad with Broad Beans, 202
   Vegetable Extravaganza, 176
rainbow sprinkles
   Confetti Cake, 406
rapini
   Rapini Pesto, 258
   stripping, 256
red beans
   Adas Polo, 158
red wine vinegar
   Creamy Oregano Dressing, 125–27
   Marinated Gigante Beans, 161
   Marinated Roast Beetroot, 248
   Marinated Shell Bean Salad, 235
   Roquefort Dressing, 135–37
   Torn Charred Courgettes with Chillies and Mint, 239–41
Refried Beans, 161
Relish, Spicy Meyer Lemon, 81
rice
   cooking, 151–54
   Vanilla Bean Rice Pudding, 430
   varieties, 150–51
   water ratios, 153
   yields, 153
   See also basmati rice; brown rice; jasmine rice
rice vinegar
   Creamy Sesame-Ginger Dressing, 119–21
   Gingery Roasted Cabbage Wedges, 259
   Green Sauce, 51

rice vinegar (cont'd):
    Kid Crudités, 91
    Marinated Roast Beetroot, 248
    Peanut-Ginger Dressing, 176
    Quick Cucumber Salad, 221
    Sesame-Soy Dressing, 174–76
    Smashed Cucumber Salad, 221–22
    Whipped Baba Ghanoush, 100–102
ricotta
    Courgette and Pesto Lasagne, 358
    Creamy One-Pot Pasta with Ricotta and Peas, 182
    Creamy Spinach Lasagne, 355–58
    Ricotta Custard Pancakes, 145
    Whipped Ricotta, 66
    Winter Squash Lasagne, 358
Roast Chicken and Potato Dinner, 265
Roast Chicken with Bread Salad, 94
Roasted Almonds with Fried Sage, 98
Roasted Aubergine Parmesan, 225
Roasted Aubergines, 223
Roasted Parsnips, 260
Roasted Summer Squash, 241
    in Summer Squash au Gratin, 241
    in Sweet and Spicy Courgettes with Meyer Lemon, 241
Roasted Sweet Potatoes, 268
Roasted Tomato Sauce, 244
    in Creamy Tomato and Goat's Cheese Pasta, 244
    in Shakshuka, 244
    in Tomato-Poached Fish, 244
Roasted Vegetable Salad Matrix, 272–75
rocket
    Roast Chicken with Bread Salad, 94
rockfish
    Saffron and Tomato Fish Stew, 186
    Tomato-Poached Fish, 244
roll-cutting, 32
Rolls, Oat and Honey Bread, 381–84
romaine lettuce
    Autumn Chopped Salad, 137
    Chicken Kabob Wraps, 134
    Classic Chopped Salad, 127
    Spring Chopped Salad, 124
    Roquefort Dressing, 135–37
        in Autumn Chopped Salad, 137
rosemary
    Marinated Goat's Cheese, 74–75
Runner Beans with Tomatoes and Aioli, 236
Russian Honey Icebox Cake, 399–401

S

saffron
    Golden Chicken Soup, 293–94
    grinding and blooming, 37
    Joojeh Kabob Roast Chicken, 284–86
    Saffron and Tomato Fish Stew, 186
    Saffron-Flecked Crispy Rice, 156
    Sautéed Greens, 256–58
    Stewed Clams with Tomatoes and Saffron, 185–86
    White Bean Stew with Tomatoes and Saffron, 186
sage
    Roasted Almonds with Fried Sage, 98
    Winter Squash Lasagne, 358
salads
    Autumn Chicory Salad, 118
    Autumn Chopped Salad, 137
    Baked Goat's Cheese Salad, 75
    California Citrus Salad, 266
    Chickpea Salad with Cucumbers and Dill, 163
    Chicories Caesar with Focaccia Croutons, 131
    Chilli Crisp Chicken Salad, 313
    Classic Egg Salad, 149
    Classic Chopped Salad, 127
    Corn Salad, 213
    Crunchy and Refreshing Green Salad, 118
    Crunchy Cabbage Slaw, 121
    Crunchy Shaved Pepper Salad, 230
    Elote-Style Salad, 213
    fattoush, 245
    Greek Salad with Farro and Souvlaki-ish Chicken Skewers, 127
    Grilled Summer Salad, 229–30
    Herb Salad, 218
    Kale and Farro Caesar Salad, 131
    Marinated Shell Bean Salad, 235
    panzanella, 245
    panzanella with torn croutons, 247
    Quick Cucumber Salad, 221
    Roast Chicken with Bread Salad, 94
    Roasted Vegetable Salad Matrix, 272–75
    Runner Beans with Tomatoes and Aioli, 236
    Shaved Carrot Salad, 255
    Shaved Fennel and Apple Salad, 124
    Shirazi salad, 113, 247
    Sicilian Citrus Salad, 266
    Simple Soba Salad, 174–76
    Smashed Cucumber Salad, 221–22
    Spicy Gem Caesar with Golden Panko, 131
    Spring Chopped Salad, 124
    Spring Salad with Broad Beans, 202
    Sugar Snap Pea Chopped Salad, 205
    Summer Salad Matrix, 214–17
    Thai Pomelo Salad, 266
    Three-Bean Salad, 238
    Tomato Salad, 245
    Tomato Salad Matrix, 246–47
    Vegetable Extravaganza, 176
    Warm Potato Salad, 263
    White Bean, Celery, and Tuna Salad, 127
    Winter Citrus Salad, 266
Salmon, Slow-Cooked, 337–41
salt, about, 25
Salty Lemon Soda, 81
sandwiches and wraps
    Chicken Kabob Wraps, 134
    Chilli Crisp Chicken Salad Sandwiches, 313
    Fried Chicken Sandwiches, 310
Sarit's Ashura Cereal, 146–48
sauces
    Basil Pesto, 67
    Béchamel, 360
    Green Sauce, 51
    Lazy Sugo, 361–63
    Rapini Pesto, 258
    Roasted Tomato Sauce, 244
    Simple Tomato Sauce, 359
Sautéed Corn, 213
Sautéed Greens, 256–58
Sautéed String Beans, 238
seeds, toasting, 37
Sekanjebin (Sweet and Sour Mint Shrub), 105
serrano chillies
    Green Sauce, 51
    Mark's Giardiniera, 69–70
    Refried Beans, 161
    Summer Salad Matrix, 214–17
    Whipped Baba Ghanoush, 100–102
sesame oil, toasted

Calabrian Chilli Crisp, 56–59
Creamy Sesame-Ginger
  Dressing, 119–21
Gingery Roasted Cabbage
  Wedges, 259
Sesame-Soy Dressing, 174–76
Shoyu Chicken, 300–301
Smashed Cucumber Salad, 221–22
Steamed Kabocha with Sesame-
  Ginger Dressing, 271
Summer Salad Matrix, 214–17
Teriyaki-ish Chicken Thighs, 306–7
Toasty Whipped Tahini, 64
sesame seeds
  Calabrian Chilli Crisp, 56–59
  Chewy Sesame Flatbreads, 388–90
  Crunchy Cabbage Slaw, 121
  Roasted Vegetable Salad
    Matrix, 272–75
  Sarit's Ashura Cereal, 146–48
  Simple Soba Salad, 174–76
  Summer Salad Matrix, 214–17
Sesame-Soy Dressing, 174–76
  in Simple Soba Salad, 174–76
7½-Minute Eggs, 149
  in Warm Asparagus
    Vinaigrette, 201
Shaken Roast Potatoes, 264
Shakshuka, 244
Shallot Oil, 55
  in Chewy Sesame
    Flatbreads, 388–90
  in Refried Beans, 161
  in Sautéed Greens, 256–58
  in Shallot and Spring Onion
    Labne, 48
  in String Beans with Ginger and
    Shallots, 238
  substitutions, 39
shallots
  Autumn Chopped Salad, 137
  Calabrian Chilli Crisp, 56–59
  Crispy Fried Shallots, 55
  Curried Carrot and Coconut
    Soup, 169–71
  House Dressing, 117–18
  Sautéed Greens, 258
  Shallot and Spring Onion
    Labne, 48
  Shallot Oil, 55
  String Beans with Ginger and
    Shallots, 238
  Winter Squash and Green Curry
    Soup, 171
Shaved Carrot Salad, 255

Shaved Fennel and Apple Salad, 124
shell beans
  Marinated Shell Bean Salad, 235
  selecting, 235
  storing, 235
  Summer Salad Matrix, 214–17
  Three-Bean Salad, 238
sherry vinegar
  House Dressing, 117–18
  Stewy Harissa Chickpeas with
    Winter Squash, 166
Shirazi salad, 113
  in Tomato Salad Matrix, 247
shishito peppers
  Grilled Summer Salad, 229–30
shiso
  Herb Salad, 218
  Summer Salad Matrix, 214–17
  Sweet and Spicy Courgettes with
    Meyer Lemon, 241
  Tomato Salad, 245
Shortbread, Laurie Ellen's
  Cardamom, 417–18
Shoyu Chicken, 300–301
Shoyu Chicken Wings, 301
Sicilian Citrus Salad, 266
Silky Parsnip Purée, 260
Simple Chicken Thighs, 306–7
Simple Soba Salad, 174–76
  in Vegetable Extravaganza, 176
Simple Spatchcocked
  Chicken, 282–83
Simple Tomato Sauce, 359
  in Creamy Spinach
    Lasagne, 355–58
  in Fluffy Pork Meatballs, 335–36
  in Roasted Aubergine
    Parmesan, 225
Simple Vegetable Marinade
  in Italian-Style Marinated
    Aubergines, 225
  in Marinated Shell Bean Salad, 235
  in Sweet Pepper Antipasto, 229
  in Courgette Antipasto, 241
single cream
  Vanilla Bean Flan, 419–21
Sky-High Focaccia, 372–76
  in Barbari Focaccia, 377–78
  in croutons, 37–38
  with Sweet Pepper Antipasto,
    229
Slow-Cooked Salmon, 337–41
Smashed Cucumber Salad, 221–22
soba noodles
  Simple Soba Salad, 174–76

Soda, Salty Lemon, 81
soups and stews
  Coconut-Lemongrass Soup with
    Chickpeas, 167
  Creamy Tomato Soup, 172–73
  Curried Carrot and Coconut
    Soup, 169–71
  Golden Chicken Soup, 293–94
  Saffron and Tomato Fish
    Stew, 186
  Stewy Harissa Chickpeas with
    Winter Squash, 166
  Tortilla Soup, 295–96
  White Bean Stew with Tomatoes
    and Saffron, 186
  Winter Squash and Green Curry
    Soup, 171
soured cream
  Apricot Clafoutis, 426
  Cherry Clafoutis, 425–26
  Creamy Corn and Squash
    Sauté, 213
  Elote-Style Salad, 213
  Fluffiest Mashed Potatoes, 265
  Oat and Honey Bread Rolls, 381–84
  One-Bowl Chocolate
    Cake, 409–10
  Roquefort Dressing, 135–37
  Russian Honey Icebox
    Cake, 399–401
  Soured Cream Fudge Icing, 407
  Sparkling Banana Bread, 414
  Strawberries with Soured Cream
    and Brown Sugar, 422
  Summer Salad Matrix, 214–17
Soured Cream Fudge Icing, 407
  in Yellow Buttermilk Cake,
    402–6
  in Yellow Cupcakes, 406
Souvlaki-ish Chicken Thighs, 307
  in Chicken Kabob Wraps, 134
soy sauce
  Peanut-Ginger Dressing, 176
  Sesame-Soy Dressing, 174–76
  Shoyu Chicken, 300–301
  Teriyaki-ish Chicken
    Thighs, 306–7
Spaghetti Cacio e Pepe, 180–81
Sparkling Banana Bread, 414
spices, toasting, 37
Spicy Gem Caesar with Golden
  Panko, 131
Spicy Meyer Lemon Relish, 81
  in Roasted Vegetable Salad
    Matrix, 272–75

Spicy Tuna Pantry Pasta, 177–79
Spicy Whipped Tahini, 64
spinach
   Courgette and Pesto Lasagne, 358
   Creamy Spinach Lasagne, 355–58
   Kuku-kopita, 330–33
   Pasta Verde, 353
   sautéing, 199
   Stewed Spring Vegetables, 207
   Winter Squash Lasagne, 358
Spring Chopped Salad, 124
spring onions
   Brown Rice Bowl, 121
   Chilli Crisp Chicken Salad, 313
   Crunchy Cabbage Slaw, 121
   Gingery Roasted Cabbage Wedges, 259
   Persian-Style Herbed Rice, 158
   Shallot and Spring Onion Labne, 48
   Simple Soba Salad, 174–76
   Summer Salad Matrix, 214–17
   Tahini Sbagliato, 132–34
   Warm Potato Salad, 263
Spring Salad with Broad Beans, 202
squash. *See* summer squash; winter squash
Steamed Kabocha with Sesame-Ginger Dressing, 271
sterilising jars, 38
Stewed Clams with Tomatoes and Saffron, 185–86
   in Saffron and Tomato Fish Stew, 186
Stewed Spring Vegetables, 207
Stewy Harissa Chickpeas with Winter Squash, 166
Strawberries with Soured Cream and Brown Sugar, 422
string beans
   Blanched String Beans, 236
   Runner Beans with Tomatoes and Aioli, 236
   Sautéed String Beans, 238
   sautéing, 199
   shopping for, 236
   String Beans with Ginger and Shallots, 238
   Summer Salad Matrix, 214–17
   Three-Bean Salad, 238
   in Tomato Salad Matrix, 247
substitutions, 39
sugar snap peas
   Boiled Spring Vegetable Matrix, 208–11
   preparing, 205
   sautéing, 199

Spring Chopped Salad, 124
Spring Salad with Broad Beans, 202
Stewed Spring Vegetables, 207
Sugar Snap Pea Chopped Salad, 205
Vegetable Extravaganza, 176
Summer Salad Matrix, 214–17
summer squash
   Boiled Summer Squash, 239
   Courgette and Pesto Lasagne, 358
   Courgette Antipasto, 241
   Creamy Corn and Squash Sauté, 213
   Grilled Summer Squash, 239
   Roasted Summer Squash, 241
   sautéing, 199
   Summer Salad Matrix, 214–17
   Summer Squash au Gratin, 241
   Torn Charred Courgettes with Chillies and Mint, 239–41
   Sweet and Spicy Courgettes with Meyer Lemon, 241
Sweet and Spicy Winter Squash, 271
sweet potatoes
   Charred Sweet Potatoes, 268
   Fluffy Steamed Sweet Potatoes, 268
   Roasted Sweet Potatoes, 268
   Roasted Vegetable Salad Matrix, 272–75
sweetened condensed milk
   Pressure Cooker Dulce de Leche, 432
   Vanilla Bean Flan, 419–21

t

tahini
   about, 30
   Chilli Crisp Chicken Salad, 313
   Spicy Whipped Tahini, 64
   Tahini Sbagliato, 132–34
   Toasty Whipped Tahini, 64
   Whipped Baba Ghanoush, 100–102
   Whipped Green Tahini, 64
   Whipped Tahini, 63–64
Tahini Sbagliato, 132–34
   in Chicken Kabob Wraps, 134
   in Roasted Vegetable Salad Matrix, 272–75
   in Summer Salad Matrix, 214–17
tarragon
   Herb Salad, 218
   Vibrant Beetroot Labne, 248
tearing ingredients, 32
tenderstem broccoli

Roasted Vegetable Salad Matrix, 272–75
   sautéing, 199
   Spring Chopped Salad, 124
   Vegetable Extravaganza, 176
10-Minute Eggs, 149
   in Classic Egg Salad, 149
   in Crème Fraîche Deviled Eggs, 149
Teo's Brisket Chivis, 346–48
Teo's Chivi Spice, 348
   in Arroz Rojo, 154
   in Chivi Spice Chicken Thighs, 298–99
   in Crispy Snacking Chickpeas, 165
   in Frijoles con Todo, 161
   in Teo's Brisket Chivis, 346–48
   in Tex-Mex Thighs, 307
tequila
   Sekanjebin, 105
   Vin de Pamplemousse, 108
Teriyaki-ish Chicken Thighs, 306–7
   in Brown Rice Bowl, 121
Tex-Mex Thighs, 307
Thai chillies
   Chilli Vinegar, 76
   Coconut-Lemongrass Soup with Chickpeas, 167
   Pickled Thai Chillies, 76
   Piri Piri Chicken, 287–89
Thai Pomelo Salad, 266
Three-Bean Salad, 238
thyme
   Chicken Stock, 314–15
   House Dressing, 117–18
   Marinated Goat's Cheese, 74–75
Toasty Whipped Tahini, 64
Tofu, Mara's, 187
tomatoes
   Arroz Rojo, 154
   Chicken Braised with Apricots and Harissa, 302–5
   Chicken Kabob Wraps, 134
   Chivi Spice Chicken Thighs, 298–99
   Classic Chopped Salad, 127
   Confit of Little Tomatoes, 242
   Creamy Tomato and Goat's Cheese Pasta, 244
   Creamy Tomato Soup, 172–73
   fattoush, 245
   Greek Salad with Farro and Souvlaki-ish Chicken Skewers, 127
   Grilled Summer Salad, 229–30
   heirloom varieties, 242
   Lamb Tagine, 305

Lazy Sugo, 361–63
Marinated Shell Bean Salad, 235
panzanella, 245
panzanella with torn croutons, 247
Peperonata, 230
Roasted Tomato Sauce, 244
Runner Beans with Tomatoes and Aioli, 236
Saffron and Tomato Fish Stew, 186
Shakshuka, 244
Shirazi salad, 245
Simple Tomato Sauce, 359
Spicy Tuna Pantry Pasta, 177–79
Stewed Clams with Tomatoes and Saffron, 185–86
storing, 242
Summer Salad Matrix, 214–17
Teo's Brisket Chivis, 346–48
Tomato Salad, 245
Tomato Salad Matrix, 246–47
Tomato-Poached Fish, 244
Tortilla Soup, 295–96
White Bean Stew with Tomatoes and Saffron, 186
Torn Charred Courgettes with Chillies and Mint, 239–41
Tortilla Soup, 295–96
tortillas
  Crispy Open-Faced Quesadillas, 168
  Teo's Brisket Chivis, 346–48
tuna
  Spicy Tuna Pantry Pasta, 177–79
  White Bean, Celery, and Tuna Salad, 127

v

vanilla pods and extract
  about, 30–31
  Vanilla Bean Flan, 419–21
  Vanilla Bean Rice Pudding, 430
  Vanilla Extract, 31
  Whipped Vanilla Cream, 410
vegetables
  bias cutting, 36
  Boiled Spring Vegetable Matrix, 208–11
  boiling, 194–95
  Brown Rice Bowl, 121
  Kid Crudités, 91
  peeling, 32, 35
  Roasted Vegetable Salad Matrix, 272–75
  roasting, 196–97
  roll-cutting, 32
  sautéing, 198–99
  Stewed Spring Vegetables, 207
  Summer Salad Matrix, 214–17
  Vegetable Extravaganza, 176
  See also specific vegetables
Vibrant Beetroot Labne, 248
  in Roasted Vegetable Salad Matrix, 272–75
Vin de Pamplemousse, 108
Vin d'Orange, 106–8
vinegar, about, 26. *See also* specific vinegars
vodka
  Noyau Extract, 438
  Vanilla Extract, 31
  Vin de Pamplemousse, 108
  Vin d'Orange, 106–8

w

waffles
  Amy's Bacon Waffles, 393
  Buckwheat Waffles, 393
  Marion's Yeasted Waffles, 391–93
walnuts
  Autumn Chicory Salad, 118
  Roasted Vegetable Salad Matrix, 272–75
  toasting, 37
Warm Asparagus Vinaigrette, 201
Warm Nocellara Olives, 87
Warm Potato Salad, 263
Whipped Baba Ghanoush, 100–102
Whipped Green Tahini, 64
Whipped Ricotta, 66
  in Boiled Spring Vegetable Matrix, 208–11
  in Creamy One-Pot Pasta with Ricotta and Peas, 182
  in Pasta with Broad Beans and Mint, 202
  in Pasta with Long-Cooked Broccoli, 252
  in Roasted Vegetable Salad Matrix, 272–75
  in Summer Salad Matrix, 214–17
  in Sweet and Spicy Winter Squash, 271
Whipped Tahini, 63–64
  in Boiled Spring Vegetable Matrix, 208–11
  in Roasted Vegetable Salad Matrix, 272–75
  in Summer Salad Matrix, 214–17
Whipped Vanilla Cream, 410
  in Passion Fruit Parfaits, 429
white beans
  White Bean, Celery, and Tuna Salad, 127
  White Bean Stew with Tomatoes and Saffron, 186
white wine vinegar
  Butter Beans Braised with Artichoke Hearts and Goat's Cheese, 162
  Classic Caesar, 128
  Classic Egg Salad, 149
  Fava's Caesar, 128–31
  Mark's Giardiniera, 69–70
  Piri Piri Chicken, 287–89
  Sekanjebin (Sweet and Sour Mint Shrub), 105
wine, red
  Lazy Sugo, 361–63
wine, rosé
  Vin de Pamplemousse, 108
  Vin d'Orange, 106–8
wine, white
  Lazy Sugo, 361–63
  Prawns with Calabrian Chilli Butter, 343
  Stewed Clams with Tomatoes and Saffron, 185–86
  Vin de Pamplemousse, 108
  Vin d'Orange, 106–8
Winter Citrus Salad, 266
winter squash
  Dark-Roasted Winter Squash, 271
  Roasted Vegetable Salad Matrix, 272–75
  Steamed Kabocha with Sesame-Ginger Dressing, 271
  Stewy Harissa Chickpeas with Winter Squash, 166
  Sweet and Spicy Winter Squash, 271
  Winter Squash and Green Curry Soup, 171
  Winter Squash Lasagne, 358

y

Yellow Cupcakes, 406
yogurt
  Basic Crispy Rice, 155–58
  Homemade Labne, 29
  Joojeh Kabob Roast Chicken, 284–86
  See also labne

PHOTO: ROBBIE JEANNE

SAMIN NOSRAT is a cook, teacher, and author of the James Beard Award-winning #1 *New York Times* bestseller *Salt Fat Acid Heat*. She was named one of *Time*'s 100 Most Influential People and Chef of the Year by *Eater*. She is the co-host (with Hrishikesh Hirway) of the *Home Cooking* podcast, a former columnist at *The New York Times Magazine,* and the host of the Netflix original documentary series based on *Salt Fat Acid Heat*. She lives in Oakland, California.

AYA BRACKETT is a photographer whose work has appeared in many publications, including *The New York Times, The Wall Street Journal, Bon Appétit,* and *Dwell*. She has also photographed several cookbooks, including the James Beard Award-winning *Bitter* and the James Beard nominees *Rintaro* and *Japan: The Vegetarian Cookbook*. She is based in Oakland, California, and is, in fact, Samin's neighbour.